The
Eternal
Garden

Other Books by Sally Wendkos Olds

The Working Parents Survival Guide
The Complete Book of Breastfeeding (with Marvin S. Eiger, M.D.)
Psychology (with Diane E. Papalia, Ph.D.)
Human Development (with Diane E. Papalia, Ph.D.)
A Child's World (with Diane E. Papalia, Ph.D.)
The Mother Who Works Outside the Home
Raising a Hyperactive Child (with Mark A. Stewart, M.D.)
Helping Your Child Learn Right from Wrong: A Guide to Values
    Clarification (with Sidney B. Simon, Ed.D.)

The Eternal Garden

Seasons of Our Sexuality

Sally Wendkos Olds

𝕿𝖎𝖒𝖊𝖘 BOOKS

All rights reserved under International and Pan-American Copyright Conventions. Published in the United States by Times Books, a division of Random House, Inc., New York, and simultaneously in Canada by Random House of Canada Limited, Toronto.

Library of Congress Cataloging in Publication Data

Olds, Sally Wendkos.
    The eternal garden.

    Bibliography: p. 301
    Includes index.
    1. Sex. 2. Youth—Sexual behavior. 3. Middle age—
Sexual behavior. 4. Aged—Sexual behavior. I. Title.
HQ21.039 1985   306.7   84-40433
ISBN 0-8129-1159-8

Designed by Doris Borowsky
Manufactured in the United States of America
9 8 7 6 5 4 3 2 1
First Edition

To David
husband, lover, best friend

Acknowledgments

EVERY AUTHOR HAS an extended literary family, without whom it would be impossible to sit down, day after day, to face a blank sheet in the typewriter. Mine for this book includes Ned Chase, former vice president of Times Books, who one day sounded out a friend on the idea of a book about "sexual passages throughout life." The friend, literary agent Julian Bach, recognized the theme as an important one. As my agent he knew my work and my interests, and he called me to ask whether I was interested in speaking to Ned. I was, I did, and you hold in your hands the result. My editor at Times Books, Kathleen Moloney, consistently supported the project with her enthusiasm; her good judgment saved me from some of my indulgences, and her good heart allowed me others.

I would like to express my deep appreciation to those eminent people who took the time to read parts or all of this book in manuscript, and whose valuable suggestions helped me to improve it: Mary S. Calderone, M.D., Robert N. Butler, M.D., Edward M. Brecher, and Shirley Zussman, Ed.D. While the book is better for their contributions, they are not, of course, accountable for the final result.

I am grateful to the many researchers, therapists, teachers, fellow writers, and representatives of professional organizations who gave generously of their time and their expertise. While many of the persons who helped me are cited somewhere in this book, some—whose contributions were just as valuable to the development of my thinking—are not. They all have my thanks.

I am, of course, especially indebted to the individuals who shared their own personal histories with me. I hope that they will be gratified to know that, in addition to the direct help they gave me, telling their own personal truths is bound to help others who read about them. While the limitations of space prevented me from telling all the stories I heard, the ones I didn't tell are, by and large, as fascinating as the ones I did. They all contributed to my understanding of the sexual milestones experienced by people in the 1980s.

Finally, let me say how fortunate I am in my friends and my family, who talked with me about issues I was grappling with, who encouraged me when I was stricken with anxiety at the audacity of this undertaking, and who rejoiced with me at its conclusion. I hope the work proves worthy of the efforts and the interest of so many people.

Sally Wendkos Olds

Contents

*The
Eternal
Garden*

Introduction

A CHILD ENGAGED in a game as innocent as any other—and being harshly scolded and shamed for it. Another child learning to love her body as her parents allow her to pose nude for a book of art photographs. An adolescent fascinated by the sight of a boy and a girl fondling and kissing each other. A college student distinguishing "falling in lust" from "falling in love." A young man in love for the first time and uncertain about marrying the woman he cannot bear to be parted from. A new mother full of the urge to parent, empty of the urge to couple. A divorcee discovering a vibrant sexuality that had been dormant during an unsatisfying marriage. A man who cannot attain an erection, a woman who cannot achieve orgasm seeking sex therapy for the dysfunction that has suddenly become intolerable. A couple married fifteen years tasting the joys of a lusty "second honeymoon." A middle-aged spouse feeling like an out-of-control teenager in the heady delights and miseries of an extramarital affair. The survivor of a life-threatening onslaught on health, grateful to be alive but saddened by sexual losses. A widow who would like to be sexually active but feels

3

frustrated by the lack of a partner. A septuagenarian experiencing a robust sexual rebirth.

These are just a few of the people who have shared with me some of the turning points in their lives that shaped the way they now feel, think, and act about their sexuality. All of us have had such pivotal experiences, through the events or the people we encounter. Often, we don't fully appreciate the impact of such episodes at the time they happen. We may not perceive their import for years, until we examine ourselves from the perspective of the people we have become, not the ones we were. Then as we open the history books of our lives, we search for and often find those discoveries and those decisions that have changed us from the people we once were.

Sometimes it is only through such hindsight that we can understand why some of us have always thought of sex as something shameful while others celebrate the delights of the flesh, why some of us use our sexual attractiveness as a weapon while others cherish it as a God-given gift, how sex became so important to some of us that it eclipsed other pursuits while it's been a low priority in the lives of others.

For more than a decade and a half I have been writing about the human condition—our hopes and our dreams and our efforts to realize our goals through work, through love, through caring for our children, through caring about our parents, through the entire range of caring relationships. When my search for the answer to a professional question drove me to look back at my writing over the years, I could not miss hearing the importunate rhythms of several major themes, themes that obviously throb in my work because they are clamorous in my life. As so often happens in professional decisions, my choices of subject matter have frequently grown out of deeply felt (although not always consciously acknowledged) personal needs. One of the most insistent leitmotifs in my work turned out to be the interrelationship between sexual development and virtually everything that happens in a human life.

In two college textbooks, I have written about physiological, intellectual, and emotional development throughout the life cycle; the sexual melodies that play a compelling role in this development assumed a prominent place in these books. Furthermore, in many of the magazine articles I've written and in every one of my other books—whether they have dealt with breastfeeding, the clarification of values to live by, the life of the working parent, hyperactivity in children, or the basic tenets of the science of psychology—sexuality has emerged as a major counterpoint to the prime topic of the work.

Struck by the constancy of this refrain throughout my writing, I realized that my own sexual development, my parents', and then my husband's and children's, had informed the paths of my own life far more deeply than I had ever acknowledged. I began to wonder about this development. Were the kinds of events and influences I had experienced unique to me and my family? Was I "normal"? What is normality? Why were some times in my life weightier in impact than others? How unusual were the "sexual turning points" in my life, those pivotal periods that seemed to mark the times when my life and the lives of the people I knew proceeded in a different direction from earlier paths?

I felt that the search for answers to these and similar questions would constitute the basis for a fruitful research and writing project. It would help me understand myself and would also, I felt sure, speak to others who, in our eroticized society, also have unanswered questions about their sexuality. I thought I would delve into the research literature, contact prominent authorities, and build my exploration on a powerful understructure of research and theory. I would flesh out this framework by telling the stories of individuals who would confide in me their own histories of sexual turning points in their lives.

When I consulted the social science literature, however, I received a rude shock. Few researchers or theorists had conceptualized such sequences in people's lives. Of course, there was Sigmund Freud. And after him there was Erik H. Erikson, both major figures in delineating the times of life when certain aspects of sexual development normally take place. And there was a plethora of papers on narrow aspects of different kinds of experiences, common to different times of life, which *could* constitute turning points.

But Freud didn't even admit of the possibility of sexual development once we were out of adolescence, and Erikson emphasized the social aspects of developmental crises rather than the sexual. No one in recent years had attempted the kind of long-term research focusing on the sexual development of adults such as that more general developmental research conducted at Yale University by Daniel Levinson and his colleagues, at Harvard University in the form of the Grant study, and on the West Coast by Roger Gould. The findings from these studies had formed the armature on which Gail Sheehy constructed her book *Passages*.

All of these contemporary studies of adult development dealt with many issues related to sexuality—breaking away from one's family, developing a long-term relationship, getting married, having children, going through a midlife crisis. The research, however, touched only lightly on the sexual ramifications of these passages. Furthermore, these studies omitted the important beginnings and endings of the life cycle, saying virtually nothing about childhood, adolescence, and old age.

So I went to people living their lives today and asked them to tell me about the crucial turning points in their own sexual development. These are the people who make "cameo" appearances throughout this book. Who are they? They are men and women in every stage of adulthood. The youngest person I interviewed was twenty years old at the time; the oldest was eighty-three. The cameos in the chapters on childhood and adolescence were filtered through the memories of the adults who had such vivid recollections of them.

I came to these speakers in many ways. A very few were personal friends who dared to reveal some of their most intimate thoughts and experiences to me, trusting me with their secrets in the knowledge that I would not betray their trust. Some were friends of friends or clients of professional colleagues—counselors, therapists, and researchers. Others were reached through my attendance at workshops, conferences, and meetings on various aspects of sexuality.

All the voices in this book are authentic. The words attributed to people describing their intimate experiences and their feelings were actually spoken to me. The events were described to me. The essence of every history is firmly grounded in a foundation of truth. The only deviation from this truth is in the use of pseudonyms for almost all the individuals and in the alteration of just enough of the details of their lives to prevent their being recognized by employers, neighbors, even their immediate family.

I particularly chose to keep my interviewees anonymous since I felt this would be the route to greater candor. I sought to explore the sexual turning points in the lives of people like the ones most of us are likely to know—people who are not "professionally" sexual, who don't publish erotic magazines, who don't found sexually adventurous retreats, who don't work in massage parlors, who don't trumpet their sexuality even though they live by its rhythms. In this anonymity many people dared to share with me information and opinions that they had never shared with anyone else.

The people you'll meet in these pages probably acknowledge more deeply than the average person the centrality of sexuality in their lives. Sometimes this acknowledgment has come from a sustained history of sexual interest and sexual activity. Sometimes it has come from a specific crystallizing experience.

As in any research project that depends on volunteer informants, the people in this book do not represent a cross section of the general population. An interminably repetitious refrain that has greeted every major (and many a minor) research project on sexuality has been the complaint that the people relied upon for information were not "typical," that they were more sex-oriented than average and that, therefore, they could not tell us much about ourselves. But who among us is "typical"? We are all individuals, each of us holding our own precious and particular and peculiar view of the world and our place in it. You, the reader, are likely to identify and feel empathy toward some of the voices you'll hear and to feel alien from others.

I sought to make my group of informants more representative of a wider population by actively seeking out people from different parts of the country, from communities that ranged from big cities to rural outposts, from different socioeconomic levels, from different racial, religious, and ethnic backgrounds. It was remarkable, however, how little influence these factors had. While some large-scale surveys have found considerable demographic differences according to region and social class, others have found very little.

In these days of global communication, the same viewpoints being broadcast in New York and Los Angeles also reach people in Weirton, West Virginia, Ajo, Arizona, Xenia, Ohio, and every other pocket of the country. So it's not surprising that it always comes down to the individual. Some of my most conservative informants were from the "wicked" coasts, while some of my most adventurous ones harkened from sleepy little inland hamlets. In some cases I looked for individuals who had undergone specific experiences; in others, I encountered interesting people and dug to discover the pivotal influences in their lives. I had to do quite a bit of persuading to get some people to talk to me. Others sought me out.

In a few cases, when I interviewed both members of a couple or people who knew each other, I was able to get corroboration of accounts. Sometimes, while the facts seemed the same, the perceptions of the two individuals differed widely. Most of the time, of course, it was impossible to corroborate the truth of what people were telling me, forcing me to rely on my respondents' versions of what had happened. This rarely posed a problem, since I got the sense that most of the interviewees were speaking sincerely, in large part because they were using these interviews as opportunities to order their own thinking about their sexuality. Many of the people I spoke to told me how much they had gained from our talks, in which they explored, sometimes for the first time in their lives, some of the feelings and experiences that had been significant in their sexual development.

In the end, then, I took the stories that people told me, of the experiences and events and life circumstances that affected their sexual development, and I interviewed professionals in the field, and I pored over reports of studies and analyses of their meanings, and I drew my own conclusions about the ways our lives affect our sexuality and our sexuality affects our lives. Sometimes I devoted a great deal of space to one kind of turning point because it seemed important to substantial numbers of people. Some kinds of experiences I barely mentioned. Others didn't make it into these pages at all simply because there wasn't enough space to include the multiplicity of experiences that color the human tapestry.

As I heard people describe—sometimes haltingly, sometimes regretfully, sometimes joyously—the events that delineated their sexual journey through life, I was confirmed in my belief that such sexual turning points are often a function of the time and place in which a person lives. While puberty is obviously a physical turning point for everyone, it carries more of a sexual aura in those societies in which it signals a young girl's or boy's readiness to engage in sexual activity, or even to marry and have children. In our society, in which pubertal youths are still children by every measure other than biology, physiological blossoming often outpaces psychological maturity.

A major difference in turning points within our own culture over the span of one generation is evident in regard to marriage. The commitment to marry signals a major change in many facets of both people's lives, of course, but today that change is less *sexually* significant, when newlyweds are likely to have been lovers before marriage, with each other as well as with other partners. Marriage was more frequently cited as a turning point by older persons, who were more likely to have been virgins on their wedding nights. Several of the women over forty and several of the men over fifty who spoke to me owned up to having been virgins until marriage in their early or middle twenties, while none of the younger women and men related this pattern. The only women under forty who were virgins till marriage, and there were only two of these, had married while still in their teens.

Hearing so many intimate accounts, and reflecting upon my own life and the lives of those close to me, I was also struck by how often we create our own turning points. Sometimes, of course, an event happens to us over which we have no control—a child is molested, a young woman raped, a man taken ill, a parent or sexual partner dies. Such events often carry the seeds for our future sexual development, and the only control we have over them is how we care for and harvest those seeds once they have been sown in the soil of our lives.

At many other times, however, we are clearly the agents right from the start; we initiate the change that becomes a turning point. Something impels a woman to leave the convent, and the leaving itself becomes the turning point. A man makes the decision to go into therapy, and he attributes the changes in his life to the therapy when, in fact, they may occur because he is allowing the therapy to serve as the catalyst. Or we invest someone with the qualities we seek—as Andrea did with her Ron, with whom she became sexually entranced for no other reason than his presence in her life at a time when she was undergoing inner changes that drove her to seek a sexual partner outside her marriage.

Our own control over our sexual turning points also shows up in the way we choose to remember some incidents in our lives and to forget others, and in the way we impose our own meaning, filtered through our personal belief system, on everything that happens to us. This personal stamp upon the records of our lives does not, of course, invalidate outside influences on us. It shows, instead, the power we hold to interpret events and to govern our lives according to the constructions we put on them.

One truth that has emerged from these tales of turning points gives cause for optimism: very often a turning point that at first blush seems unrelievedly negative has turned out to have a happy ending after all. The trauma of a heart attack, for example, is often followed by a new appreciation of life and love, and a closer bond between partners. And the cataclysm of divorce, with all its pain, often leaves in its wake a strengthened individual personality and a never-dreamed-of sexual blossoming.

As so many of those whose stories unfold in these pages have demonstrated, the quest for the marker events in our lives can be richly rewarding, yielding a fuller knowledge of ourselves as sexual beings. We can learn from each other. The more each of us knows about the turning points experienced by other people, the better we can understand those that have occurred or will occur in our own lives. And the more we know about the turning points we ourselves have already undergone, the better able we are to anticipate those to come and the more expertly self-guided we can be as we complete our sexual journey through life.

In the process of writing this book I underwent profound changes in my own thinking. I clarified some of my values. I changed facets of my behavior. I came up with answers to some of the questions that had perplexed me, and these answers in turn spurred new questions.

My life came together in a new way for me, as I saw how I was shaped by being the adored little sister of two older brothers; as I realized how I had achieved the necessary independence from my mother over a sexual battleground; as I appreciated a sensuality in her that I had, in her lifetime, never dealt with; as I saw the distance my father maintained with me (along with his unquestioned love) to keep our relationship "pure"; as I acknowledged falling in love with a man who looked enough like my brother to be mistaken for him, and whose character and personality, in many subtle ways, were very much like my father's; as marriage took me away from my family geographically, forcing still more independence and forging a new strength that I hadn't known I had; as I embraced the sensuality of motherhood. Ultimately, I realized how much of my dance through life was continually being choreographed by the powerful force of my sexuality.

I now saw that sex is like the sea. The huge, uncharted realm in which all life began. Not only a gift of nature, but the essence of nature itself. As such, it assumes different faces, different moods—now raging, now tranquil; now shimmering, now dark; now shallow, now plunging to unplumbed depths.

Yet this basic drive, which is with all of us from the cradle to the grave, has rarely been recognized simply as the natural function it is. It has seldom achieved the kind of acceptance that would enable it to be an energizing life force rather than a source of shame and doubt. It has been trammeled by fearfulness that has resulted in hypocrisy, in repression, in denial.

I hope, then, that some of the insights presented in these pages, both my own and those of the individuals and the professionals who shared their lives and their expertise with me, will help readers unravel some of their own sexual riddles, and that understanding this aspect of themselves a little bit better will help them to see their own personal truths more clearly and to lead more richly fulfilling lives.

Prologue:
A Sexual Cameo

Sex for me has always been enjoyable, and with everybody besides Anne it's been just fun and games, and I could always keep it that way. Until Eileen. There's something special about her that made me fall in love with her. And now here I am. I can't give her up and yet I still love Anne. I don't know what to do. I hate the idea of what I'm putting both of them through. I'd kill anyone else if he did to either of these women what I'm doing.

TONY

I FIRST MET TONY and Anne Rocco at a dinner party in Shaker Heights, Ohio. I wasn't really "working" that night; my husband and I were visiting old friends. But in another sense, I was *always* working. Throughout the germinating stage and the research stage of this book, I kept raising the topic of its concept and its overriding theme—the inter-relationship of sexuality and the other aspects of our lives—everywhere I went. I talked to clarify my own thinking, I listened to expand my focus, and—always—I was on the lookout for people who would be willing to speak to me on a more intimate level about the special experiences in their lives.

Even when nothing further came of these conversations, they definitely raised my appeal as a dinner guest. My hosts and hostesses found that once I mentioned the topic of my book, any worries they had about keeping the conversational ball rolling quickly evaporated. For most people like to talk about sex. They like to talk philosophically in global terms, they like to talk specifically about what their friends and neigh-

12

bors are doing and how they feel about it, and they like to talk about sexual rights and wrongs.

Every conversation took off from the same point, but since every combination of individuals is unique, each conversation had its own special flavor. Most often, the verbal currents led us into the shallow impersonal shoals of an exploration of "sex in America today," but occasionally I was invited into the deeper waters of intimate thoughts and feelings.

On this particular evening, I caught an immediate signal that my topic had special significance for at least two of the guests. I saw Tony and Anne exchange a glance, the way couples often do when they have an especially meaningful secret between them. Neither of them said much at the dinner table, but they were both listening intently to the rest of us. I wondered how I might find out their special interest in the topic of my book.

I didn't have to wonder for long. At the end of the evening, Tony took me aside and said, "If you're looking for people to interview, we'd be happy to talk to you." Anne smiled and echoed Tony's invitation.

A couple of days later I find myself in the Roccos' comfortable living room on a winding street in a development of ranch houses on half-acre lots. Anne and I are sitting on the gracefully carved chairs in front of the fireplace. She and I are to talk alone for a couple of hours before Tony comes home, the three of us will have dinner together, and then while Anne goes out to a class Tony and I will talk.

"I don't know where to begin this," Anne says, a new tentativeness showing. "I don't even know why Tony and I decided to talk to you. But I don't have anyone else I can really talk to, so maybe this will help me get my thoughts in order. I just hope I can get through this without crying on your shoulder. That's not why we invited you over. Do you want more coffee? Cookies? Anything?"

As I shake my head to all her offerings, she runs out of ways to put off what she has to say and plunges in.

"One night, about ten years ago, the ice cream man came jangling down our street—we were still in Akron—and Lisa came running in for money. She was frantic that he'd drive away before she got her Popsicle, so instead of going upstairs for my purse I reached into the pocket of Tony's jacket, which he'd left lying on the couch when he went out to play tennis.

"As I fished out change, a folded piece of paper fell out. It was the really good kind of notepaper—that you get at Potter and Mellon—thick and creamy, with an embossed monogram on the front. I handed Lisa some silver and as she skipped off, I read the note. I couldn't believe what I was reading. I can still see it in front of me—the round, neat handwriting, the kind almost like printing."

Anne fixes her clear green eyes on the wall behind me and recites the words that invaded her safe little nest:

Tony darling—

I am desolate without you. I live only when you are with me, only when I feel your arms folded tightly around me, your skin breathing warm against mine, your wonderful cock entering me, coming home where you belong.

Till next time—when you make me live again.

Your own
E.

"I had thought we were so happy together," Anne says, her chestnut hair falling across her cheeks as she bends to gulp the now-tepid coffee in the translucent china cup. "We had the children, we had just bought a little house, we had loads of fun together, and we had a wonderful—and very active—sex life. So who was 'E'? And where did she fit into Tony's life?"

When Tony came home and Anne showed him the letter, he made a full confession, telling her about all the other women who had been in his life over the years. The first time Tony had gone to bed with another woman had been fourteen years before, when Anne was pregnant with the first of their four children. Since then, he had been with one woman after another. Most were faceless, nameless blurs in his memory. But Eileen was different.

"I was dumbfounded," Anne says. "I still am. I can't believe the man's energy. We have always had an active sex life. We make love

14

just about every night. I don't know how he finds the time or the energy for all these other women. But he finds it somehow.''

This affair was different. Tony admitted to Anne that he was in love with Eileen. He had never fallen in love with any of the others. He started to cry as he told Anne, and he promised to give up Eileen. He never promised to stop seeing other women, and Anne didn't ask him to.

"I sort of accepted the fact that this was very important to him. I didn't like it—I didn't want any other men and I couldn't understand his need for other women—but I felt if it was just sex, like all the other women, it wouldn't threaten our marriage, so I forced myself to accept it. After every one, he would come back and tell me about her. He never saw any of them a second time, and it was never anyone I knew and so they never seemed to affect our life together. Which has been really good.''

As if for confirmation, Anne looks around the neatly appointed room, the comfortable, well-made furniture, the Christmas tree bedecked with ornaments, the family pictures of children and grandchildren on the wall behind the piano, the new car parked in front of the big picture window. But then she fixes her eyes on me, and I see them fill with tears.

"Now I think we're in trouble," she finally says, when she trusts her voice. "Because now he's in love. Again. Or still. Because Eileen is in the picture again. She had married and moved away, but now she's split from her husband and she and Tony found each other again. He came home and told me she's the sun and the moon and the stars to him. Tell me, how can I compete with the sun and the moon and the stars?''

Anne draws a deep breath. "You've talked to a lot of people. You must have heard stories like this one before. It's nothing new, God knows. But what do other people do? I don't want a divorce. I'm not even sure Tony wants a divorce. But I can't live like this, knowing he's living with me and loving somebody else. I don't know what to do.''

I don't know what to say. I don't presume to give Anne any advice. I am neither a professional counselor nor a close friend. So I murmur some words of sympathy, let her know she can say whatever she wants—that nothing will go into the book without her permission—and go on listening.

Tony's breakup with Eileen that first time served as a major turning point in his life. He had been unhappy in his job in a tire factory in Akron, but, unwilling to risk a secure job, he had never wanted to take a chance on doing what he really wanted—go into business for himself as a contractor. Now that both Tony and Anne wanted to be a safe distance away from Eileen, it made sense to leave Akron. And to take a flier on that contracting business.

That decision, precipitated by the affair with Eileen, probably changed Tony's and Anne's life together more than any other they had made during the past thirty-one years. After a few struggling years, Tony's business picked up, until now he's one of the most successful home building contractors in Cleveland, sought after by wealthy homeowners who want the very best work and are willing to pay for it.

During those early lean years, Anne put to work the secretarial skills she had picked up in high school but hadn't expected to use except in case of emergency. Despite all the difficulties in finding child care for four children, Anne loved working. She enjoyed the excitement of the busy advertising agency, she liked the heady feeling of earning her own money and having more of a say in family financial decisions, and while to all outward appearances she was still the submissive wife who catered to her husband's every wish, her working had brought about subtle changes in the balance of power between Tony and Anne. And they both knew it.

Little by little, Anne learned more about the advertising business, until now she's office manager of the agency, which had become so successful that it opened up branches in Chicago, San Francisco, and New York. It's clear to me that Tony's and Anne's professional successes came about as the direct result of their moving, not only *to* Cleveland, but away *from* Akron. There, the pressures from their families might well have kept Tony at the job in the same tire factory where his father and brothers still work, and would almost certainly have kept Anne in the role of housewife. Far enough away from Akron so that they were not dependent on their families (and not comfortably close to Eileen), yet close enough to retain important ties, Tony and Anne built a good life in Cleveland.

16

Their relationship flourished. In the soil of their commitment to the marriage, they gradually rebuilt the structure of their life together. Tony was so frightened that he even stopped seeing other women for the longest stretch of sexual fidelity in his life—about a year. Anne regained her trust in him, enabling her to allow him his sexual "fun and games" when they resumed, even though she had no such interests herself. These past ten years had been good to the Rocco family.

But what about now? Tony and Anne are obviously in the midst of another crisis, one that could have even greater ramifications for their future, especially if Tony should decide to leave Anne—or if she should decide to throw him out.

"I don't know what to do," Anne tells me. "Eileen wants Tony to leave me and marry her. I insisted on speaking to her one night when she phoned here for Tony. She's ready to give up everything for him— her job, her apartment, even her child.

"She told me, 'Tony's unhappy with you. If you really loved him, you'd let him go.' I *do* really love him, but I'm not at all sure he's as unhappy as *she* says he is. He *couldn't* have been acting all these years. We're best friends. We can talk about everything with each other, even this. In fact, we've been talking and talking and talking. We've hardly left each other's side all week. We even stayed home from work a couple of days, just to talk.

"I feel we have too much going for both of us for me to give him up now. We've had a lot of fun and been through a lot together over these thirty-one years. When Amy goes to college next year, we'll be alone again. After sacrificing for so many years because of the kids and because of money, now that things are easier for us and we can enjoy life together, I'm not ready to turn all of that over to some other woman. Besides, Tony means so much to me. He's my strength. I would be different without him. I would be wishy-washy, but he stands up for me and he makes me stand up for myself.

"And yes, I'm terrified of being alone. I know I *could* survive on my own, but I don't want to. I'd have to make a whole new start, because I wouldn't stay in this house, this neighborhood. This house means nothing to me without him to share it with. And I like my job, but I don't *love* it. What I really want to do is to work with Tony in his business, to live with him, to love with him, and to have us go on with our life together. Deep down, I think that's what Tony wants, too. And that's why I'm hanging in.

"He's going through his own private hell. He tells me how different he feels when he's with Eileen and how much he loves her. But then he tells me he loves me, too."

At that moment, Tony strides in the door. A big man with a booming voice and bulging muscles, he fills the room. He seems too big for this one-story house, towering over his tiny, delicate-boned wife and dwarfing everything around him.

There are just the three of us for dinner. The three older children are already out on their own, and Amy is spending Christmas week in Florida with a friend. As we sit down to a dinner of Anne's version of her mother-in-law's famous lasagna, I expect only small talk until I speak with Tony after dinner. Instead, both of them speak openly and unselfconsciously to me about their dilemma.

Tony's first words to me at the dinner table are a shamefaced "I guess Anne told you what a mess I've gotten us into." At that point he looks not so much like a middle-aged grandfather as like a penitent seven-year-old caught with his hand in the cookie jar.

After Anne leaves, I sit at the kitchen table while Tony loads the dishwasher, cleans up, and then joins me over more coffee, which he made. At dinner they joked about his newfound domesticity.

"You know, I never thought this would happen to me," he says ruefully. "I never believed that two people are mated for life and that neither should ever have any other sexual activity. Sex for me has always been enjoyable, and with everybody besides Anne it's been just fun and games, and I could always keep it that way. Until Eileen. There's something special about her that made me fall in love with her. And now here I am. I can't give her up and yet I still love Anne. I don't know what to do. I hate the idea of what I'm putting both of them through. I'd kill anyone else if he did to either of these women what I'm doing."

As Tony talks, I can see his confusion. Loving Anne as the best friend whom he can talk to about anything—even about Eileen; as the mother of his children, as the woman who often looks after him like a mother, and also as the woman who still turns him on sexually. But then there's Eileen. Ten years younger, voluptuously round in contrast to Anne's doll-like delicacy. Different not only from Anne, but from all those other women—the

18

hundreds whom Tony has bedded over the past thirty years. Exciting to him in innumerable ways that he tries to capture for me.

"It's not so much *what* we do when we make love. There are just so many things you can do in bed with one other person, and I guess I've done with other women just about everything I've done with Eileen. But with her it's very different. A big part of it is the feedback I get from her. The way she cries out, the way she looks at me while we make love instead of just lying there with her eyes closed. We can look at each other and our glances touch and we smile at each other and I feel like I'm in heaven.

"She shows me how much she loves whatever we do. It's like—with oral sex. I've had a lot of women go down on me and it's always great. Most of the time I have the feeling that they're doing it as a favor to me, because they think I'll like it, and that's okay as long as they don't act like they're disgusted. But when Eileen takes my penis in her mouth, it's like she's doing it because this is the one thing she wants to do more than anything else in the world, that this is her great joy in life, that I'm granting her a special favor to *let* her do it. I know this because the same thing happens with me. When I eat her, that's how I feel.

"But this is just part of it. Sex for me used to be very different. It was a boost at having someone respond to me, to feel that I was in control, I was running things. The thrill of the chase. Like making that sale, getting that big contract. The ego stroking was a big part of it. But with Eileen I don't need that because I know she loves me and I don't need to prove anything. So I can just let myself feel. And I can sense what she's feeling. So it's a whole different ballgame from any sex I ever knew before. And as much as I try to get this with Anne—and I do try because I do love her and I don't want to give up all that we have together—I can't get to that same point. This is what I can't give up about Eileen. So I don't know what to do."

As I leave the Roccos' house that evening, I don't know which door Tony will open—the one to the lady or the other one, to the tiger. I feel that I've been privy to a classic crisis in these times, the midlife affair that has the power to turn at least three lives upside down and to spread outward to affect lives on the peripheries of all the principals. I am to learn eventually which door Tony opened—but more about that later.

The more I learned about Tony and Anne, and the more I delved into the issue of sexual turning points throughout life, the more I realized how these two people's lives epitomize the importance of such pivotal events. From Tony's early interest in sex, which led to his first intercourse at age thirteen, through Anne's unplanned pregnancy that led to their marriage at eighteen (a typical time of transition, often tied in with moving out of the parental home), to Tony's first infidelity toward the end of that pregnancy (a not unusual reaction to pregnancy), to the timing of both his involvements with Eileen—the first at thirty-nine and the second at forty-nine—to Anne's increasing assertiveness associated with her job success and with a common midlife shift in personality characteristics between men and women, to the surprising (even to them) route that Tony and Anne took to save their marriage right after their fiftieth birthdays, these two people lived through many of the turning points we'll look at in the chapters to come.

As we examine these turning points—the universal ones that almost all of us experience and the idiosyncratic ones that only some of us undergo—we'll see how our experience of them owes so much to the times we live in, the families we come from, the people we meet, the adventures we have, the people we are. We'll see how sexuality is like a shining thread interwoven throughout the fabric of our lives.

Chapter 1

Sowing and Gleaning: Sexuality Throughout the Life Span

There are particular times in people's lives that are especially significant, but it's the weight the individual gives them that makes them important. One landmark might be of consequence to one individual and not at all to another.

WILLIAM H. MASTERS, M.D.

ALTHOUGH IMMENSE FORESTS have been stripped to print the mountains of words that have been written about sex, there is still a vast unexplored terrain in this perpetually absorbing area of our lives. Our sexuality permeates our lives in a constantly oscillating push-pull, as our sexual development influences virtually every other aspect of our lives and almost every element in our lives influences our sexual development. For most of us, this part of our lives continues to be charged with wonderment and excitement—and agonies, doubts, dilemmas, and colossal confusion. Even in these relatively enlightened days, in a society so eroticized that sex permeates our public as well as our private lives, few of us have gotten our sexual act together.

The sexual revolution that plunged our society into ferment over the past couple of decades did not fulfill the promise many of us expected of it. It brought sexual freedom but failed to bring the sexual happiness many of us had assumed would come with that freedom. True, it did vanquish some of the repressive moralistic despotism that had been keeping people from the normal, healthy expression of their sexuality.

At the same time, however, it imposed its own rules, which in their militant insistence on "free" expression substituted new pressures. The very insistence on hypersexuality may be largely to blame for the hyposexuality so many sex therapists are seeing these days, as lack of desire has soared to the top of the therapeutic charts as the nation's number one sexual complaint. Furthermore, the demolition over so short a period of time of so many long-held taboos has left many people adrift in sexual anarchy.

As long as the revolution focused only on genital sexuality it was destined to fail, because the sex act does not deal with the most problematic realm of sexuality, the relationship. Most sex is still, as it has always been, firmly embedded in a bond between two people. And since there are no easy answers for achieving the idyllic attachment, there will never be easy answers for all our questions about sex. Often we don't even know what questions to ask.

We wonder what good sex is and whether we're having the best. We wonder what it means to be a good lover and whether we're considered one. We wonder whether we want sex too much or too little and engage in it too often or too seldom. We wonder what's normal and what's abnormal and where we fit in.

Until fairly recently, most students of human nature thought of growth and development as phenomena that exist during childhood and that stop abruptly at the end of adolescence. According to this view, sexual development will have ground to a halt at just about the time most people have barely begun to express themselves as sexual beings. The truth, as wise people throughout history have always known and as the academic and research communities have finally recognized, is that virtually every kind of human growth (except, of course, for a few physiological markers) takes place throughout the entire life span. As long as we live, we are in the process of becoming something other than what we were.

Thanks to a number of recent studies of development in adulthood, we now accept the notion that there are certain predictable patterns in our development throughout life. Such patterns, highlighted by specific experiences and decisions, are especially significant in charting our sexual development. The psychoanalyst Erik H. Erikson, in delineating eight major crises in development throughout life, maintained that growth comes only from the resolution of these crises. This seems to hold true for sexual flowering as well as for evolution in other spheres of our life. For just as we have certain physical and intellectual goals that are appropriate to different stages in life—such as learning to walk and read and empathize with other people—each period throughout the life cycle has its own program of sexual goals as well.

In connection with our attempts to achieve these goals, we often come to a turning point—an event or experience that has a pivotal impact on our sexuality. It marks a place at which we turn ourselves around sexually. The way we react at these times determines our attitudes, our feelings, and our actions from that time on. All of us have many such turning points, since our sexual development is so intertwined with every aspect of our lives.

Fortunately, human beings are not automated; no one can prescribe a timetable for the achievement of any task. Nor does the failure of a specific turning point to arise in an individual's life mean that that person is not developing normally. While most of us become concerned if we take part in certain life events much earlier or later than most of the people we know ("What's wrong with me?"), this kind of asynchrony is not necessarily a sign of trouble. If you go through your Age 30 Transition at age twenty-five or thirty-five or forty or never, you may be marching to the music that you alone can hear in the rhythm that you move to best. While it's often helpful to recognize that the patterns in our lives resemble those in the lives of others, it's dangerous to impose these patterns arbitrarily.

Sexual turning points vary, too. Some are universal, while others are as individual as a fingerprint. Even those turning points that are common to many lives all occur differently, in each individual context. Still, despite our differences, the similarities among us construct a common roof that shelters us all. There are definite relationships between our stages in life, in society, and in history as they relate to who we are sexually. Furthermore, everyone alive today has been affected by technological and sociological changes that have vastly altered how we feel and what we do sexually. And always, of course, there is our biology.

Some experiences are universal—and universally seen as significant. There's the first time a girl menstruates and a boy ejaculates, the first time either engages in sexual intercourse, the first time a man and a woman learn they have conceived a child, the first awareness that one's sexual powers are not what they once were. Each of these events has its own special meaning for each person, depending on the context in which it occurs, the manner of its occurrence, and the way the individual views the experience.

As pioneer sex researcher William H. Masters, M.D., told me, "There *are* particular times in people's lives that are especially significant, but it's the weight the individual gives them that makes them important. One landmark might be of consequence to one individual and not at all to another. For example, if the first coital activity is a disaster—if a man ejaculates too rapidly or has trouble maintaining an erection and can't achieve penetration—this individual will give a great deal of importance to this landmark. For another, the first time he goes outside the marriage might be more important."

So for Tony Rocco, his first foray into sexual intercourse, in the closet of his eighth-grade classroom with a girl he hardly knew and didn't care about, was not nearly so significant as the events that occurred during his adulthood, which shook the very foundations of his life. For Robin, whom we'll meet in the chapter on adolescence, her first sexual intercourse—at almost the same age—had far-reaching ramifications.

It's easier to see the distinctive *individual* nature of salient turning points when we look at those that are influenced by cultural standards rather than physical ones: the first date, moving in with a lover, the wedding day, an extramarital affair, a divorce, the public avowal of homosexuality, adjusting to being deprived of a sexual partner after widowhood.

The way we enter into each of these events and the way we react to them are apt to be different for those of us living in the 1980s from the way it was for people who lived in earlier times. It's also vastly different for people in a volatile, individualistic Western society from the way it is for those in a stable, tradition-governed tribal one on the other side of the world.

This book will limit itself to looking at such turning points as they're experienced by people who are living in the decade of the 1980s in the United States. Some of the stories in the cameo roles acted by this cast of "sexual actors" re-create events that took place more than half a cen-

24

tury ago; others were still being written even as they were being narrated to me. In all cases, the people who related them were very much alive in this decade and often able to recognize the impact of early events upon the course their lives followed afterward.

While some of these sexual turning points commonly take place at certain times in life, when the challenge of specific sexual goals almost demands their occurrence, we continually need to remind ourselves that the sexual goals described for each life stage are not prescriptions but descriptions. Not how things have to be but how they often are.

This book is organized chronologically, from the buoyant hopefulness of the cradle to the final resignation of the grave. While the sexual goals don't always fit neatly into age frames, they do tend to find their psychological levels in the life span, and so I've described them in the time periods in which they're most likely to occur. Since many other books about sexual development have focused primarily on the first fifteen or twenty years of life, this book will cover only the highlights of these ages and report new findings and new perspectives. The bulk of the book is about adulthood.

"The entire universe is our potential erotic turn-on," says the Reverend William R. Stayton, assistant professor of psychiatry and human behavior at Thomas Jefferson Medical College in Philadelphia, whose evangelical mission is to achieve the acceptance of sex as the most positive life-giving force in the world. "We are commonly aroused by spiritual experiences, autoerotic ones, and experiences with nature, animals, and inanimate objects. Yet we live in a world that believes sex is a negative force and that devotes a tremendous amount of energy to repressing it. Restricting sexual expression is one of the most powerful controls exerted by religions, culture, and government.

"Instead of asking, 'What causes homosexuality' or 'What causes heterosexuality,' or some such, we should instead ask, 'What keeps us from being sexual in all the dimensions of our life?' "

This question is the key, for our sexuality is elemental, one of the capabilities that differentiates us from other mammals. The outspoken sex educator Mary S. Calderone, M.D., describes the three intrinsically human attributes as "mind (including communication and reasoning powers), body (upright posture and appositional thumbs and

25

fingers), and sexuality (our mating is not governed by the length of the day, or by our state of nutrition, or by seasonal changes but is at all times elective, no matter that the bases for such election vary among individuals).''

Our upright posture displays our sexual signals—such as the female's breasts and her distinctive rounded contours, the male's penis and his distinctive triangular physique. The way our hands are constructed makes them sensitive participants in our sexual encounters, as we use them to caress, to arouse, to intimately sense our partner. And our intellectual powers play such a large role in our sexual lives that it has become a truism to say that the most erogenous organ in the human body is the brain. The British man of letters Malcolm Muggeridge is reputed to have said, ''Throughout the Western World, we have all got sex on the brain, which apart from any other consideration, is a most unseemly place to have it.'' Not unseemly at all. We become sexually aroused by our thoughts, by the meanings we give to situations and people, by the associations we form throughout life. The reverse is also true, that our thoughts respond to our sexual experiences in ways that radiate outward to every corner of our lives.

This, then, is what emerges from these pages—the powerful rhythms of sexuality as it sets the patterns for our lives and is in turn affected by the other chords we play. Throughout our days on earth our lives encompass many melodies—needs for survival, for safety, for love, for achievement, for self-fulfillment. Many of these are fulfilled through pursuits that are on their face nonsexual but that owe their power to that sexual life force within.

Here are some of the questions I'll be raising and seeking answers for throughout this volume:

- How have advances in birth control, such as the Pill, vasectomy, and improved abortion methods, affected the sexual expression of both the married and the unmarried?
- How has the trend toward more casual sexual activity affected marriage? Do people who engage regularly in ''recreational'' sex devoid of emotional commitment get it out of their system and then remain more content in monogamous marriages? Or have they set up patterns of sex with multiple

26

partners that they will carry with them through life? Are they
now committed to promiscuity?

- Why, in our sex-oriented culture, when the motto often
seems to be "If it feels good, do it" and the widely heralded
sexual revolution has plucked our inhibitions from us, is today's most common sexual problem a lack of desire?

- What is the truth about homosexuality? Is it a normal variation of sexuality? Or is it pathology? Are homosexuals born
or made? Do their sexual development patterns parallel
those of heterosexuals? How are they similar—and how are
they different?

- Are people meant to be monogamous? Or is that a restriction
that goes as counter to basic human needs as Prohibition
did? Is there really a "seven-year itch" or is that just folk-
lore?

- What happens in sexually open marriages in which both
partners have the agreed-upon freedom to have relations
with others? Do they last as long as monogamous unions (or
ostensibly monogamous unions in which one partner is having a plain, old-fashioned secret affair)? Do they remain
open, or is openness a developmental stage in these marriages?

- How does parenthood affect sexuality? What are the consequences of pregnancy and the presence of small children?
What are the implications of the inability to conceive? What
happens when the presence of teenage children reminds parents of their own sexual awakening? How is a couple's relationship affected by the emptying of the nest?

- What are the special problems of newly single adults? Especially when they are now parents? Should they keep their
sexual involvements a secret from their children? How are
they affected by their choice of openness or privacy?

- How does sexuality contribute to the midlife crisis—and how
is it affected by it?

- What role do sexual attitudes and activities play in determin-
ing whether old age will be a fulfilling or a depressing time of
life?

As we explore the interplay between sexuality and the wide canvas of our lives, on which so many events are painted, we'll look at the influence of the times we live in, the culture we live with, the people we encounter. We'll examine some of those turning points that are universally perceived and some of the ones more idiosyncratically affected by our social and sexual mores.

You won't find instructions or suggestions for the sexually "right" way to be. For the one truth that has emerged from my explorations into sexuality is that there is no right way. There are many ways to express this vital life force—including the asexual choice that looks like a refusal of expression but which may have deeper, important meanings to the individual who chooses celibacy. While monogamy and fidelity may express for one person the ultimate in sexual fulfillment, another may achieve a new level of relatedness through joining with many partners.

Each of us must draw up our own moral universe, but we are on dangerous ground when we attempt to tell others how to live. Their lives are not ours, their histories are not ours, their feelings are not ours. Yes, there *are* some basic, universal, absolute criteria for sexual morality that most reasonable people could agree on: Don't force or coerce anyone into doing anything, don't take advantage of someone more naïve or more vulnerable than you, and don't mislead your partner. Beyond these basic tenets, however, I believe it's up to each of us to draw up whatever other moral codes apply to us. Only after a careful consideration of the multiplicity of options available in a pluralistic society and of the values we hold important and intend to live by, can we make those choices appropriate to the goals we'll address throughout life.

Chapter 2

The Sensual Seedling: Infancy and Childhood

Whenever I get angry with my parents for something I feel I didn't get from them, I have to shake myself a little and remind myself of some of the really important gifts they did give me. . . . Probably the greatest gift was an easy comfortableness with my body.

—STEPHANIE

"MY EARLIEST MEMORY is one that in retrospect feels very sexual, but of course at the time I didn't know that. I couldn't have been more than two or two and a half, because I was still in my crib, and I went into a big bed when I was three. I remember having a white sheet over me, on a warm summer day, and hearing the voices of my parents' guests coming into the house. The sexual feeling is that there was something warm and all-engulfing and there was a bright light. As that little tiny child, I felt very connected to everyone and everything around me and very much inside the radiance of that light."

Juliana, the thirty-four-year-old woman who shared this recollection with me, remembers more than most of us do about our very early sexual feelings and experiences. Perhaps this is because the beauty of that cherished moment was so outweighed later in her life by the seductive father who exploited Juliana's innocence that she needs to hold on to what she sees as the real truth of her sexuality, that infant ecstasy. Another early memory of Juliana's is of her grandmother playing with her sexually.

"She would stroke me and rub my back and do other physical things that were arousing to me, including fondling my genitals. But at other times, when I would wrestle with my father, she would start a whole ruckus about him doing sexual things to me. I loved fooling around with my father when I was little, and the first time she said that, I remember being so stunned it was like someone hit me over the head. I didn't know what she was talking about. But it raised a question in my head: Can I trust my father or not? Later on, just before I got into my teens, my father did get very seductive with me. So maybe my grandmother saw something even then that nobody else in the family was aware of. Or maybe it was just that she saw sexuality in everything."

Everyone knows that we are sexual beings from the very beginnings of life. Even those people who express the greatest horror at any "contamination of the innocents" know this. Otherwise, why would they be so afraid that children could be induced to have "impure" thoughts or to engage in such sexually satisfying activities as masturbation?

The popular wisdom is that Sigmund Freud discovered infantile sexuality. However, mothers and grandmothers were fondling infants' genitals to quiet their crying hundreds of years before Freud's birth, as we know from pre-Renaissance art and from the reports of anthropologists. Such practices are still common among some peoples around the world.

It takes a concentrated effort at repression to deny what anyone who spends a great deal of time around babies must see—that when babies of either sex are allowed to remain unclothed, they discover their genitals and learn how pleasurable it can be to handle these parts of their anatomy. Even before birth, as we have learned from ultrasound photographs of a fetus only twenty-nine weeks old, baby boys have cyclic erections, and after birth they have them regularly, both asleep and awake. Newborn baby girls lubricate vaginally.

Still, we don't know what sexuality means to babies. They don't have the vocabulary to describe their feelings even to themselves. By the time they get the words, most will have repressed and then forgotten the sensations, even if they had been sufficiently aware of them at the time. And despite Freud's great contribution—for which he was publicly vilified as a "purveyor of filth"—in insisting on the fact of infantile sexuality, no one has yet made systematic observations of children's sexual behavior. This is understandable, because of the difficulties and the ethical dilemmas such an undertaking would present, but it's also regrettable, because it leaves us with a molehill of knowledge and with mountains of theorizing.

What *do* we know? We know that these early years are crucial for the development of healthy sexual attitudes and values. During the first few years of life, children need to become aware of themselves as sexual beings and to become comfortable with the sexuality that is an intrinsic part of their personalities, their very nature. They need to feel good about their bodies, to appreciate their beauty and the pleasure they can give them. Babies are born needing to be touched in warm, sensual ways by a loving caretaker. Masturbation and early sex play with other children are both common and normal ways to develop this pride and pleasure in themselves; the feelings a child develops about these activities reach far into the future of the adult the child will become.

Children need to develop healthy sexual attitudes if they are to feel comfortable within their own gender identity. This sense of comfort may well determine whether a child will act in appropriate male or female patterns and how that child will feel about his or her total self. Children learn these differences between themselves and others by exploring their own bodies and by seeing those of other children and of adults. They develop a sense of what sexuality means, of its relationship to love, to conception, to pleasure. And they learn their culture's standards for sexual behavior.

If these early sexual goals are not fulfilled in a healthy, satisfying way, we continue throughout life to try to make up for any interference with our healthy sexual development. For most of us growing up in twentieth-century America, our sexual development has been hindered by ignorance, naïveté, and embarrassment that get passed down from generation to generation. For some who are even more unfortunate, development is further distorted because of such childhood traumas as molestation or incest. Such events leave scars that people may spend the rest of their lives trying to obliterate.

Since childhood sexual development is covered extensively in other books, especially those for parents, and since the major focus of this book is on sexual turning points in the adult years, we'll touch only upon those facts and issues that are either new or of such importance in

31

understanding sexual development that they have to be here. Definitely in this category are the theories of Sigmund Freud, the Viennese physician who first conceptualized sexual development as a series of turning points from one stage to another.

While Freud did not discover infantile sexuality, he set it into a theoretical framework that emphasized its importance in the development of personality. Many of Freud's theories were—and continue to be—controversial, and the most controversial of all has been his viewpoint on sexuality. No other concept of his has ever given rise to the political, personal, and ideological attacks on the man as has his insistence on the sexual drive as the primary motivating force for behavior throughout life, starting in infancy.

There may be some truth to charges that Freud overemphasized sex by attributing to it the motivation for virtually all human behavior. Still, no one else has ever had the impact that he had in forcing us to recognize the vast importance of our sexuality and the way it permeates and is itself affected by every other aspect of our lives. In the tightly repressed Victorian world in which he lived and worked, Freud dared to emphasize the vital role of sex.

Freud acknowledged sexuality as the major force in his global view of personality, which he saw as being made up of three different parts—the id, the ego, and the superego—whose development is intricately bound with sexual maturation.

The id, present at birth, consists of the life instincts that direct all human behavior—hunger, thirst, and sex, all fueled by a form of energy called the libido. The id operates on the "pleasure principle," which demands immediate gratification: "I want it—and I want it NOW!" When the infant realizes that she will not always get what she wants when she wants it, and that she may never get it unless she figures out a way, the ego develops. This part of the personality operates on the "reality principle," by which a person works out a plan and then takes action to test the plan to see whether it's likely to work.

The last part of the personality to develop is the superego, which appears in early childhood and operates by what we could call the "perfection principle." The child aspires to be perfect—to embody all the ideal moral values that society instills, first through parents and then from other cultural institutions. The superego is the conscience, the moral taskmaster. It tries to prevent the id from acting out its impulses, especially the sexual and aggressive ones, and tries to divert the ego from its emphasis on how something *can* be done to a consideration of whether the act *should* be done. It does this through a carrot-and-stick approach: the carrot is the good feeling we get when we feel we're doing the right thing and will get approval for it; the stick is the guilt we know we'll feel if we go against our own standards.

Freud maintained that these three constantly warring factions of personality develop separately, through five stages—oral, anal, phallic, latency, and genital—which begin in infancy. People whose needs are not met at any one stage or who are, at the other extreme, overindulged in a certain stage may become fixated, with lifelong effects on their personalities.

In the oral stage, the baby's erogenous zone is the mouth: the sensual pleasures of eating, sucking, and biting. In the anal stage, the child recognizes the pleasure he gets from moving his bowels and from having control over his body. The phallic stage begins when the child feels pleasure in the genital region and lasts from about age three to six. This is the time of the Oedipus complex, a psychic conflict in which a little boy lavishes love and affection on his mother and thus competes with his father for the mother's love and affection, and the Electra complex, in which a little girl desires her father, fears her mother, represses those feelings, and eventually identifies with her mother.

Freud called the years from six to puberty the latency stage, considering this a time when children are relatively uninterested in sex. In fact, during these years children do continue to engage in sex play, masturbate, ask sexual questions. As Calderone and Johnson write, however, in *The Family Book About Sexuality,* by this time children "have learned that the grown-up world does not approve of children's sexuality, and so they hide it. There is general agreement among psychological researchers and theorists today that the latency period described by Freud simply does not exist." The last Freudian stage is the genital, which lasts from puberty on, marking mature sexuality by the forging of heterosexual relationships outside the family.

Since it's impossible to discuss in a few pages the complex theories that took Freud volumes to express and that have taken other volumes to refute, we'll concentrate on what Freud considered to be the most crucial turning point in childhood, the resolution of the Oedipus and Electra complexes.

"Freud reduced everything to the Oedipus complex, the notion that adults become neurotic because as little three-year-olds they wanted to get into bed with Mommy, have sex with Mommy and kill Daddy," New York psychoanalyst David Tribich told me. "I don't deny that when we grow up we may color our reminiscences with feelings of this sort, but I don't think this is the child's nature. I think if the child actually feels this, it's because of pathological dynamics going on in the family. If the child does want to sleep with Mommy, it comes from Mommy. Mommy is the one who sends off seductive signals. When I say Freud had it backward, I think the Oedipus complex, if you want to call it that, exists in the adult set.

"There's no question about the amount of incest that does go on—more prominently between father and daughter than between mother and son. Freud was faced with abundant evidence of the sexual seduction of young girls by their fathers, but he had great difficulties coming to grips with the fact that adults have sexual feelings for children."

The recent decision by Freud's heirs to publish many of his letters and other documents that had been withheld up till now sheds new light on his thinking about this early sexual crisis—and raises questions about the influence his own family played in the development of his theories. One speculation is that Freud ignored the role parents played in creating their children's emotional problems and insisted on blaming the children themselves because he detected neurotic symptoms in his brothers and sisters and would then have had to blame his own father for having been seductive.

Whether or not the Oedipus complex is the definitive turning point that Freud maintained it was, his impact on our thinking about infantile sexuality continues to be profound. Both followers and critics alike agree that what happens in early childhood is extremely important for healthy personality development, including, of course, sexuality.

"Childhood is our first view of what the world is like," says Dr. Tribich, speaking earnestly not only as a professional psychoanalyst but also as the conscientious father of two small children. "If you have unloving parents, you're going to be unloving yourself and have a hard time finding love in the world.

34

"If you have bad relationships early on, it's going to be very hard to find good relationships later on in life. If you feel unlovable, you may turn a good relationship into a bad relationship because you can't tolerate the intimacy or for any one of a number of reasons. But I do think that later on is definitely important, too. It's not childhood or nothing. Even if you're very badly wounded from your early relationships, I think you can have a good relationship later on."

This optimistic attitude holds out hope to untold numbers who suffered sensual deprivation in infancy, a deprivation that goes against the basic laws of nature. One such deprivation is the lack of the vital warmth of physical contact, first known by most people in the loving touch of nurturing parents. This touch initiates the lucky among us as sensual, sexual beings, and its absence stunts the sexual development of the less fortunate.

"I don't ever remember my parents touching me when they didn't absolutely have to," Robert, a fifty-two-year-old social worker, tells me. "I don't ever remember seeing them touch each other, either. I guess it's possible that when I was a baby they played with me the way any normal parents would play with a baby. But I don't know. I had younger brothers and I don't remember the kind of closeness I'm talking about going on with them, either. There was a stiff, arm's-length quality to life in our house. Even a handshake was a big deal.

"At first I just thought that this was how all families were, but then when I would go to my friends' houses I would see how differently other people lived. But I still didn't realize how affected I was by this hands-off atmosphere I grew up in. It took a failed marriage and a rotten relationship with my own children to realize how much I missed, how much I was furious about, and how much work I had to do just to be a normal human being."

Robert's painful memories, which still intrude themselves into his continuing struggle to overcome the climate he grew up in, attest to the void in people's lives when that vital experience of a loving touch is absent. Babies need to be touched and held as much as they need to be fed, and when they are deprived of this vital nurturing care, the consequences can be grave. Research done in the 1940s by psychiatrist René Spitz found that babies and small children who spend a great deal of time in a hospital or other institution where staff workers didn't make a special effort to provide a lot of touching and holding developed abnormal behavior like head banging or rocking movements.

Spitz compared children being reared at home with babies who were being cared for in two different institutions. At the end of the first year, the home-reared children and the babies in one of the institutions (called "Nursery") were normal, healthy babies. In stark contrast were the babies in the other institution ("Foundling Home"), who were undersized and underweight and much more likely to get sick, and sometimes even to die. Furthermore, the intelligence levels of the Foundling Home babies, which had started out at an above-normal average of 124, sank to 75 by the end of the first year and plummeted to 45 by the end of the second.

On the face of it, you would expect the babies from Foundling Home to have done better, since they came from a variety of backgrounds, some very favorable, while the backgrounds of the babies in Nursery were mostly "disadvantaged." They were the children of delinquent girls, many of whom were retarded or emotionally disturbed. Why, then, did these babies thrive more than the others?

The answer seems to lie in the kind of personal attention the babies got. The ones in Nursery were cared for by their own mothers or individual full-time mother substitutes, while in Foundling Home one nurse had to care for eight babies. There just doesn't seem to be any substitute for picking up babies, holding them close, crooning to them, and letting them sense physically the love that flows from another human being.

Institutionalized babies are not, of course, the only people who suffer from what University of Massachusetts educator Dr. Sidney B. Simon calls "skin hunger." There are all those people who live in cold, distant families, who suffer from the same kind of emotional starvation. The hunger for contact with another person through touching and being touched drives some people to sexual promiscuity, renders others unable to form sexual relationships, and reverberates into every aspect of their lives.

It's just as important to meet children's needs to be touched as it is to meet their needs for food and shelter. This is so not only for healthy sexual development but for healthy development in other areas as well.

For example, people who experience an abundance of physical pleasure tend to be less prone to violence, thus demonstrating a vital link between sexuality and other aspects of life. James W. Prescott, a neuropsychologist with the National Institute of Child Health and Human Development, compared forty-nine different cultures and found that those societies that lavish the most physical affection on their infants have less theft and violence among adults. This stands to reason, as Dr. Prescott points out when he says, "The hypothesis that physical pleasure actively inhibits physical violence can be appreciated from our own sexual experiences. How many of us feel like assaulting someone after we have just experienced orgasm?"

While Robert was never beaten as a child, he is still struggling to overcome emotional abuse. "My father was a sadistic man who never missed a chance to tell me that I'd never amount to anything and who put me down for everything I did," Robert remembers. "Now I wonder how much of his anger was linked to what I'm sure was an extremely repressed sex life. He squelched any display of spontaneity in my mother. If she would walk around the house in her underwear or greet him affectionately at the door, he'd make some scathing remark that would absolutely wither her."

The inverse relationship between sexual pleasure and violence, by which the presence of one discourages the other, is dramatically obvious in the research on parents who abuse their children. Dr. Brandt F. Steele and Dr. C. B. Pollock, psychiatrists at the University of Colorado, have studied child abuse in three generations of families. One of their findings was that parents who mistreat their children had been deprived of physical affection during their own childhoods. Furthermore, Steele found that women child abusers were nonorgasmic and the men tended to find sex unsatisfying. These parents were, by and large, perpetuating the same kind of abnormal upbringing they had had themselves. Mistreated or neglected in their own early lives, they were now visiting the sins of *their* fathers and mothers upon their own children.

All of this research confirms one of the most compelling reasons to breastfeed a baby, even now when formula-feeding is convenient, nutritious, and generally safe. *Nothing* can duplicate this first physical joining of two human beings. The breastfed baby of a mother who is nursing because she *wants to*—not because she feels she *should*—gains a unique sense of security. Right from birth, the nursing baby luxuriates in the safe feeling of being held close to the warm, sweet-smelling flesh of its mother's body and associates intimate skin-to-skin contact with the warm sensation of being cared for.

For years psychiatrists have written about the emotional benefits of breastfeeding; in recent years the American Academy of Pediatrics has taken an active stance to promote it; and now more and more parents are showing their commitment to this ancient means of nurture, as breastfeeding rates in the United States and Canada have been soaring in recent years, especially in better-educated, higher-income families. With the right kind of support and encouragement, 95 percent of all women can nurse their babies. If a woman is in the other 5 percent or if she feels uncomfortable with the idea of nursing, her baby can still, of course, grow up to be a healthy, psychologically secure, sexually well-adjusted individual—*if* both mother and father hold the baby lovingly during feedings, *if* they resist temptations to prop the bottle no matter how busy they are, and *if* they offer many chances for the baby's un-clothed body to touch the parents' bare flesh.

"I made my first communion when I was seven and after that I had to go to confession every week," remembers Juliana. "Before we would go, all the little children in my first-grade class would put our heads down on the desk and contemplate about what we had to confess. Meanwhile, the nun would walk around the room and in a melodious voice she would rattle off a list of things that had to be confessed. One was masturbation. I had no idea what it meant, so naturally I never confessed it. A couple of years later I learned how to use a dictionary. I finally figured out how to spell that word and I looked it up. And then I thought, 'Oh, no! You mean I can't do that anymore?' It had been something wonderful for me, but now that I knew it was a sin I knew I had to stop. Also, I knew I would be too embarrassed ever to confess to the priest that I did *that*.

"But I guess I kept doing it, because I worked out a phrase to use in confession—that I 'committed the sin of sex in thought, word, and deed.' The priest always glossed over it and never asked me to go into any detail. So I just kept doing it—and kept on confessing it."

"Infantile masturbation is the child's first behavior that parents recognize as sexual," writes psychoanalyst Warren J. Gadpaille in *The Cycles of Sex.* Usually, therefore, the first time parents find their child masturbating marks the first opportunity they take to show their attitudes toward sexuality and the pleasures of the flesh. This is another turning point in early childhood, when the child gets one of two messages: The body is good and you are supposed to enjoy it; or it is bad and you are supposed to ignore it.

It is an extremely moving experience to hear, as I did not too long ago, an outspoken, courageous, beautiful woman in her seventies speak publicly of one of her most painful childhood memories. Tears came to my eyes as I heard physician Mary Calderone tell of the aluminum mittens her mother had made her wear. "She had found me masturbating, and, convinced that dire harm could come to me from that habit, somehow she got hold of these metal horrors and forced me to wear them to sleep every single night of my life until I was about seven or eight years old."

Later, when we spoke privately, Dr. Calderone told me about some of the devices parents attached to the bodies of their young sons. "There were gadgets that went around the penis, closed the circulation whenever the penis swelled, and then rang a bell in the father's room. We've been very brutal about this. No wonder we have sexual problems!"

While few parents—especially in these relatively enlightened times—take so extreme a position, few openly encourage their children to masturbate. Most typically, parents will either move a child's hands away from the genitals or will pretend not to have seen the act. Their discomfort shows in their tone of voice, their facial expressions, or a stiffness in their own bodies. The child, being exquisitely sensitive to parental cues about what is approved of and what isn't, will learn that masturbation is bad.

Research has shown that babies who get the best care from their mothers are more likely to masturbate before their first birthday than are babies whose mothers have personal problems that interfere with their ability to nurture their children. Furthermore, research has shown that masturbation is not only not harmful, it is good for us. Adults who masturbated before engaging in sexual relations know their own bodies

39

better, learn how to have orgasms, and can then help their partner bring a sexual experience to a mutually satisfying conclusion. Back in 1953, in the landmark study *Sexual Behavior in the Human Female,* Alfred Kinsey and his colleagues pointed out that women who had had orgasms by any means, including masturbation, before marriage were able to reach orgasm in marital sex three times as often as those who had not.

Yet despite the almost universal inclination toward masturbation and the beneficial nature of the practice, almost all the individuals who spoke to me directly confirmed what is in the research literature: that relatively few people have had the kind of body-positive experiences reported to me by Stephanie, a forty-year-old social worker, who gives much of the credit for her vibrancy and comfort with her body to her parents.

"Whenever I get angry with my parents for something I feel I didn't get from them, I have to shake myself a little and remind myself of some of the really important gifts they did give to me, which I know now are rare and precious," she tells me. "Probably the greatest gift was an easy comfortableness with my body.

"When I was a little girl, my mother took me to the country house of a photographer friend of hers who was putting together a book of art photos. My sister and I posed nude, and I remember it as a delicious experience. I have this picture in my mind of the two of us running outside on a grassy place with no clothes on and an immense sense of freedom, with no embarrassment at all." She shows me that beautiful little book celebrating the human body.

"Another way in which this comfort about my body came about was in the way I felt about masturbation," Stephanie continues. "My sister was two years younger, and we shared a bedroom for years. When I was about nine years old, we used to masturbate together. I don't know whether my parents ever saw us or ever said anything, but if so they must have conveyed their approval, or at least their acceptance, because both my sister and I felt very comfortable. Also, I think that the fact that we were *both* doing it made it okay.

"The fact that I had enjoyed and felt comfortable about masturbating helped me stay a virgin until I got married—and then helped me have a terrific sexual relationship with my husband. I could tell him—I

40

could *show* him, for example, that rubbing round and round my clitoris made me go up the wall. And then he was free to tell me how he liked me to stroke his penis. This kind of openness led to all kinds of goodies for us both.''

Learning to masturbate is often a major sexual turning point in a person's life—his or her discovery of the pleasures the body can yield. If this discovery is followed by a sense that these pleasures are wrong, an ambivalence about sexuality arises that can dominate a person's entire life. What happens when children learn principles that they have to unlearn later on to become successfully functioning adults? Says Dr. Gadpaille, who urges parents not to teach children anything they will have to unlearn later, ''Children who are taught that it is bad to pursue sexual pleasure must learn as adults that now sexual pleasure is good—a difficult and sometimes insurmountable task.''

It's clear that we're living in a period of history that could be described as sexually permissive or even ''sex-obsessed,'' depending on your personal attitudes. Medical and psychological views about masturbation have made a complete about-face from what they were a century ago, when professionals in these fields were issuing dire warnings about the evils that would arise from the practice. Today, such respectable organizations as SIECUS (Sex Information and Education Council of the U.S.) are saying publicly that masturbation is good for us. Every well-regarded child-rearing book on the market today communicates the message that parents should accept children's masturbatory practices as a healthy, normal part of growing up. Highly respected professional sex therapists—physicians, psychologists, and educators— incorporate into their practices the teaching of masturbation methods to nonorgasmic adults.

Dagmar O'Connor, a psychologist and director of the sex therapy program at the Outpatient Psychiatric Clinic of Roosevelt Hospital in New York City, told me about the success she's been having with the therapy groups she conducts for women who have never had an orgasm. A key element in the success of these groups, says O'Connor, are the regular homework assignments teaching these women to masturbate. The first woman sex therapist in New York, she had been trained in St. Louis by sex therapists William H. Masters and Virginia Johnson to treat couples. She soon realized, however, that women who had

41

never had orgasms needed to deal with their own bodies first before they were ready to include a partner. So she began to conduct groups for women only. "These women need to know they have permission to masturbate—and permission to have an orgasm. The group—and I—give them that permission."

, By the end of treatment, more than 90 percent of the women have reached the first orgasm of their lives, through masturbation, and many then go on to be orgasmic with a partner. Most sex therapists maintain that people who have learned about their bodies through pleasuring themselves enjoy sex more as adults and are better sex partners.

And yet one major link between contemporary attitudes and behavior has not yet been made. No one—not the most progressive sex educators or therapists, not even the courageous Mary Calderone—is suggesting that parents teach their children how to masturbate. Dr. Calderone, probably the most outspoken advocate of masturbation in the country, maintains that it isn't necessary—that all normal children will find ways to give themselves sexual pleasure and that all parents have to do is not spoil it for them. She urges parents to acknowledge clearly and positively the pleasure children get from self-stimulation. She suggests that parents let their babies spend time naked, that they smile and show approval when children explore their bodies (instead of trying to distract them or ignore the activity), and that they teach their children to bathe themselves with the soap in their hands rather than with a washcloth. Parents can let their children know that it's good to touch themselves, while also getting across basic socialization— decorum: that this is something to be done in private; and safety: that they should never insert any object into the vagina or rectum—just as they should never put foreign objects into mouth, ears, nose, or any other body part.

This approach, however, waits for the child to take the first step, showing a reticence seen in few other aspects of modern child-rearing advice. What if a parent never sees a child exploring his or her body? Generally, when parents think something is important for their children to learn, they themselves take the initiative. If masturbation is indeed as important a preparatory activity for fully realized sexuality as most contemporary sex therapists maintain, why should we wait until people have gone through adolescence and young or even middle adulthood before teaching them how to do it?

This question is especially important in view of the many people who have learned to masturbate in "dead-end" ways that don't lead to smooth transitions to lovemaking with a partner. Most men stimulate themselves in a way that resembles the kind of stimulation experienced in intercourse—by encircling the penis with the hand and stroking up and down. Others, however, use techniques that touch only the glans or provide a kind of touch absent in intercourse. As a result, they cannot climax in coitus. For many men, the goal of masturbation is to reach orgasm as soon as possible, reminiscent of the "circle jerk" that many teenagers engage in, competing to see who can ejaculate the first and the farthest. Kinsey found that most men climax within a minute or two after starting to touch themselves and that some need only ten to twenty seconds of self-stimulation before they ejaculate.

Sex therapist Dr. Bernie Zilbergeld points out that this approach tends to carry over into lovemaking, leading a man to hurtle toward orgasm, when more prolonged activity would be more satisfying and more sensual for both partners. If boys learn at an early age that the real winner in masturbation is the one who delays ejaculation as long as possible, the prize will eventually go both to them and their partners.

Some women, on the other hand, masturbate with objects they can't very conveniently bring into bed with their lovers—faucets or shower sprays or the armrests of chairs. If they had learned how to give themselves pleasure with their hands, they could then teach their partners what kinds of movements arouse them the most, a shared knowledge that would enhance both partners' lovemaking.

If masturbation is as normal and healthy as the research seems to indicate, why should we feel that we're doing our duty as parents by reacting instead of acting? By waiting until we see our children doing it and then giving an appropriate response? Why don't we openly encourage and teach our children how to masturbate, the way we encourage and teach them how to do other things we think they should learn, like swimming, reading, riding a bicycle, and using graceful table manners?

Contemporary sex therapists appear unanimous in their conviction that there's nothing harmful about masturbation, but it's not hard to understand why no one has come out urging parents to teach their children how to do it. This *is* a sensitive area fraught with troubling questions that even the professionals don't yet have answers for. First of all, research has shown that most adults in our society experience more anxiety in talking about masturbation than any other apsect of sexuality. Furthermore, even those of us who have come to accept it as healthy and good still wouldn't know how to go about teaching this essentially private activity. If we demonstrated on our own bodies, wouldn't this be seductive (as well as embarrassing)? If we guided our children's hands, wouldn't that be intrusive (and border on abuse)? If we used diagrams or anatomically correct dolls, wouldn't that be didactic (and take the fun out of the whole enterprise)?

Most parents, of course, do not exploit their children sexually, even though they have unlimited opportunities to do so while bathing them, undressing them, putting them to bed, even just watching TV with them. Most parents do have their children's best interests at heart. They want to do what's best for their children. Chances are, then, that, with a little encouragement and help from sex educators, parents could give their children guidelines for healthy self-pleasuring as effectively as they carry out other parental responsibilities. If done in the right spirit—to emphasize the naturalness of the pleasure we can get from our own bodies—there's no reason why such teaching need be any more seductive, intrusive, or didactic than any of the other guidance that parents offer.

It seems that it's about time for some forward-thinking professionals in the field to disseminate the research findings about the desirability of early masturbation to help parents prevent the problems that arise from inhibitions against any self-stimulation at all, or from the development of techniques that interfere with normal sexual development rather than enhance it.

It's ironic that most parents tell their small children about baby-making, which they probably won't be doing for another twenty years and won't need to know about for at least another ten, but very few tell them anything about the kind of self-pleasuring they could be—or are already—doing right now.

"Both my mother and father were very comfortable about their own bodies," Marcy, fifty, told me. "I could walk into my mother's room and if she was there naked, that would be all right—she wouldn't scurry to cover herself. I first learned about menstruation when I was about five years old, and I saw my mother get dressed, standing in front of her closet with a piece of absorbent cotton stuck between her legs.

"In the mornings, my father and I would share the bathroom. He had no sense of embarrassment about being naked, or urinating, or having a bowel movement when I was in the room. And I didn't, either, about doing the same things when he was there. And my mother would walk in and out constantly. There was no seductiveness, only a very easy naturalness. I was surprised when I married a man who had never seen his mother undressed and thought it was disgusting to do anything having to do with elimination in front of the person you loved. So my children never had the experience I had had. I think it's too bad."

As children begin to move out of the egocentric stage of life, when they consider themselves the center of the universe, they look around at other people. The first people most children see are their parents, but because many adults are not comfortable with their own bodies or have been cowed by psychoanalytic tenets on the psychic dangers of children seeing their parents' unclothed bodies, many people in Western society have grown up without ever having seen a naked adult.

According to traditional psychoanalytic dogma, children suffer severe emotional trauma from seeing their parents' genitalia, which are so much larger and more impressive that they dwarf the children's own small organs, making the children feel inadequate. In many places around the world, however, adults walk around naked in front of everyone, and children seem to grow up as well or better adjusted sexually than children in more repressive cultures. Apparently, those psychoanalysts who are so concerned about the emotional harm that could ensue from a child's sight of adult genitalia have drawn their conclusions on the basis of persons who were severely troubled to begin with.

In any case, many professionals now disagree with this viewpoint. According to a recent survey, 44 percent of five hundred psychiatrists polled feel that an occasional glimpse of unclothed parents would have little effect on children, 28 percent feel that it's healthy, and only 25 percent feel that the children might be aroused or frightened. The study of sexually well-adjusted adults, even in Western society, reveals many people like Marcy, who, as Dr. Gadpaille points out, "frequently recall the bodily freedom of their parents during their early years as a major source of their comfortable acceptance of their own physical sexuality." He concludes, "Both common sense and authoritative reasoning lead to the conclusion that casual and natural parental nudity is not only harmless but beneficial."

The trouble comes when parents who are self-conscious about their bodies pretend not to be. Turning the home into a nudist colony in which everyone walks around in the altogether won't work if uncomfortable parents are straining hard to throw off old attitudes and teach their children new ones that the parents themselves don't yet have. Parents who try this are bound to be embarrassed and to end up teaching their children just the opposite of what they want them to learn. It's far better for such parents to wear clothes around the house and keep bedroom and bathroom doors closed most of the time, if that's how they feel most comfortable. They can save their major efforts for those occasions when their children come upon them unexpectedly. If at these times they can act so casually that they avoid making a child feel as if she or he has committed a major social blunder or has caught them at some shameful activity by seeing them dressing or bathing, they can communicate the message that while they prefer privacy, still there's nothing shameful or dirty about the naked human body.

Few people remember their first sight of their parents' bodies. Since most people do see them at some time or another during the course of growing up, the fact that they don't remember may mean that it occurred so early or so naturally that it wasn't experienced as a marker event of childhood.

This is generally not so for the early sight and exploration of other children's bodies. Many people hold on to memories, however shadowy, of this early sex play for the rest of their lives. All too often this satisfaction of natural curiosity was contaminated by adults who discovered the children in this perfectly normal activity and imbued them with a sense of guilt, making them feel as if they were bad and as if the human body were a shameful sight.

From the hundred or so interviews I conducted for this book and from reading some 250 pseudonymous sexual autobiographies from college students at the University of Puget Sound in Tacoma, Wash-

46

ington, I identified a common element that runs through so many people's lives that it has become the typical childhood experience. This is the confusion and bewilderment felt by small children when their parents scold or punish them for the almost universal "You show me yours and I'll show you mine" exploration. "I couldn't understand what I had done wrong" is the refrain I kept hearing and reading.

This repressive attitude toward childhood curiosity and sex play has been a prime suspect for the prevalence of sexual dysfunction in our society. Around the world, those cultures that are permissive toward childhood sex play are generally more successful in raising adults who enjoy fulfilling heterosexual relationships and who are relatively free from dysfunction and deviation.

Why are parents so shocked when they come upon their children doing the same thing they probably did themselves as children? Professor Ernest Borneman, an Austrian sex researcher, attributes this shock to a phenomenon he calls "pubertal amnesia," by which young people forget their early sexual experimentation. This forgetting may well come about because of the guilt the parents themselves felt when they were children. And so the pattern persists in a never-ending chain from generation to generation, despite the fact that this kind of "show-and-don't-tell" activity is not at all like adult sexual overtures, but is part of children's search for identity, in which they seek to determine who they are and who they are not.

In our society, few people are as fortunate as four-year-old Kathryn, whose mother, Leslie, called me recently to ask for suggestions on handling the exploratory sex play that was going on between Kathryn and her five-year-old friend, Sean. Kathryn has always run around freely in the nude in her own home, showered with both her parents, and expressed great interest in helping her mother diaper her little brother. There is a comfortable casualness in her home about the human body.

The day before Leslie's call to me, however, she had just become aware of a new activity going on in Kathryn's room. "Sean showed us his wiener!" Kathryn told her mother after Sean went home. Leslie expressed about the same amount of interest she usually shows in Kathryn's other reports, adding only, "You know, some people think that penises and vaginas are private." When Kathryn retorted with "We

47

don't!'' Leslie dropped the subject. Until that evening, when she noticed that Kathryn's vulvar area was bright red.

''Why is your vagina so red?'' she asked. ''Were you touching yourself hard?''

''No,'' Kathryn answered. ''Sean was putting some things from my doctor kit in it.''

Leslie, to her credit, stayed calm, being careful not to impute wicked motives to either Sean or Kathryn, yet saying what had to be said: ''I know you and Sean like to learn about each other's bodies, and that's fine, but you have to be careful. It's dangerous to put things inside any part of yourself—you could hurt yourself badly. Remember when you stuck the knitting needle in your ear and you had to go to the doctor? So don't you put things inside yourself—your ear, your nose, your vagina, anyplace. And don't let anyone else do it, either.

''And always remember that your vagina is part of *your* body. It belongs to you. You don't ever have to let anyone else touch it if you don't want them to. And if anybody ever tries to make you do something you don't want to do, you come and tell me.''

And this wise young mother was asking *me* for advice? Clearly, she had said it all, said it right, and was helping her child develop a healthy attitude toward her body and her sexuality.

In the spring of 1975 I took part in a five-session ''Female Sexuality Awareness Workshop,'' a consciousness-raising seminar for women. Each session opened up with a ''go-around,'' during which each of the seventeen women present shared her experiences about the topic of the evening. I vividly remember the evening when one of the group's co-leaders, Flo Walden, a teacher of courses in human sexuality at a Long Island college, asked each of us what word we used to describe our genitals. What did we say? Several of us used slang words like ''pussy,'' ''sissy,'' or ''cunt.'' One Hispanic woman offered ''cho-cho,'' while a Jewish woman said ''shmootzkie.'' Several of us used the word ''vagina'' to refer to all the female genitalia, including the vulva, labia, and clitoris. Two women said only ''down there,'' and one said, ''I don't call it anything, because I never talk about it.''

After we had all talked about our own and each other's vocabulary, Flo held up her hand. ''What is this?'' she asked in her soft, gentle voice. This time there was unanimity rather than variety. Everyone said, "A hand." "Why is it," Flo asked, "that we all use the same word for this part of our body, but we all use different nicknames for our sexual parts?" Why indeed?

An important turning point in early childhood is the time when children learn about their sexual organs. If they learn words for them as simply and as naturally as they learn the terms for their other body parts, they learn that these parts, too, are perfectly acceptable pieces of physical equipment. If not, they get the unspoken message that there is something wrong with these elements of their bodies. Somehow they don't belong with the rest. By ignoring the sexual parts of children's bodies, parents transmit the signal: "This is something you have to be ashamed of."

Just as the naming of sexual parts can mark a turning point in childhood, that evening at the workshop marked a turning point in my adult life. I realized how negligent I had been in helping my three children negotiate this early linguistic passage in their childhood. I remembered the delight I used to take in playing a naming game with my daughters even before they could talk. As we would sit together—perhaps as I was dressing or toweling them dry—I would ask, "Where is your nose? Your eyes? Your mouth? Your chin? Your belly button? Your hand? Your foot?" They would smile wide grins of self-satisfaction as they pointed to each body part in turn. Never, though, did I ask them, "Where are your nipples? Your vulva? Your clitoris? Your vagina?"

Even if I had posed these questions, my baby girls would not have known what I meant. For I, who considered myself the Perfectly Modern Parent, did not use those words with my little daughters. I didn't use the correct words until the girls were about nine or ten and we had started to talk about menstruation and reproduction. By then, the foundation of their sexual attitudes had been laid.

Unfortunately, most parents are just as tongue-tied as I was. Even today, only eight girls in 100 learn the correct names for the female genitalia in childhood, and most girls learn the right words for the male sex organs sooner than they learn the words for their own. Clearly, something is wrong here.

This, of course, is just one aspect of early sexual learning and just one way children pick up parental and societal attitudes relating to sexually explicit language, and to all the other issues in this chapter. How do the parents feel about nudity, theirs or their children's? What do they communicate, by words or gestures or complete silence, about masturbation? What do children sense of their attitudes toward exploratory sex play with other children?

The single most important bit of early sexual learning, according to most sex educators, may well be the feeling that children get about their parents' relationship with one another. Or, if they live in a single-parent home, their mother's or father's attitudes toward the other parent and the other sex in general. Do children get a sense that men and women like each other? Do they see parents being affectionate together? Kissing and hugging? Cuddling in a chair? Patting each other's behind? Showering together?

Parents are the most influential models of behavior that most children will ever know. While they can, of course, learn ways of relating to people other than the ones they saw played out before the screen of their childhood, the attitudes they became familiar with then become the norms to which all other ways are compared.

It isn't surprising, then, that Robert, who never saw his own parents show affection toward each other, grew up handicapped in his ability to show it to anyone else. It isn't surprising that Robert, painfully shy with the girls and young women he knew in adolescence and early adulthood, did not know how to approach them. It isn't surprising that Robert remained a virgin until the age of twenty-six, when he married a woman as sexually constricted as he was. Nor is it surprising that he suffered from premature ejaculation and a constant feeling of inadequacy through sixteen years of a sexually disastrous marriage. The miracle is the way Robert was able to write a new script for himself and the life he's now leading, as we'll see in Chapter 7.

The abiding effects of childhood sexual traumas are sadly apparent in the life story of Mae, a seventy-seven-year-old former librarian who agreed to speak to me at the urging of Donald, the man she has been in love with for more than fifty years, whom she has seen only during the intervals between his two marriages to other women. Mae herself never married.

When I interviewed Donald the day before, he told me of a recent conversation with Mae. "Do you like to fuck?" she had asked him, and then, to his nod, had said, "I *love* to fuck. I love to fuck more than I love to do anything else in the world—even eat. And I *love* to eat!"

When I first set eyes on Mae, however, I have a hard time believing that this is the person Donald told me about—a sweet little white-haired lady wearing a neat paisley dress. Her washed-out-looking sea-green eyes peer at the world unframed, under almost nonexistent pale eyebrows. She cheerfully takes me out to the redwood deck in the woods behind Donald's house, where we sit under the trees on this Indian summer day in October.

"I don't know what I'm doing talking to you," she says. "I've *never* talked about my love life to anyone but Donald. Not even to my closest friends. But Donald asked me to, so here I am."

I smile and begin the interview the same way I have begun so many. "Are there any experiences in your life that you would consider turning points in your sexual development?" I ask, tape recorder running and pen poised.

"I don't want to talk about it," she says quickly. "There is one in particular, but I never talk about it."

"Okay," I say. "You don't have to talk about anything you don't want to." And I prepare to go on to a more fruitful question. Before I can, Mae's face contorts in pain and her hands fly up to her face.

"Every time I think about it I cry," she says through the trembling hands shading her face. "It happened seventy-two years ago, and it still makes me cry." I want to take her into my arms, but I'm afraid she might consider my touch an intrusion. So I speak soothingly and give her a tissue.

And then, with no prompting from me, her story comes out. The story of a child who had trusted and of an adult who had betrayed that trust. The story of an incident that a little girl couldn't understand, couldn't explain except to think that somehow she had been to blame. The story of an incident that had reverberated throughout her life, making her feel too frightened ever to trust, too defiled ever to marry.

She had been in the kitchen, sitting on her grandfather's lap on an old rocking chair, when this man she adored reached into her underpants and began to stimulate her genitals with his hand. "He must have hurt me or something," Mae says between sobs, "because I

51

struggled to get away from him and I couldn't. I remember that time as always trying to get away. I finally did. I didn't tell my father and mother until about a week later, when I saw him coming around the hill to our house and I started to cry and scream. I told my mother then and she faced him with it and he said he'd never done it. My mother said, 'She's too young to make up anything like that,' and he never did it again—he'd be too afraid of my father. Nobody ever talked about it again, not to me, not to anyone else.

"From that time on, I felt I was contaminated. Maybe if they had talked it out with me to make it clear that it really wasn't my fault, I might have felt differently. But this was more than seventy years ago and people didn't know those things then. I've told it to myself so many times over the years, but it doesn't make any difference. I didn't have any intention of telling you that, but now I'm glad I did because that was probably the most important sexual thing that ever happened to me and the thing that had the biggest influence on my life."

The universality of the incest taboo declares the strength of its temptation (we don't have taboos for activities that don't entice us), and, indeed, current research shows that incest is much more extensive than most of us have dreamed. The American Psychological Association reports that 10 to 13 percent of American women—or some 12 to 15 million individuals—have been victims of incest with an older male relative, ranging from sexual molestation to full sexual relations. About one-quarter of these women have been victimized by their fathers, another quarter by their stepfathers, and the rest of the cases involve brothers, uncles, grandfathers, and other relatives. A recent study reported that one-third of the sexually abused children in one Midwestern mental health center were males. Only one-third of all incidents of child molestation occur at the hands of a stranger; the rest are committed by relatives, neighbors, or people who work with children—teachers, day care workers, scout leaders, clergymen. Furthermore, incest occurs across the entire socioeconomic scale.

In recent years some sexologists have suggested that incest can in some cases offer positive benefits and that any trauma that results is caused by the shocked reactions of those who discover the adult-child sexual episodes and then fill the child with fear, guilt, or shame. However, research conducted with incest victims vigorously contradicts this theory. The emotional fallout from incest persists not only through one lifetime but usually into the lives of the next generation as well.

The most harm seems to come from mother-son relations, while the least arises from those between brothers and sisters. One study in Maryland found that about 80 percent of incest victims judged the long-term effect of the experience as marked or severe, and another in California indicates that about 90 percent suffer from depression and are likely to block out their incestuous memories by such self-destructive means as alcohol, drug abuse, or even suicide. Studies of prostitutes, especially those who began as adolescents, have found a high degree of incest in these women's histories. And mothers in incestuous families were typically sexually abused themselves in childhood, and often become severely dependent—both emotionally and financially—on their husbands, leading them to try to keep the family intact at any cost.

Even though some children do emerge from an incestuous childhood to form healthy attachments in adulthood, this does not mean that the incest was good for them. The flaw in the pro-incest argument—that this is one way for children to receive love and affection, and a healthy way, given children's innate sexuality—is that a relationship between a child and an adult is never one between equals. There can be no such thing as "mutual consent." The child almost always knows intuitively that there is something about the relationship that is wrong, that needs to be kept secret, and yet, because of her (or his) vulnerability and dependence, is not in a position to reject inappropriate overtures.

Anne Eriksson (her real name) told me about her childhood, a distressingly typical story. When she was two years old, her father regularly bathed and put her to bed at night. He would lie down next to her because she "had trouble falling asleep"; as they lay in her bed he would fondle her. Before she was six the fondling had escalated to oral sex (he would sometimes put ketchup on his penis and ask Anne to lick it off) and to simulation of intercourse without penetration, which continued until she was twelve, when she finally told her mother.

"One of the worst things about all of this was that it took both my parents away from me," Anne says, stuttering as she has from the age of twelve. "I couldn't trust my father because he was doing something I knew was wrong. Even though he may have loved me, I couldn't use

53

that love. It was spoiled; there was something wrong with it. And I couldn't be close to my mother because, first of all, by permitting this to be going on she wasn't taking care of me, and I now understand that I was angry with her for that. Besides, I was her rival. I always knew that I was involved in a relationship that should only have been between her and my father.

"I can remember, when I was five, telling her in front of my father, 'We don't need you in the house' and her just sort of sitting around smiling. I'm sure she was aware of the situation on some level, but I think she didn't know how to handle it. When I finally did tell her, very quietly, that Daddy had been bothering me, she didn't ask what he did. She didn't have to. I'm sure she knew. She said she would talk to him, and about a week later she came back and said she had and he wouldn't bother me anymore. And he didn't. After that, he never came close to me. He died when I was nineteen without my ever having discussed it with him.

"It wasn't until many years later, when my husband—now my ex-husband—was psychologically 'incesting' our children, that I had some understanding of what my mother had gone through. I think she was trapped in a marriage that she felt she had to stay in for her own security. I feel that she felt totally overwhelmed. I had that feeling myself in my own marriage. My theory is that these marriages are never really marriages to begin with. You're in no shape to marry somebody you really like. You don't think you deserve anyone decent. But you want to be loved and be married like everyone else, so you make yourself available to somebody even though you know he's all wrong."

Anne's history repeated itself in her daughter's life. While her husband was not as overtly physical with his daughter as Anne's father had been with her, he was seductive in many ways. He would regularly "forget" his towel in the shower and ask his daughter to bring it to him. He would form a series of alliances with each of the children against his wife so that it would be the two of them against her.

Despite her own history, Anne was not labeling this as the psychological incest she now feels it was. "I felt it had nothing to do with me. I couldn't say anything to him, mostly because he was blaming me for all the other family difficulties. So I'd just be uncomfortable inside and keep going on, like a zombie. I wasn't there as a wife, I wasn't there as a mother, I wasn't there as a person. I got into almost a catatonic state.''

This continued until Anne's daughter ran away, at the age of fourteen. To deal with her problems, the entire family went into family therapy. When her daughter applied for foster care, Anne came to understand how the events of her childhood had led her into this unhealthy alliance, marshaled the strength to confront her problems, and made her husband leave the household. She subsequently divorced him. Meanwhile, the daughter, whose acting out was seen by the therapist as a courageous effort to save her mother, went into individual therapy, which, Anne hopes, may help her break the cycle she had been mired in. Anne's sons continue to have emotional problems, a troubling sign that they, like their father, may possibly try to meet their unfulfilled emotional needs in the same unhealthy way he did.

Happily, Anne is a survivor. When I spoke to her again a year and a half after our initial interview, she told me how she had met her present husband, Erik, at a meeting of the organization she was instrumental in founding, the Incest Survivors Resource Network, International. She and Erik are now co-chairing the organization and traveling all over the world together to help other survivors. They asked me to use their real names in this book, in their conviction that only when incest victims ''go public'' will more survivors gather the courage to speak out about their histories.

When we spoke on the phone, I was struck by the fluency of Anne's speech. She doesn't stutter anymore. She also told me that the sexual problem she had in her first marriage—her inability to be responsive—has disappeared. ''It's all in the head,'' she said, laughing. ''It's all a matter of trust.''

Molestation in childhood can leave many different imprints. It's a common pattern in the childhood of sex offenders, with some research showing such a history in as many as eight out of ten rapists. Pat, whom I met through the psychologist who led group sessions for convicted rapists at the prison from which Pat was released two years before, is, at twenty-nine, a boyishly slender man with good features behind a sallow, pockmarked complexion. I can see the ghost of what must have been a beautiful little boy.

At the age of two Pat had been taken away from his parents, both al-

55

coholics, and for the next thirteen years he lived in institutions. "I was a little kid who had never done anything wrong, and there I was doing time for no reason at all," Pat tells me as we drink coffee at a roadside bar.

"Here I was in a place where people were supposed to be taking care of me, and instead I would get beat up or put in a closet or something for no reason at all. When I was eight and a half this enormous guy, a unit leader—he must have been six foot two, 250 pounds—took me into the kitchen off the main hallway, told me to pull my pants down, and sucked me off. The next time he tried it, I wouldn't submit, so he grabbed me by the neck and put me in the isolation room. That happened a few times until I finally gave in and did whatever he wanted me to. He would give me extra food and stuff when I did. This went on for years. I didn't tell anybody, because who was going to believe a kid? Then finally he got caught with somebody else and he got fired.

"Then when I was about twelve there was this woman—a rough and tough type about thirty or so, who really freaked me out. This was a lot worse because she would make *me* be the one who did things, and I was scared and nervous and I didn't know what to do. She used to make me come to her room and touch her boobs and other areas. I didn't want to—I thought it was really weird—and she would take my hand and place it on her. I used to hide from her all the time but she would find me, and this went on for about eight months or so until she was transferred someplace else."

While so much in Pat's childhood went against him, it seems clear that the sexual molestation had a particularly strong impact. It seems implicated in much that followed—his shyness with girls as a teenager and young man, the low sexual appetite that was a source of discord in his short-lived marriage, his generalized anger against women that finally exploded the night he got drunk and had a fight with a sometime girlfriend ("I didn't really like the broad. All I used her for was screwing"), pushed her out of his moving car, picked her up, bruised and bloody, and raped her in the back seat. Pat is what psychologist A. Nicholas Groth, director of the Sexual Offenders Program at Somers State Prison in Connecticut and a specialist in the study and treatment of sex offenders, calls an "anger rapist," someone who uses sex, along with violence, to express his anger at women.

The rape constituted a turning point in Pat's life. Although he had been arrested and jailed dozens of times for assault and disorderly conduct, it hurt him to be convicted as a rapist. He hasn't had a drink for five years, nor has he been arrested during that time. He's holding down a job as a garage mechanic and working part-time with drug and alcohol offenders. He's planning to marry the woman he's been living with for about a year.

The heartening thing about Pat's story, as about Robert's, Anne's, and so many of the others that I've heard, is that while early sexual experiences can push a person down an unrewarding path in life, life keeps presenting us with opportunities to change goals, to reverse directions, to turn ourselves around. Conclusive biographies are not immutably written in childhood.

Chapter 3

The Budding Bough:
The Adolescent Years

Here I had given him something that I thought was really precious—and to him it was just one more notch in his belt.

—ROBIN

OF ALL THE MARKER periods along the life cycle, the most dramatic sexual turning point comes very early in our lives. Sometime around the age of ten, or twelve, or fourteen, or so, the biological determinants of our sexual flowering awaken to some mysterious message and gradually proclaim our emerging womanhood or manhood. The little girl's chest, till now identical to her brother's, begins to bud; her straight lines begin to curve; the genetically programmed timing mechanism deep inside her begins the twenty-eight-day cycle that will prepare her body for motherhood. The boy experiences his own changes. His legs lengthen, his shoulders widen, and one morning he wakes up to find a spot on his bed, evidence of his new ability to ejaculate semen when he is sexually excited.

While sexuality is an intrinsic part of our essential being from infancy on, childhood sexual response is very different from the kind we're capable of once we achieve the physically evolved stage of development that comes with adolescence. This crossing of the threshold of biological maturity is so apparent that it forces recognition of our differ-

58

ent status by those around us. It also, of course, creates a maelstrom of novel feelings within us.

The sexual goals of adolescence are all based on this immense change in our bodies and the psychological changes that accompany it. First we have to come to terms with the fact that we're now sexually mature. This implies an acceptance of our physical changes—what we look like and what we're capable of. Our new sexual capabilities of ejaculation or ovulation signal our untried fertility. These capabilities usually bring a more intense level of sexual responsivity, which may express itself at this time in masturbation, petting, and possibly sexual intercourse. While we're coming to terms with what we look like and what we can do, we also need to come to terms with our sexual identity. This is the time of life when young people actively establish their sexual preference—usually heterosexual, sometimes homosexual; when they think seriously about their sexual values, deciding which of their parents' values they agree with and which they want to supplant; and when they think about being sexually competent.

The implications of reproductive maturity pose other challenges. Girls need to overcome their ignorance about their own bodies, along with any fear of being penetrated. The first gynecological examination may help them accomplish these tasks—or it may traumatize them, depending on how it's managed. Both boys and girls need to know about birth control so that they can be prepared for their initial experiments with sex. They also need to consider sex within the context of a relationship as they begin to date and to become romantically involved. All of this is a fairly tall order for people still only in the first quarter of the life cycle.

Freud considered this genital stage of mature adult sexuality a reawakening of the sexual urges of the phallic stage, which can now be directed into "socially approved channels"—that is, heterosexual relationships with people outside the family. Because of the undeniable physiological changes of sexual maturation, adolescents can no longer repress their sexual urges. They may express them in solitude, with only their fantasies as partners to masturbation, or with other adolescents feeling the same nascent desires, or, occasionally, with adults who assume the role of teacher.

When I spoke with sex researcher Wardell B. Pomeroy in his office at the Institute for the Advanced Study of Human Sexuality in San Francisco, I asked him which marker events of human sexuality he felt had been ignored over the years. As the right-hand man to Alfred Kinsey in his ground-breaking surveys of the 1940s and 1950s as a respected researcher in his own right, and as the author of several books about sexuality and sex research, Dr. Pomeroy would know whereof he spoke. His immediate answer: "First intercourse."

"The effects of first intercourse are irreversible," Dr. Pomeroy said. "Are you a virgin or not a virgin? In our society—and in probably every society around the world—this experience has significant ramifications as a turning point in people's lives."

The obviousness of this statement makes it all the more remarkable that I have been able to turn up no research on the significance of the first experience of sexual intercourse upon subsequent sexual development. Most individuals, of course, consider it among the important events of their lives. And everyone remembers his or her "first time." While some hold it in memory more vividly than others, not one of the more than one hundred people I interviewed for this book answered my question about their first sexual intercourse with a vague "I don't remember." Everyone knew how old she or he had been, who the other person was (even though not everyone could remember the name), where it happened, what led up to it, and how they felt afterward.

It certainly had its effect upon Robin, the youngest of four children of two professors at a small college in Oklahoma. We can see the intermingling of identity and sex in Robin's tale of one major turning point—first sexual intercourse—tumbling right on the heels of another sexual turning point—puberty.

Robin looks so very young as she sits, legs tucked under her, that at times I feel as if she is the thirteen-year-old Robin of the story she is telling me, not the twenty-year-old of today.

"Ever since I had this experience, I've felt like a very different person," Robin says, a shadow of sadness belying her smile. "At thirteen, I was kind of shocked into adulthood.

"I used to hang around with a bunch of girls from school and some guys from around town who were a little older. One day when we were all standing around at the candy store, Jimmy walked over and said hello to one of the guys. I loved his looks—he really was tall, dark, and handsome, and there was something sort of devilish about him. When Jimmy was in a crowd, he just took over. He told the best jokes, he had the best ideas for doing stuff, and he was just fun to be around. Plus, he really turned on the charm for the girls. When he would talk to you, you felt like you were the only girl in the world. I didn't know then that he was always like that with a new girl. All I knew was that this great guy was treating me this way, and by the time I went home for dinner I was in love with him.''

Like so many teenage romances, Robin's was fueled by her family's opposition (what one team of research psychologists has called the "Romeo and Juliet" effect). The more her parents and her older brothers and sister told her what they didn't like about Jimmy and her involvement with him, the more her attachment to him grew. Her eighteen-year-old brother asked, "What do you think a seventeen-year-old boy wants from a thirteen-year-old girl?" Her sixteen-year-old brother told her stories he had heard of the trouble Jimmy had got into before he dropped out of high school. Her sister, fifteen, didn't try to hide her disgust at the antics of the "baby of the family," who was hanging out with "a bunch of zeros" instead of doing her schoolwork. Her parents were troubled by Robin's youth, her neglect of school and piano practice, and Jimmy himself. They expressed their disapproval of the relationship but, being "modern," never tried to forbid Robin from seeing Jimmy.

Robin smiles wryly, tossing her long hair behind her shoulder. "Here were my parents—the big liberals who had taught me that everyone was equal—now telling me that I shouldn't go out with Jimmy because he came from a family that 'didn't share our values.' What I figured they meant was that Jimmy was poor, but later—a lot later—I had to agree with them that there was more to it. I probably wouldn't have listened if they had tried to make me stop seeing him, but I still think they should have done *something* to protect me.''

For the next five months Robin's thoughts revolved around Jimmy and her fantasies of marriage, children, and a little house. Their activities were typical of teenagers in small towns all around the country. About ten or fifteen boys and girls would get together every day after school and on weekends. While the boys played basketball, the girls would watch from the sidelines. At night they'd usually gather at the house of someone whose parents weren't home or cluster around the local candy store.

"For all those five months, we made out a lot—you know, just necking and petting. Jimmy never pressured me to go any further. One day, after we'd been making out on my living room couch for a long time when nobody was home and he could tell I was really excited, he asked me whether I had ever done anything with a guy, and when I said I was a virgin and I just didn't know if I should and I wasn't ready, he just smiled at me and kissed me and said, 'Okay. When you're ready you tell me because I want to make love to you, but I don't want to push you.' I kept thinking how great that was, how it showed how much he respected me.

"Then after about three months, I think what really went through my head—this was kind of sick—was that I was starting to feel like I was kind of losing him. I felt like I was maybe too much of a baby for him and maybe he was tired of playing this stupid game because I knew about sex and I knew guys are supposed to really like it and maybe I would have to or I would lose him. He never said anything like that— this was all in my head and in books I read and movies I saw. And then they would sleep together and be in love forever and he would marry her. So I figured this was the way to make my fairy tale come true.

"I can't believe I was so dumb. I planned the whole thing, feeling like some heroine from a book. I bought myself a set of black lace underwear, and the next afternoon when Jimmy picked me up at school I asked him if anyone was home at his house. He shook his head and I said, 'How about going over there, then? You asked me to tell you when I was ready. And now I am.'

"So we went into his room and got on his bed and he undressed me just the way I had read about in books and we fooled around a little— and then it happened. He was real gentle with me and it didn't hurt at all, which surprised me because I had expected a lot of pain. I can't remember exactly how it felt physically, but emotionally I was in heaven. Mostly, I just loved the idea that I was really *doing it* with the guy I loved, and it was all so romantic.

"Afterward Jimmy asked me if I was okay and he kept telling me how much he loved me. When we went outside and I was walking kind of bowlegged, he put his arm around me and helped me. It was real romantic. He always opened doors for me, he always lit my cigarettes for me, and now he was being superromantic.

"I went home floating on air. I looked at my mother and my sister and I felt as grown up as they were, more than my sister, actually, because I was sure she was still a virgin. I wasn't a little girl anymore. And the best thing was that I had 'become a woman' with the guy I loved." Robin's tone is gently self-mocking as she looks back at that innocent of seven years ago. Then tears well up in those clear hazel eyes as she relives the pain she still has not overcome. "The very next day he broke up with me. The very next day."

Robin falls silent, drifting back into that lost, bewildering time.

"What happened then?" I ask.

"I really freaked out. I was in hysterics. A couple of my girlfriends saw me crying and they said, 'Oh, don't take it like it's you. Jimmy is just a shit. He told you he loved you and he was going to marry you, right? That's what he tells everybody. Even while he's seeing other girls at the same time. That's probably what he's telling Mary Ann right now.' It turned out he had been seeing Mary Ann at the same time he was seeing me. It also turned out he liked to break in virgins. Some kind of macho thing with him. Here I had given him something that I thought was really precious—and to him it was just one more notch in his belt.

"I was in complete, total shock. Just to think I had just made love to him—and I didn't take it lightly. I figured *making* love means you're *in* love, you're going to get married, you're going to have kids. I wasn't used to having bad things happen to me. I was used to everybody being nice to me and everybody loving me. As far as I knew, nobody had ever lied to me before.

"I just grew up overnight. Now I knew that people could be nasty and horrible and manipulative. They could get what they wanted from you—and then zap you. I felt like a thousand knives hit my body when Jimmy broke up with me. For a long time I hated him, but then I started to feel sorry for him because I knew he'd never be happy.

"I hated my parents for telling me the world was a pretty place. I hated my brothers and sister. Sure, they had warned me against Jimmy, but they hadn't told me how *much* I could get hurt. And nobody had *done* anything to keep it from happening. How come everybody set me up for such a fall? I just went crazy. I started doing drug after drug and screwing as many guys as I wanted whenever I wanted. I ran away from home, and I finished high school only because my parents found me and dragged me back. Now I'm glad they did.

"Now I don't do drugs much anymore, mostly because I'm too scared. I hate cheap sex—you know, with some guy you meet and you think he's cute, and you talk and you like him, and you go to bed with him. In fact, I don't have much of a sexual drive for anybody, even if I really get to know and like him. I think I'm afraid of everything now. I'm afraid of falling in love because I just know it wouldn't work out and I'd get hurt again. I'm afraid to get married because I know I would end up getting divorced. I'm afraid of having children because I couldn't stand seeing a daughter of mine go through what I've gone through.

"So I don't know where my life is going these days. I'm in college and I'm doing okay, but I don't know where it's taking me. I get along okay with my parents, but when you're twenty years old your parents just aren't that big a part of your life. I have a hard time making girlfriends and I think that's because I never got over the fact that girls I considered my friends and I trusted were going out with my boyfriend behind my back. And as far as guys are concerned, forget it.

"It's funny—with all the hurt I had after what happened with Jimmy, I still look back on those early months when we were going out, with a nostalgic feeling. It was so wonderful being in love like that. I've never felt the same kind of excitement with anyone else since, and I'm just worried that I never will."

A sense of sadness hangs in the air as Robin's voice trails off. She is still so very young and vulnerable, giving the lie to the common myth among the young that emotional maturity goes hand in hand with sexual maturity. A myth that's particularly significant today, when the age for first sexual intercourse is getting younger and younger all the time.

One of the most dramatic sexual shifts in our society has been the lowering of the age of first intercourse. Adolescents have always had sexual stirrings. This is only natural, since the principal physical changes in adolescence are those hormonally produced ones associated with the reproductive system. In times past, however, teens tended to repress these urges more, or to express them in slowly progressing stages of hand holding, necking, and petting before they eventually engaged in intercourse. These days fewer teens pet to orgasm. If they're aroused sexually, they usually see no point in stopping short of intercourse. Today's sexually active teenagers are more likely to go right into a coital relationship. Even though most adolescents are not promiscuous and are sexually active with only one person at a time, the fact that they begin their sexual careers so early means that they will, over their teenage years, have more sexual partners than their parents did.

This is not the only change that has been cleaving the generations with a confusing and disturbing intensity. The biggest changes have been among girls, who are now acting more like boys in expressing their sexuality. The main difference is that girls are more likely to have their first sexual intercourse with a steady boyfriend, while boys are more likely to have theirs with someone they know casually. (Boys are far less likely than in generations past to have that first experience with a prostitute.) Overall, boys and girls of today are acting more like each other than like their same-sex parents. But in this rush to cast off the mantle of the double standard, many girls, boys, *and* parents blot out of their minds the defining difference between the sexes: girls are the ones who get pregnant. And they're doing so at an alarming rate, despite all the recent advances in birth control. If current trends continue, four out of ten of today's fourteen-year-old girls will become pregnant while still in their teens.

Between 1925 and 1965, about 10 percent of girls in their last year of high school were no longer virgins. By 1973 the nonvirgins accounted for 35 percent, and by 1979 more than 80 percent of seventeen-year-old white girls and 86 percent of seventeen-year-old white boys had experienced sexual intercourse. The incidence among black teenagers is even higher, but by a smaller margin than in years past. Furthermore, the age for first intercourse has been dropping steadily. By the age of fifteen or sixteen, about one in four white boys and girls, half of black girls, and nine out of ten black boys have given up their virginity. Among the nation's thirteen- and fourteen-year-old boys and girls 20 percent have already had intercourse.

What does this mean when youngsters barely over the pubertal threshold enter into the sexuality of adulthood? Often, the kind of bewildered grief and trauma that has followed Robin over these past seven years—and that will probably continue to follow her unless she can resolve the issues that drove her into Jimmy's bed and made her act out her nonsexual concerns in a sexual way.

65

In his delineation of eight stages of psychosexual development throughout life, the psychoanalyst Erik H. Erikson maintained that people are not ready for genital sexuality until early adulthood. Not till then, he proposed, when a person has achieved a sense of identity and knows who she or he is, is anyone ready to give up that self in the kind of fusion that orgasmic intercourse calls for. Caught up as they are in their struggle to define themselves as adults, adolescents want to make commitments of love but are not ready to do so.

Some teens do recognize their unreadiness for a sexual relationship and decide to wait, either until they feel more mature or until they enter into a serious loving relationship. As Nick, a virgin at nineteen, told me, "I want my first time to be special, and with a girl I know well and greatly admire, rather than a one-nighter." And while Maureen admitted her embarrassment about still being a virgin at eighteen, she plans to wait until she feels mature enough to handle a sexual relationship. The most recent information indicates, in fact, that the tide may be turning. While the percentage of women undergraduates at Ohio State University who said they'd had premarital sex rose steadily through the 1960s and into the 1970s, reaching 80 percent by 1975, the proportion dropped to only 50 percent in 1980.

Robin's involvement in the relationship with Jimmy bespoke a conflict of which she herself was not yet aware—the need to define herself within her family and to gain independence from it. Jimmy was the vehicle she seized to shed her status as the "baby," to achieve a sense of self-esteem, to feel valued for herself. How better could she dissociate herself from her "goody-goody" achieving older sister, from the competent brothers she felt she could never catch up with, from the parents who seemed to have found their answers in life when all she had were questions?

Robin does not, of course, exemplify all young adolescents who enter into sexual activity, some of whom do seem able to handle such a relationship and even grow from it. In our society, however, few people at this early age are ready, as Robin herself came to realize.

"I wouldn't advise other people to have sex as early as I did," she told me. "I'm happy when I hear a lot of my friends didn't lose their virginity till they were sixteen, 'cause by then you know more about people. You've been ripped off once or twice, you've had a girlfriend or two lie to you over one dumb thing or another, and you've had a boyfriend spread rumors about you or let you down some other way. You've had enough bad things happen so you have some defenses up, guards—you know, feelers out. Not the way I was, with nothing.''

A moving story like Robin's brings to life the warnings against premature sexual activity that come from many sectors of society. Such warnings come not only from religious leaders and ultraconservative moralists but also from more surprising quarters. Like the controversial birth control evangelist Sol Gordon, director of the Institute for Family Research and Education at Syracuse University, who's been vilified in many quarters for being ''too liberal, too permissive.''

''Sex for teenagers is a health hazard,'' said Dr. Gordon, in an impassioned speech to his fellow sex educators when they gave him the American Association of Sex Educators, Counselors and Therapists 1982 award for outstanding contributions in the field of human sexuality. ''I don't speak for all sex educators, but I speak for most of them who say we don't think it's a good idea for teenagers to have intercourse. We have 1.3 million pregnancies each year among teenagers, several million new cases of venereal disease. Teenagers are too young, too vulnerable, too available for exploitation. They don't know that the first experiences of sex are usually grim. Almost no girl will have an orgasm. The guy gets his orgasm three days later when he tells the guys about it.''

What do we do, then, about all these children who are rushing into the sexuality of adulthood when they still have years of growing up to do? Recognizing that most teens start to date because their friends are doing it, not because their sex hormones are pushing them into the arms of the other sex, a ''new'' (if familiar-sounding) philosophy is emanating from even the most liberal homes, schools, and communities.

A recent article by *Boston Globe* columnist Ellen Goodman in *Ms.* magazine quotes prominent sex educators on their conviction that parents need to make age distinctions and flatly tell their children, ''Thirteen is too young. Fourteen is too young.'' The Emory/Grady Teen Services Program, a family planning program in Atlanta, Georgia, calls its new approach for thirteen- to fifteen-year-olds ''Postponing Sexual Involvement.'' This series differs from most sex education programs in two crucial ways. It starts with a given value: ''You ought not to be having sex at a young age,'' and it discards the idea of encouraging young people to make their own decisions about the time to become sexually active, bombarding them instead with all sorts of activities designed to motivate them to wait and to help them do it.

The outspoken, much-picketed Sol Gordon has, with his wife, Judith, written a book with the surprising title *Raising a Child Conservatively in a Sexually Permissive Society*. This conservative approach does not mean limiting access to contraception. As Dr. Gordon thundered out in the Grand Ballroom of New York's Grand Hyatt Hotel, ''I know that half of all young people are going to have intercourse whether we like it or not, and whether they like it or not. So we have to say to them, 'If you're not going to listen to us, at least use birth control.' Those are the messages we're going to have to get across. And I'm tired of all this research that says the reason girls get pregnant is because of an unresolved Oedipal complex. Or because they can't understand moral development. Or because they have all this peer pressure, or because they want to get pregnant.

''I know why teenage girls get pregnant—if you listen carefully, I'll tell you. They get pregnant because they have sexual intercourse.''

Much of the time, they have that sexual intercourse unaccompanied by any form of birth control. Why? Often because planning ahead for sexual activity would shatter the fragile fiction that they are not sexual persons who want and enjoy sex, but instead are romantics who would do ''that'' only under the sway of a grand, irresistible passion. They cannot admit to themselves that if they meet a boy who appeals to them, they'll go to bed with him even if he is *not* the great love of their life. This is why most adolescent pregnancies occur to sexually inexperienced girls, within the first six months of their sexual activity. Furthermore, the guiltier they feel about sex, the more likely they are to get ''caught,'' a sad irony we'll talk about in the next chapter.

Parents and teachers need to get the facts across to young adolescents in a way that will encourage them to wait or to use contraception. Harsh facts like the reality that almost 90 percent of all teenage boys who make their girlfriends pregnant abandon them. Biological facts that attest to the efficiency of their reproductive systems—yes, you can get pregnant the first time; yes, you can get pregnant doing it standing up; yes, you can, you can, you can. Happy facts like the finding that waiting till the late teens results in better sex.

When David L. Weis of Rutgers University's Cook College asked

130 undergraduate women about their first experience of sexual intercourse, he found that the ones who felt best about their first time had, as it were, rehearsed for this personal drama. By having done a fair amount of dating, kissing, and petting before moving to intercourse, they had come to know themselves as sexual beings and to feel more comfortable with their sensual feelings. Among these young women, whose ages at first intercourse ranged from nine to twenty-one, those who had waited the longest had the best experiences.

The other all-important element was the other person in this small cast. It's not surprising that the young woman whose first lover was loving, tender, and considerate is much more likely to have good feelings about the entire experience than the one who gave herself to someone who acted unloving, rough, and inconsiderate. Surprisingly, the depth of commitment between the two didn't seem to matter: some women whose first lovers were their fiancés still felt exploited and uncared for.

Another recent study, one among 116 male and female college students, was carried out by Daniel P. Murphy of Creighton University in Omaha, Nebraska. Dr. Murphy found that the experiences of those who had given up their virginity at thirteen, fourteen, or fifteen were different from those who waited till they were eighteen or older, with the differences especially marked for girls. The older a girl was at time of first intercourse, the more aroused she became and the more she enjoyed it. The older "first-timers" of both sexes were also more likely to feel that this new kind of sexual intimacy strengthened their relationship.

Virtually every woman I've spoken to who remembers long hours of petting on the living room couch or in a car parked on some dark side road treasures her memories of the feverish pleasure to be found in gradually reaching a peak of sexual excitement. The pleasure was, of course, often frustrating for both her and for whatever high school or college boy was her passion of the moment, but there were also countless times when both of them climaxed in a deeply satisfying orgasm.

For many women those orgasms experienced in the first flush of sexual awakening were more spine-tingling than any achieved in sexual intercourse in the years afterward, no matter how many lovers they eventually took in efforts to recapture those early thrills. The fortunate ones learned from those hours of exploring each other's mouth with tongue, lips, teeth; of discovering the magic places in their own and the other's body with their hands; of moving their body in concert with another to reach ever higher levels of sensuality. The sexually impoverished ones are those whose entire concept of sexual contact still revolves around intercourse as the be-all and end-all. The sad thing, in these supposedly liberated times, is that many young people, in their frantic search for the fulfillment of adult sexuality, go too far too soon and miss the delights to be had along the way, thus planting the seeds for sexual problems later on.

If young adolescents learn how much they have to gain from putting off sexual intercourse until they've warmed to the fires of sexual arousal in other ways, until they've found a partner they care for and trust, and until they can consummate their passion in a setting that's comfortable for them, they're likely to postpone that first time until they feel truly ready for it. Making the decision themselves, based on this kind of information, will demonstrate a much more mature involvement than if they're only reacting to the moralizing of parents, teachers, and religious leaders.

If a young couple are reaching orgasm from petting, why should they go on to coitus? No reason at all. They'll be running no risk of pregnancy and a sharply reduced risk of venereal disease, and they're apt to become far better lovers if they learn how to bring each other to orgasm without intercourse. It is not only the girls who gain; waiting also has benefits for males. The most favored treatment these days for impotence is a return to the courtship patterns of an earlier day—as therapists urge partners to enjoy the sensuality of being with each other and giving each other pleasure, while stopping short of intercourse.

While more repressive approaches to sexuality left many bruising legacies, adolescent male sexual dysfunction was apparently not one of them. But over the past ten years California psychologist James E. Gardner has noted an increase from "zero" problems of sexual dysfunction in teenage boys (except for gender identity and homosexual problems) to about one out of every three new cases in this age range. The problems are often due to a boy's anxiety in the face of what he feels is pressure to perform like an expert.

In his 1982 book *The Turbulent Teens*, Dr. Gardner introduces Don, a shy, handsome fifteen-year-old, who describes the first time he tried to have intercourse. A girl came up to him, asked "Want to get it on?" took him into a bedroom, and tore off her clothes, standing naked before him.

"Like that," Don said. "That quick. I wasn't ready. I didn't know what to do. . . . I just know I didn't get hard. I was ashamed."

The burden shifts. In times past, a boy would "make a pass," with little expectation of success. The girl was expected to sit back passively and rebuff any sexual advances, no matter how much she wanted them. Today, with the awareness that girls too are sexual beings, more of them are taking the initiative. This change is healthy, but it's hard on boys, because our mores haven't yet shifted to giving males the option of saying no. The mystique that a real man is always ready for sex, at any time, with any woman who'll have him, lives on, and the boy who is shy, inexperienced, or just not interested is put on the spot. With any luck, this pressure will be just an artifact of rapidly shifting mores, and in due time a boy's lack of sexual interest will be accepted just as readily as we accept a girl's expression of interest.

Postponing first intercourse will not, of course, protect teenagers like Robin from having their hearts broken by uncaring, exploitive partners. But there would be some protection. It's always painful when an adolescent's love affair breaks up, but if the couple haven't engaged in intercourse together, the final step hasn't been taken and the parting can be accepted more easily. Somehow, when sexual intercourse isn't part of the relationship, less of a commitment is implied. Virginity can be given away only once in a lifetime, and sex is a heavily charged facet of any relationship. After people have been to bed together, they feel closer to each other; when they break up—as most teenage romances do—the parting is more wrenching, especially when one or both partners are so young that they haven't had time to build up the necessary defenses.

Is this emphasis on urging teenagers to wait a repudiation of the advances that have come with the sexual revolution—the lowered emphasis on guilt, the discarding of the view of sex as evil, the new focus on sex as a natural expression of vitality and affection? No. It just recognizes that with every revolution there are casualties. In this one the casualties too often are our children.

Many of these casualties are, of course, young girls who become pregnant. A first pregnancy is always a turning point. When it's planned, in the context of a loving, stable relationship, it can be the affirmation of mature womanhood and the tangible evidence of an intimate bond with the

71

father of the child. When that pregnancy comes prematurely, before either partner is ready to assume the responsibilities of parenthood, it can change the course of their lives—especially the girl's—forever.

It's obvious how pregnancy affects unmarried mothers who keep their babies, who are likely to drop out of school, end up on welfare, or become even more dependent on their parents at a time when their classmates are achieving separation from theirs. It's clear how the responsibility for taking care of a child will affect all future decisions involving school, work, and relationships with men. (In most cases, the relationship with the baby's father ends either before or soon after the birth.)

Even among those women who solve their problem with an early abortion, the pregnancy is usually a major turning point in their lives. As Christie, twenty-five, now a junior executive with a Chicago bank, told me, "Of course I had an abortion. At fifteen I knew I couldn't have this baby. My parents put a lot of energy into my education. As the only daughter of the most successful black businessman in East St. Louis, Illinois, I knew that getting pregnant before I graduated from college was a no-no. I was a straight-A student, and my family had a lot of expectations for me. And I had them for myself.

"Rick—my boyfriend—was great. He borrowed half the money—I paid my half from savings from a summer job—and he stuck by me all through it. But a few months later we broke up when I realized that we were going to go very different places in life. I see him occasionally now, and I feel sorry for him because he hasn't really gone anywhere and I've had a lot of great opportunities. But, you know, I haven't had a really close relationship with a guy since. I don't know how much the abortion had to do with it, but all I know is that every time I start to get close to someone I start to get all these dreams about the baby."

Even when an abortion comes a little later in life, it can have serious repercussions, as we'll see in the next chapter. For most young girls it's a better solution than continuing the pregnancy—but it's still an ordeal full of both emotional and physical pain. With the high current rate of teenage pregnancies, it seems likely that we'll be seeing more and more girls opting for abortion.

So far we've been talking about sexual turning points in the lives of young people who seem well anchored in heterosexual waters. Teenagers whose currents of sexual orientation swirl toward members of their own sex also experience major turning points, since adolescence is usually the time when homosexuals first acknowledge and act upon their sexual preferences. While Freud believed that homosexuality was a mark of immaturity, contemporary sex theorists generally concede that the sexual awakening of adolescence applies just as strongly to people with a homosexual orientation, marking their entry into adult sexuality.

This was certainly true of Ted, who tells me, ''When I was fifteen, in tenth grade at high school in Edina, Minnesota, I didn't realize that one night at the house of some girl, whose name I can't even remember anymore, would still stick in my mind as a major turning point. But here we are, twenty years later, and of thousands of times in my life, this is one of the most vivid memories I have.''

Ted, a trim, muscular, sandy-haired man of medium height, is speaking to me in the parlor of his North Georgetown townhouse. On the book-lined shelves stand a dozen or so framed photographs—of Ted with his parents, his brothers, his sister, his nieces and nephews. A couple of the pictures show him with young women.

''I was pretty well liked in junior high and high school,'' Ted says, leaning forward on the maroon velvet loveseat. ''I was vice-president of the student body and an honor student. I was also a good dancer, which got me invited to a lot of parties and stuff. I could do everything— swing, ballroom dancing, the twist, whatever. Both boys and girls were always after me to teach them how to dance. I loved to do it. It was my way to shine.

''I tried going out for sports—not because I particularly wanted to but because I felt it was expected of me because my brothers were such good athletes. I shouldn't have bothered. From the time I was a little kid, I was a dud. I could never make a baseball team, and even when I tried to play kickball or whatever the kids were playing at recess, I was a wash-out.

''I wasn't like other boys in a lot of ways. I stayed around the house a lot, watched the little kids, helped my mother with the ironing and cleaning. She always used to say how proud she was of me, how I was the one she could count on. Naturally, my brothers and the other kids on the block teased me a lot. They used to call me a 'sissy' and a 'Mama's boy,' and, sure, it bothered me. But the minute music played, I was in my element, and this was what saved me when I got into adolescence.

"There was this very rugged guy in school—a football player, John. He was a couple of years older than I was, and his senior prom was coming up, and as big and tough as he was, he was terrified. So I'd been teaching him how to dance with a girl without crushing the breath out of her. John took a liking to me. He was definitely a big man around school. All the girls fell all over him. He decided it was time I did more with girls than dance with them. So he called up whatever little creature was mooning all over him at the time and he asked her to get a cute girlfriend, and we went over to her house one day after school. The four of us were all alone in the house.

"We sat around and talked for a while, and we danced, and everything was supposed to end up that we were supposed to make out. I was fascinated by the way John was so into his girlfriend and the way he carried on with her. I was more interested in watching them than in doing anything myself. They were all over each other on the couch, kissing each other and putting their hands everywhere. And I was just not moved by it at all, and I felt very awkward. I liked this girl I was with— she *was* cute and she was a good dancer and she was nice enough, but I had no more desire to do with her what John was doing with his girl than I would have had to sit down and do the multiplication table. I didn't feel scared—I just couldn't see the point. She seemed a little puzzled by my lack of interest, but the only thing I felt bad about was that I thought I was probably letting John down."

That day was the first of many such dates, when Ted felt he wasn't doing what the other guys were doing. They were mostly double dates with friends, and eventually he did a little of the necking and petting that went on in drive-ins, on side roads, and in living rooms all around Edina. But it was always like going out for sports—an activity he took part in more because he felt it was expected of him than because he got any pleasure out of it.

"I knew I wasn't like the other boys," Ted says. "But I kept telling myself it was because I was so religious. I came from a devout Catholic family, I had been an altar boy, and I was thinking seriously of becoming a priest. It wasn't until many years later that I saw how I was using religion as an escape. Sure, I was excited about the idea of entering the seminary, but I think a big part of the excitement lay in the fact that I knew it would be an all-male environment. I had felt a certain excitement around men—my uncles, or strange men at the beach—since I'd been about seven or eight years old, but I sort of pushed that to the back of my mind and never told anyone about it."

Meanwhile, Ted was earning the money for dances and movies by bagging groceries at a supermarket about five miles away from home. A fresh-faced and appealing sixteen-year-old, he never had any trouble hitching a ride back and forth, and many of the rides came complete with offers of money from the men who picked him up.

"Most of the men were very cautious. They didn't lay a hand on me at first, but I could tell they wanted to have sex with me, just by the way they looked at me or the things they would say. In the beginning I was very frightened, especially when I would notice a man's hand inching closer to me on the seat and then feel it land on my knee. But I was intrigued, too, and I definitely felt more sexual stirrings with these strange men than I ever had necking with a girl. Still, though, I denied that I was interested."

Then one day Guy, a well-built, handsome man in his mid-thirties, picked Ted up, told the boy he was gay, pulled off the road and parked in a little wooded area, and *showed* Ted what being gay meant. "I was jumpy as a cat," Ted recalls. "And Guy was sensitive to that. He had a really calming voice and he just talked down my worries while he put his hands lightly on my shoulders, my arms, my thighs. By the time he asked me to unzip my jeans, I trusted him, which was crazy, because I had never set eyes on him till twenty minutes before, but somehow I knew—and I turned out to be right—that this man would never hurt me.

"I had never felt anything so delicious in all my life as the feelings that went through me when Guy took my penis into his mouth. I was concentrating so hard on what I was feeling that I didn't realize at the time—not for a long time later—that he was getting just as much of a charge out of bringing me off as I was getting from what he was doing. But that's typical among gays. For some reason we get a lot more pleasure out of giving pleasure than most straight people seem to do. Who knows why? Maybe because we feel so guilty about what we're doing— and that helps allay the guilt."

"Do you still feel guilty?" I ask Ted, by now the age that Guy had been then.

"I don't now," he says slowly, thoughtfully. "But I sure did then. I did when I was dating this girl—Italian and Catholic like me. My family loved her and everybody was sure we'd get married, everybody but me. I was gay and I never told her. I was able to hide behind my religion, act like the perfect gentleman to keep us both pure. But finally she wanted to get married and I couldn't pretend anymore, so I told her. She was very understanding and she said, 'Don't worry about it—I can change you.' But I didn't want to change. I decided that I'd better get out of Edina and go to live someplace where I *could* be myself. And so I came here to Washington, where anything—well, almost anything—goes."

Ted gets up, walks over to the window, and looks out over the quiet street. "I think it was my guilt that kept me from realizing for such a long time who I really was—and kept me from recognizing that there were other boys like me. Guy was a very important influence in my life and not just because he was the first man I had sex with. Sure, that was a major turning point for me. But his importance to me was much broader than that. He helped me to accept myself. Here was this very masculine guy, successful in business, someone I could look up to and respect. If he was gay, well, that couldn't be such a terrible thing to be. By being able to say to myself, 'Okay, this is who I am and this is the way I want to be,' I was able to form other relationships with people closer to my own age. I've had some wonderful attachments over the years."

Fern, too, recognized her homosexuality in early adolescence, as the outgrowth of an obsessive unrequited attraction that made her life miserable for years. Then she met the woman she is now happily "married" to after a ceremony conducted at her Unitarian church. Fern is a tall, big-boned, sturdy-looking woman of thirty-five dressed the way so many women dress nowadays—jeans, blouse, sweatshirt, pea jacket, tousled brown hair cut short and boyishly.

"The year I turned fourteen things started getting real crazy for me, and they've stayed crazy ever since," Fern says, laughing. That was the year her family moved to the suburbs from their St. Louis home, the year she transferred from a parochial girls' school to a public coed high school, the year she met and fell wildly in love with Tommie. "I had never seen anyone as beautiful in my entire life," Fern said. She found a way to meet Tommie and then took to waiting for her after school, inviting her home to play and sleep over, going to her house from time to time. Unaware that this "crush" would remain with her for some twenty years, Fern continued to be close to Tommie even as she dated boys.

It wasn't for another couple of years that Fern realized the sexual component to her obsession. It happened on the afternoon when she complained to Tommie that all that her current boyfriend wanted to do was French kiss. Tommie said, "You don't have to French if you really know how to kiss. You want me to show you how to do it right?" Tommie pushed Fern against the bedroom door, enfolded her in her arms, and kissed her passionately. Fern, who didn't at the time understand what was happening—except that it felt good—now says, "Of course, I was in climax right then and there. And that's the way it started."

Both Ted's and Fern's stories are typical in many ways of the early lives of homosexuals. During the 1970s the Alfred C. Kinsey Institute for Sex Research conducted a major study in which researchers interviewed almost 1,000 homosexual men and women and almost 500 heterosexual men and women living in the San Francisco area. Among the questions they asked were those having to do with the respondents' early lives. It took more than a decade to analyze this information, which Alan P. Bell, Martin S. Weinberg, and Sue Kiefer Hammersmith published in 1981 in *Sexual Preference*.

This study showed that the single factor associated most strongly with adult homosexuality was having been different from other children of the same sex. Like Ted, a great many homosexual men had felt different from the other little boys—effeminate, sissyish, not masculine. They had enjoyed playing house, hopscotch, and jacks much more than baseball and football, in contrast with boys who turned out to be heterosexual. The gays told the interviewers such things as "I just didn't feel I was like other boys. I was very fond of pretty things like ribbons and flowers and music," and "I wanted no involvement in sports where you have to prove your strength. I hated phys ed and sports."

The same pattern showed up among the homosexual women in the study, who as little girls were more likely than the girls who grew up to be heterosexual to have enjoyed activities like climbing trees, playing baseball, and taking part in rough-and-tumble games. As Fern told me, "I had my Ginny dolls, but I would rather climb a tree with the boys on the block than sit and play with my dolls any day of the week."

As adolescents, the homosexual men and women had had as many chances to become involved with the other sex as had the heterosexuals, were just as attractive, and, in fact, had dated as often as their heterosexual classmates. Their feelings about dating, however, were much less positive. They said things like, "I could take it or leave it. It was the thing to do"; "I wanted to see if I could enjoy a girl's company. The results weren't worth the effort"; or "I was always embarrassed at the end of a date. I knew it was customary to kiss them, and I didn't want to." As Fern told me, "I had plenty of opportunities to be straight, and I even dated one guy for a long time just as a cover. But, you know, I just never had any desire for guys."

This study found that homosexuals continued to feel different throughout the teen years, but, contrary to some theories that maintain that adolescents *become* homosexual because they feel different from their peers, these researchers' findings seem to point in the opposite direction: adolescent homosexuals feel different from their peers precisely because they *recognize* that different sexual orientation in themselves.

Adolescence, then, is an important turning point for homosexuals as well as for heterosexuals. This is so not because sexual preference is set at this time of life—it is apparently determined long before adolescence, for reasons that are not at all clear—but because it is usually acted upon and recognized now. Ted is different from most men, both homosexual and heterosexual, in never having had any kind of homosexual encounter as a child or young adolescent. He differs from most homosexuals in that his first encounter with another male was not with someone about his own age. Most homosexuals are not seduced by an older man.

Another finding was that the biggest difference between young people of different sexual preference was not what they did sexually, or when they did it—but how they felt about it. Many of those who became heterosexuals had early homosexual experiences that they never repeated because they didn't find them exciting. (As Joseph, a forty-five-year-old happily married heterosexual man who had attended a residential school for the deaf, told me, "When I was in ninth grade my

English teacher—one of the best teachers I ever had—invited me into his room, gave me a drink, and introduced me to homosexuality. I kept seeing him over the next four years, until I graduated, and I enjoyed the sex—up to a point—but I always knew it just wasn't my dish of tea. I was never drawn to a homosexual relationship again.'') The reverse was true of many men and women who had early heterosexual relationships yet still became homosexuals.

Alan Bell, the chief researcher in this Kinsey Institute study, elaborates on its findings with an elegant theory using that word so scarce in sex research: ''love.'' ''Sexual preference has more to do with whom you fall in love with than with whom you have sex with,'' he states.

''The feeling that the love object is essentially different from the self in certain important, tangible ways is accepted in the cultural sense,'' says Dr. Bell. ''We all know that distance and difference fan the flame of desire, that people are attracted to the exotic characteristics of people from other societies. Familiarity leads to friendship, while novelty leads to romance.''

This theory is illustrated among the kibbutzniks of Israel. On the commune-like kibbutzim, girls and boys who've been raised together from infancy, often in quarters separate from their parents, tend to experiment with each other sexually, but hardly ever fall in love with each other. Instead, they fall for someone on the next kibbutz, someone who represents the unopened book, the unexplored continent, the unplumbed psyche. This theory also explains the familiar dilemma of the happily married couple: the better they get to know each other, the more committed they are to each other as friends, the less inclined they are to feel the fires of great passion toward each other.

''This same phenomenon holds with regard to sex-based characteristics,'' continues Alan Bell. ''Straight girls, for example, don't fall in love with their girlfriends, nor straight boys with their buddies. They fall in love with people of the other sex who look different, feel different, and, most important, act different.

''What happens, then, to the boy who plays daily with girls, who feels an affinity with them, who feels he understands them better than he understands the boys on the block? He's likely to be friendly with them, but by the time he reaches adolescence, girls are 'finished business' for him, so to speak. He's used to girls, he knows their ways, he's

79

no longer fascinated by them. And so, he'll fall in love with a boy. The same thing will happen to the girl who as a youngster feels like 'one of the boys.' She won't fall in love with the guys in her gang, but with someone as much unlike them as possible—maybe a prototypically feminine girl.''

By the time young people reach adolescence, their sexual orientation is generally set. They may not act upon it yet, driving themselves to conform to societal dictates for the ''right'' person to be attracted to, to lust after, to fall in love with. But it's now that they generally become aware of any such leanings, whether they accept them right away or fight against them for lonely years to come.

From the viewpoint of sexual development, these years from about twelve to about eighteen underscore what is for most of us the greatest metamorphosis of our life. We enter our teens as human larvae; we leave them as immature adults. But, as psychoanalyst Gadpaille writes, ''The sexual uncertainties, doubts, and experiments of adolescence do not come to an abrupt end, ever.'' While we have undergone at least one major turning point during these years—the changes of puberty— most of our sexual turning points still lie ahead.

Chapter 4

Groves of Nubility: Between Eighteen and Twenty-two

I have had plenty of close sexual relationships and have always tried never to hurt anybody's feelings. Now I am at the stage in my life where the most erotic thing is to be in love. Sex is a beautiful experience which I cherish and discuss freely with the person I love.

—CHRIS

WHAT DOES IT FEEL like to be in this sexual transition between adolescence and adulthood? It's confusing. It's being lost and knowing you can't take the same road home you used to know. It's feeling incompetent and not knowing how to educate yourself. It's aching to love and be loved in new ways and not knowing what those ways are.

It's also exhilarating. It's realizing that you know some things about yourself that your parents don't know and never will. It's discovering realms of excitement in that body you thought you knew so well. It's being pierced by the revelation that you can excite someone else. It's learning that you're capable of much more than you had ever dreamed possible.

The major sexual goals of this life stage revolve around achieving sexual independence, sexual competence, sexual responsibility, and sexual equality, all of which are intertwined and all of which are minefields full of turning points—the first sexual intercourse, the first orgasm, the first oral sex, the first love affair, the first living-together experience, the first marriage. It is an age of experimentation, an age of

81

groping, an age of discovering the sexual self buried for so long under the injunctions laid down by family and society and self.

"I had a lot of sexual hang-ups even in my senior year in high school," Lisa tells me, "and I knew that I could only get rid of them if I got away from my parents." Ironically, we are now talking in her parents' home, a spacious mansion in the prosperous St. Louis suburb of Clayton, Missouri, the house where Lisa grew up—and where she and her husband of five years have been living for the past year.

"What I didn't realize was that I'd go berserk and become a wild child in the process." It's hard to imagine this vivacious thirty-year-old woman as berserk as she graciously offers me coffee and home-baked cookies. She sees the look of surprise in my eyes and laughs. "I *was* a child of the sixties. You have to remember that."

Lisa didn't feel she had to get away from her parents because they were repressive or because she didn't get along with them. On the contrary, she felt she got along with them only too well. The adored younger child of a successful lawyer and a mother who worked part-time testing the hearing of public school children but whose real mission in life was mothering her son and daughter, Lisa was the family pet. Whatever she wanted to do was fine. The family would turn out en masse to beam at her successes—her award in fourth grade as her school's "Composer of the Year," her lead in her summer-camp musical in seventh grade, her clarinet solos with her high school band. No one ever berated her for her mediocre schoolwork the way her father sometimes did with her brother. As long as she was cute (which she was) and good (which she was), acceptance was total.

"I don't remember ever hearing that there was anything bad about sex," she muses. "I don't remember when I first heard about menstruation and how babies were born and made, so I must have been pretty young. And I never had to unlearn false information. And my parents were very affectionate with each other and with all of us. My father still kisses my brother. My husband, who comes from a much less demonstrative family, is still taken aback when my father kisses him when we haven't seen my folks for a while.

"The message I got was that sex was beautiful—at the right time. Being the daughter of Orthodox Jews meant that the right time would be when I grew up and got married to a nice Jewish boy. Until then, I felt it was something I had to avoid at all costs."

Lisa took a paradoxical way to avoid sex. The friends she chose in high school were in the "fast" crowd, the kids who smoked cigarettes and pot and drank beer and didn't care about school and had parties every Friday and Saturday night where the major activity was "making out." While Lisa went along with the smoking and the drinking, she backed off at the slightest intimation of sex. Even when a boy she really liked took her home from a party or a dance, Lisa did nothing more than give him a quick kiss at her front door.

"I felt something was terribly wrong with me because I was so uptight about sex," Lisa says. "But I couldn't help being prudish about it."

When I ask Lisa whether she ever just accepted the fact that she was not ready for sexual relationships at the ripe old age of sixteen or seventeen, she falls quiet. "You know, I never did. I never saw anything positive about it. I figured if all my girlfriends were doing it and I wasn't, then there was something wrong with me. Now, looking back, I wonder why I chose those particular girlfriends."

It's likely that Lisa chose those friends because on some level she wanted what they were experiencing. But she had also picked up the message that her sexual stirrings would not fit with her "good girl" image, and so she looked out at a tempting world from the virginal bubble in which she had encased herself. Lisa did not take her first step toward sexual independence until she went away to college.

"It still took me a while to shed my inhibitions," she says. "I did it the only way I knew how—with drugs. I took almost everything that first year—pot, of course, and hash, and uppers and downers and mescaline—and a lot of LSD. That was in the early 1970s, and all this stuff was available anytime and anyplace. But I still managed to avoid sex. Since I was so stoned most of the time, that wasn't too hard. I just got good at passing out in safe places.

"Most of my first year is a blur to me. I don't know how I got through my classes. If there had been a dean's list for just squeaking by, that's the one I would have made. I was even able to hold a part-time waitress job. I needed it for the drugs. My folks were willing to give me all the spending money I needed, but I didn't have the nerve to ask them to support my drug habit.''

It was through that waitress job that Lisa finally got up the courage to rid herself of her virginity. At the beginning of her second year of college, she responded to the overtures of the thirty-year-old manager of the restaurant. ''I was lucky. Zane was a gentle man who felt honored by the 'gift' of my virginity. He was kind to me and taught me how wonderful sex could be. He taught me to value my body because he valued every square inch of it. He had a lot of experience, so he gave me a complete course in sexual expression—positions I had never heard about, techniques for oral sex, the courage to experiment. I've never had another lover like him.

''After we went to bed, I talked myself into thinking that I was in love with Zane, but he knew before I did that I was only in lust. He also knew that we came from such different worlds that we could never keep up a relationship. After a while, when he felt he had groomed me carefully enough for the grown-up world, he gradually distanced himself from me. And then I did with men what I had done with drugs.

''I didn't go to bed with the whole male population of the town and the college. I only picked all the ones who were all wrong for me. The ones who had their own self-destructive problems with booze or drugs, the ones who were ready to use me up and throw me away. They were either losers or rats.''

It was a split life Lisa was leading in those years—a life built on drugs and sex at school, and being Daddy's good little girl again when she went home over vacations. She never told her family about her boyfriends. Aside from the fact that their characters were not the stuff of parental dreams, none of them was Jewish, a fact she knew would have pained her devout parents. They didn't pressure her about her mediocre grades because they felt she was only in college to mark time until she found a husband. And she was still cute and still good.

''Then one day I had my epiphany—my divine flash: I wouldn't have to worry about going to hell because I was already living it. I woke up in a strange bed in a strange room with a strange guy next to me. There was blood all over the sheets, because I had taken a razor to myself after a horrifying LSD trip. I woke up screaming when I saw the cuts on my arms. Luckily they weren't deep. But the thing that really brought me to my senses was this man's reaction. He looked at me as if he had never seen me before and as if he never wanted to see me again.

" 'You know, you're one crazy chick,' he told me. 'You're okay in the sack, but I got no room for you in my life.' He helped me get dressed and took me back to my dorm, and that was the last time I ever saw him. It was also the last time I ever took a hallucinogen. I suddenly realized that I didn't have to swing from one extreme to the other, and I felt very grateful that I learned this in time—before I killed myself with the wrong drug or the wrong man.''

In the inexplicable way that life sometimes saves us from ourselves, the horror of that awakening marked the end of Lisa's "wild child" stage. She gave up her self-destructive drug habit and her equally self-destructive sex life at about the same time, retreating into a period of workaholic celibacy. Only after she knew she'd get her degree and would be able to become a music therapist would she allow herself to have any relationships at all with men.

After graduation, Lisa got a job in Chicago, found an apartment—and then met Joel, the embodiment of her parents' dream son-in-law. He was good-looking, bright, ambitious, polite—and Jewish. He was going for his doctorate in neurobiology. When he finally received it, he was offered a prestigious research job in, of all places, St. Louis. So here they are in Clayton.

"Sometimes I wish that I had met Joel right after I broke up with Zane. I would have learned how to be a wonderful lover and I wouldn't have all those sordid memories in between—memories that Joel doesn't know about. He doesn't want to know. Whenever I start to tell him about my past he says, 'They didn't count. As far as I'm concerned, I'm the first man you've ever known.' "

Like most young adults, Lisa made her sexual declaration of independence privately. She didn't seek a confrontation with her parents or flaunt her new life style. Unlike many, she did credit them with good—if misguided—intentions. She didn't set out to show them how wrong they had been—if indeed it had been their fault that sex was such a problem to her. She did, however, realize that it was time she became sexually independent, time she worked out her own moral code, time she did what she thought was right.

Not all young people, of course, go through the kind of crisis that

Lisa did to achieve sexual independence. For example, Amy, a twenty-one-year-old senior at the University of Puget Sound in Tacoma, Washington, went along all through high school and most of college with her mother's admonitions "not to let a boy go too far." When Amy fell in love and entered a relationship that she felt was on a mature level, she questioned her behavior.

"I felt it was time to stop playing games to keep my 'technical virginity,' " she writes. "I did a lot of soul-searching and realized I felt ready for the responsibilities as well as benefits of sexual involvement, and that my 'stop at the last moment' approach was hypocritical. I felt guilty at getting the man I loved stimulated and then stopping him cold, and felt it was not an adequate way for adults to express the feelings we shared."

So Amy did one of the most difficult things in her life. She went alone to a family planning clinic and obtained a prescription for birth control pills. She expects to marry her lover, but if this does not occur, she plans not to engage in sexual intercourse until she falls in love again.

"I do not believe in casual sex," she says. "I guess this is my new set of moral values, which replace the ones my mother tried to give me. I still do feel guilty at the thought of how wrong she would consider my behavior, but I am trying to accept in my mind that she is trying to guard my happiness and safety the only way she knows how and that after I take her good intentions into account, I must make my own decisions."

Virgins, of course, can be sexually independent too. Just because a young person is doing something in accord with what his or her parents approve of doesn't mean that she or he is blindly going along with their wishes. Those young men and women who have considered the possibility of expanding their sexual experience and have chosen not to in deference to other goals are often showing the same kind of mature judgment that leads their chronological counterparts to choose responsible sexual activity. Just as entering into a sexual relationship can arise from mature or immature needs, so can postponing one. The decision to hold back can be a mature decision by an individual who knows that she or he is too immature to take on the physical, emotional, and moral obligations of a sexual relationship.

Adam, for example, at eighteen is barely into adolescence, not hav-

86

ing attained puberty until the late age of sixteen. He is much less experienced than his contemporaries and feels their pressures—especially the ones from women—to participate more actively in sex than he feels ready for. He liked going out with Cheryl, finding her smart and fun to be with. The fun included necking and petting—until one evening when Adam realized that if the heavy petting continued, they would go on to intercourse, a step he was not ready for.

With as much savoir faire as he could muster, Adam later wrote in an anonymous "sexual autobiography," he pulled away from Cheryl and said, "How about going to 31 Flavors? What I want right now more than anything else is a hot fudge sundae." Realizing he had brought the previous activity to a rather cold and abrupt end, Adam explained his feelings to Cheryl—that while sex was fine and good, and while sexual intercourse would one of these days be wonderful, at the time he found it an unnecessary risk.

"Is there anything wrong with me?" asked Cheryl, in a hurt tone.

"Not a single thing," Adam said, trying to reassure her. "But I'm a firm believer in Murphy's Law, with an addendum: 'If anything can go wrong it will—and Mother Nature is a bitch.' " (Afterward Adam realized he had used possible impregnation as an excuse, not feeling able to say—as a young woman might—that he just wanted to wait.)

Still feeling the pain of rejection, Cheryl sent a letter to Adam the next day, which he interpreted as "laying on a guilt trip as thick as peanut butter, because she mistook my rejection of intercourse as a rejection of her. After I got another letter sarcastically asking what was wrong with my sex drive and questioning my masculinity, I wrote back, reassuring Cheryl that I was indeed a male, that I did indeed have a sex drive, but that I did not wish to have sex yet—not with anyone—and especially not with someone as insensitive as she had turned out to be. 'Besides,' I wrote, 'I hear that some people even wait until they're married.' "

Adam is generally much less interested in sex than most other young men his age ("I masturbate about once every three months. I have nothing against the act, but I'd rather go to the movies or play Scrabble"). Adam and the many others like him provide an illustration of the variability in sex drive, which corresponds with apparently inborn differences in our other physical drives—our need for sleep, our appetite for food. In today's "do it" climate, the major problem for someone like Adam is to defend his right *not* to be sexually active.

"Until recently, I never thought I was supposed to stimulate a male by caressing his genitals. It seemed odd to me. Now I am getting a little bit more comfortable doing it, but I still feel awkward. I don't know exactly how to do it. I'm learning what stimulates men and hope to please my boyfriend. I always feel like I'm not satisfying him, which makes me feel incompetent. Especially since he stimulates and excites me and I would like to return those feelings to him. I'm learning more and wish I had learned it earlier, because maybe my inhibitions would be less.

"I know nothing about how to give or receive oral sex, which my boyfriend likes. It scares me and I feel uncomfortable with it. It has always seemed gross to me. The first time my boyfriend did cunnilingus, I had never heard of it and thought it a strange act. I didn't know what to do with my hands while he was busy down there, but after a while I did enjoy it. I have never given fellatio. My friends always talk about giving 'blow jobs,' but I feel my lack of experience and knowledge about the male genitals has a great deal to do with my hesitation in giving oral sex. If my boyfriend did ask me to, I would probably do it because I love him."

These statements, expressed by Erin, a nineteen-year-old college student, illustrate a major task of this coming-of-age period, the time when most young people confront their fears and ignorance and achieve some sense of sexual competence. The first experience of oral sex often dramatizes this sense of being competent in sex, of knowing what to do and how to do it. While people in this stage of life represent a range of sexual experience, even in these days when sexual activity starts at increasingly younger ages Erin's sense of inadequacy is all too typical. True, some women and men overcome this hurdle earlier, in their middle teens, but others still struggle with it well past their twenties.

It doesn't take much digging to figure out why it's so hard for most of us to feel confident about our sexual adeptness. We don't learn about sex the way we learn about virtually every other important and desirable activity in life. We've never been taught how to please ourselves or our sexual partners in the same ways we've been taught how to dress, how to eat, how to dance, how to play tennis. We haven't had the chance to see someone else go through a sexual experience so we could tell what the right moves are, what the accepted sequence is, what looks as if it would be fun. We don't know what to do with our clothes, our hands, our legs, our mouths. We try to figure out how "tab A" fits into "slot B," often without understanding the mechanisms of erection and lubrication.

In our culture sex is even more private than elimination. Whether such privacy is good or bad for the psyche is not even debated among us, since the answer is so implicitly assumed that no one except a few people on the fringes of civilized society ever suggest that it might not be as important as the psychiatrists say it is. In any case, it certainly does not help a young person's sexual education.

Because of this insistence on privacy and because most parents are confused about sex themselves, even the liberal ones among us usually have enough difficulty explaining what sex is to our children without trying to teach them how to enjoy it. Sex is different from everything else we learn. Most young people in the Western world learn about sex by doing it. They start out ignorant, and embarrassed about that ignorance, and yet they plunge ahead. It's either sinking in the sea of loneliness or swimming in unfamiliar waters. "This is," says California sex therapist Harvey Caplan, "the only activity in life when we—especially if we're male—are supposed to be experts at something the very first time we do it."

The achievement of sexual competency embraces an appreciation of the possibilities of sexual experience. Many people take years to stop equating sex with sexual intercourse and to learn that sex is so much more than the insertion of penis into vagina. The only time when that joining need be considered the "main event," and everything else be thought of as "foreplay," is when a couple is trying to conceive a new life. At all other times, sexuality is far more encompassing than the act of intercourse alone.

A sexual relationship includes kissing and touching, the sensuous intertwining of the bodies of lovers in sleep, the senses of sight and smell and taste. It includes bathing together and washing each other and caressing each other's body with hands and tongue. It includes stimulating many other areas of each other's body besides the reproductive

89

organs—the breasts, the buttocks, under the arms, the anus, the neck, the ears—the list is as long as the number of parts of the human body. Sexual excitement also comes from stimulating oneself with hands, vibrator, water, or in some other way, either alone or in the company of one's lover.

A single session of making love may include all of the above activities in a number of different sequences, either before or after intercourse. With a variety of stimulation, a woman is likely to reach orgasm several times before, during, after, or in the absence of intercourse. She may climax when her lover sucks her nipples, when he licks her clitoris, when he inserts his penis in her vagina, when he strokes her mons veneris, when he manipulates the slippery walls of her vagina with his finger. The man may climax during intercourse or he may prefer to move inside his lover for a while, then withdraw and ejaculate in her mouth. In this case, wouldn't we consider intercourse the "foreplay"?

A sexually fulfilling experience doesn't have to include intercourse at all. Even when a man's erection is not strong enough for penetration, it is often vigorous enough to allow him to reach orgasm in some other way, possibly in response to his lover's oral or manual stimulation alone.

If lovers allow themselves the luxury of time, when both are well rested, vigorous, and energetic, more than one climax is often possible for the man as well as the woman. In such cases, the original orgasm may occur through intercourse or manual or oral stimulation; the second and possibly subsequent ones may be in response to the same or some other form of sexual activity.

Many women—possibly as many as 70 percent—do not experience orgasm from intercourse alone. Therefore, calling every other form of sexual expression "foreplay" denigrates those activities that are more satisfying to such women and makes them feel as if there's something wrong with them. The term "foreplay" connotes a goal-oriented, typically masculine work ethic that pays reverence to the *end product*, not the *process* of creating it. It's as if an artist denigrated the process of putting paint on canvas, turning the clay, chiseling the stone, or weaving the fibers, and looked only at the final creation. What about the time and the thought and the originality that went into conceiving and actually producing that final work of art? In the artistry of sex, too, process is at least as important as end product, if not more so.

People who think in terms of "foreplay" mean getting a woman "ready" so that she'll then be able to receive the penis. In these terms, a sexual encounter is a failure if both partners don't reach a climax. More sophisticated lovers generally recognize that, as ecstatic as orgasm is, the sexual enjoyment of our bodies offers many other delights in addition. We need not measure success or failure by whether or not "the big O" occurs every single time. A further burden was assumed by the "end product" crowd ever since Masters and Johnson established scientifically what many women already knew—that women are capable of multiple orgasms. Now, too many couples have a new barometer of success: not only do both partners have to reach orgasm, but she has to reach it again and again and again.

To counter this attitude, which sabotages many otherwise gratifying sexual experiences, one sex therapist compares making love to taking a vacation. "Suppose you have only two weeks' holiday time," Dr. Jacqueline Hott, director of sex therapy for the Family Service Association in Hempstead, New York, will say to a couple. "You fly to Milan, rent a car, and plan to drive to Rome. Soon after you start your trip, you reach Florence, and you fall in love with this gem of a city. You become so involved with exploring the beauties of Florence that before you know it your vacation time is over and you never got to Rome. You need to remember that you don't always have to get to Rome. You can enjoy Florence."

"We've accustomed ourselves to believing that a complete sexual experience has to include orgasm," Dr. Hott told me. "But you don't always have to have the orgasm to enjoy sex. You can enjoy the sensuousness, the sharing, loving, and giving of a beautiful experience."

Knowing that good sex does not need a "destination" is a prerequisite for enjoying the journey. It's likely, too, that there's another prerequisite—going over the same route again and again. It's possible that the early years of sexual fumbling are necessary for achieving the ultimate proficiency at pleasing ourselves and our partners. It's possible that in our culture we don't become really serious about sex until we have made the major break from the parental nest. It's possible that a

91

certain level of maturation is needed to become adventurous and experimental in sex, as in other facets of life. After all, few pre-adults are gastronomically adventurous either.

This is particularly evident with regard to oral sex, which is often the adolescent equivalent of the school child's first awareness of intercourse. "Yuk! Who wants to do *that*? You mean that's supposed to feel good?" Most people who do give it a try, though, eventually learn what all the shouting is about. Those who incorporate it into their sexual repertoire will benefit for the rest of their lives, especially during those times when intercourse may be difficult, such as during pregnancy and just after childbirth, after injury or during illness, and in the later years.

One major change over recent generations has been the increase in oral sex among young people, reflecting a greater societal acceptance of this kind of lovemaking. Oral sex has, of course, been engaged in throughout recorded history. Depictions of it are painted on friezes in Pompeii; molded in hundreds of pre-Columbian Mochica pottery sculptures filling the shelves of the Rafael Larco Herrera Museum in Lima, Peru; incised on the crumbling walls of ancient temples at Egypt's fabled Karnak. Yet this deservedly popular means of sexual expression fell from favor for years, at least in this country: in 1953 Kinsey found that only 42 percent of the women born before 1900 had experienced cunnilingus and only 29 percent had performed fellatio. Studies performed in 1977 and later, however, have found that 91 percent of women surveyed have experienced cunnilingus and 97 percent have performed fellatio. In fact, 35 percent of sixteen-year-olds of both sexes have had oral-genital experience.

Even more interesting than the steadily rising acceptance of this form of sexual activity, among all ages, all social classes, married and unmarried, conservative and liberal, is the fact that the sequence for its occurrence has changed. The traditional sexual script for heterosexual young couples in America usually dictated this scenario: First a couple kissed tentatively at the end of the evening, then they advanced to more passionate tongue-kissing for longer parts of the evening, then to light petting (above the waist, first with clothes on, then with them off), to heavy petting (below the waist, including mutual masturbation), to intercourse, and then to such refinements as oral sex.

Today, oral sex often occurs long before intercourse takes place. Oral sex offers distinct pluses to adolescents and young adults. Nobody ever got pregnant from it, but practically everyone experiences orgasms from it. Many women reach orgasm from cunnilingus even when they don't from intercourse. So the couple who want to be sexually intimate but don't want to use birth control or don't have access to a reliable method can make this kind of love to their heart's content.

Furthermore, young women who want to remain virgins for the time being can please both themselves and their partners through oral sex without taking the irreversible step of breaking that little piece of skin that some cultures hold so important. As one college woman describes her first experience of performing fellatio on her boyfriend, ''I wanted to keep my virginity, and I felt sorry for him because he had nowhere to put his penis.''

Despite the embarrassment some young women feel about being licked (''What do I look like? What do I smell like? What is he feeling? What do I do with my hands while he is down there? Will I have to kiss him afterward?'') and the reluctance some men feel (''I don't like getting hair between my teeth. The smell turns me off. Something perverted about it''), many men sing paeans to cunnilingus.

What do young men love about it? They talk about the sexy thrill they get from being able to see, feel, hear, and taste their partner's orgasm. They talk about the sense of their own power in the certainty they'll be able to bring their partner to orgasm. They talk about how great it is to give as well as receive. One twenty-two-year-old student at the University of Puget Sound writes: ''When I first heard about 'eating out' a girl, I felt sick to even think about it. I couldn't imagine how anyone would enjoy putting their face in a girl's vagina. But enough of my friends had survived it, so I gave it a try. When I found out how aroused *I* could get I was amazed!''

Writes another: ''I would wonder about the sanity of anyone who didn't enjoy it and want it as frequently as intercourse. Oral sex is a great builder of the whole act of sex, making it last longer and feel better. I am fascinated with each woman's unique gift, the vagina. I love the salty taste, and I will often become lost in a probing with my tongue as I help my lover reach her orgasm.''

And fellatio? ''Just being able to watch a woman suck my penis and at the same time feeling that warmness and wetness around it brings me as near to heaven as I could be without being dead. A woman who can perform fellatio well can have me as her slave." Other men find that they can delay ejaculation better with fellatio than with intercourse.

How, then, does a woman learn to "perform fellatio well"? How does a man learn to bring a woman to orgasm through cunnilingus? How do young men and women learn what coital positions are most satisfying to them and their partners? How do they learn to feel confident performing various sexual activities? Mostly, the same way you get to Carnegie Hall: "Practice, practice, practice."

"When I was a sophomore in high school, I was dating a college freshman. Soon after we met I went down to Planned Parenthood and had an exam and they put me on the Pill. I am still taking it now," says eighteen-year-old Sheila. "It was quite an emotional experience for me to go on the Pill, because I had to admit to myself that I would probably be having sex regularly from that point on."

"It was hard for me to deal with the responsibility that intercourse involves," says eighteen-year-old Garrett. "I think each individual should be responsible enough to deal with a pregnancy should one arise and a relationship should be strong enough to deal with surprises. This takes open communication, trust, respect, common sense, and love. My girlfriend and I have had a very good relationship over the past three years. We have explored almost all aspects of each other's sexuality, trading roles as teacher, student, dominant and passive partner. During all of this we have been very open and honest with each other."

The achievement of a responsible attitude toward birth control is a distinct turning point in the attainment of maturity. Whenever we take responsibility for the consequences of our own actions, we are showing a new level of maturity. When, as in contraceptive decisions, we are also taking responsibility for our sexuality, we are showing an acceptance of self that is essential for healthy sexual development.

Sexual responsibility is multifaceted. It involves being true to our own moral values, being scrupulous about not exploiting our partners, and being honest about our sexuality without feeling the need to flaunt it. It also, of course, implies a responsibility toward the life that could be conceived. Some of us become sexually responsible while still in our

94

early or middle teens and others not until our twenties or later (or never). Most often, though, it is during this time between adolescence and adulthood that we begin to fully appreciate the implications of the sexual course we have been charting.

Most of us learn the facts about the relationship between sexual intercourse and the conception of a baby long before we're ready to engage in the former or care for the latter. By the time we're physically able to reproduce, we usually know the risk we're taking by unprotected intercourse, even if we try to deny it to ourselves. We don't become mature in an emotional and intellectual sense, however, until we realize that it's up to us whether to conceive or to prevent conception.

With the technological revolution in birth control that has taken place during our lifetime, it's much easier to be responsible today. Before using a contraceptive, however, a person has to acknowledge his or her sexuality. This is a major problem for many young women, who are unable to say to themselves, as Sheila did when she went to the family planning clinic, "I am a sexual person. I will probably have sexual intercourse. I can decide with my eyes wide open whom I'll have sex with and when. I don't have to be swept off my feet. Planned sex can be just as gratifying as spontaneous sex—and a lot safer."

Many young women are not able to say this to themselves until they have been sexually active for a long time—or until they've already had a pregnancy scare. Why? Because they feel too guilty about even having sexual desires, much less acting on them. A considerable body of research has shown that the guiltier a young woman feels about sex, the less likely she is to seek and use a reliable method of birth control. Ironically, it's usually the least experienced and the most anxious women who suffer the consequences.

How does guilt sabotage contraception? The guilt-ridden woman often won't even read about birth control, and when she does, she won't remember what she learns. She hesitates to go to a clinic, partly from embarrassment at the thought of the internal pelvic examination that is required for the three most reliable devices—the diaphragm, the Pill, and the intrauterine device (IUD). She's reluctant to expose her body. But more important, she's ashamed to admit to anyone— including the doctors and nurses at the family planning center—that she is indeed sexually active. The phrase "family planning" (usually a euphemism for "planning not to have a family—at least not yet") does imply planning ahead for sex. And the sexually guilty woman cannot plan ahead. She has to pretend to herself that she is carried away by a sudden excess of passion, by an emotion she's powerless to resist, by a force "greater than both of us." Only in this way can she allow her sexuality to emerge.

What happens to such a woman—or to the one whose birth control method has failed, resulting in a pregnancy? Both kinds of unplanned, unwanted pregnancies are all too common, even among people who take precautions. Women in this coming-of-age transition are more likely to have an abortion than those in any other age group, probably reflecting the fact that this time ushers in a period of more frequent sexual activity, even for those women who had their first sexual intercourse as young teenagers. Every year more than three-quarters of a million women between the ages of eighteen and twenty-four undergo this experience, almost always a significant turning point in their lives—and often in the lives of their husbands or lovers as well.

No one who spoke or wrote to me about the decision to end a pregnancy has dismissed it lightly. In nearly every single case of abortion undergone by a young unmarried woman that I have heard of, the abortion was the beginning of the end of the affair. The woman becomes angry, blaming her lover. Or he blames her. Or they both blame fate—and fate assumes the shape and sound and smell of the lover. A twenty-two-year-old woman talks about the way she abhorred being touched by any man, especially the boyfriend she could no longer bear to look at, for a year after her abortion. "We've become enemies since that abortion," says a twenty-one-year-old man. Another man talks about the nervous breakdown he had after his lover and he actually *named* the embryo they had accidentally conceived and then went ahead with their plans to abort it.

The meaning of this turning point is unique for each person. Jane, an eighteen-year-old sophomore at a small Midwestern college, was buoyed by ambition and the promise of a newspaper job after graduation. David, nineteen, was at an Ivy League school preparing for his dreamed-of career as a surgeon. Though they expected to get married "someday," they were not formally engaged. They were euphorically, passionately in love. Then one day the condom broke. Jane missed a period. The rabbit test confirmed her pregnancy.

This was in 1953, before abortion was legal. David tentatively offered to marry Jane after a professor told him, "If she has the abortion, the two of you will never get married. If you really love her and feel ready for the responsibility, try to talk her into it." David did love her. But neither he nor Jane felt ready to love and care for a baby. His professor helped them find a respected anesthesiologist in New York who did careful, painless abortions for the then huge sum of five hundred dollars. Somehow—Jane never found out how—David raised the cash and brought it to her in a brown paper bag on the day of the abortion. He stayed with her, took her back to his apartment, and, late that night, he took her to her parents' apartment. About a month later, Jane sent him a "Dear John" letter.

"I felt guilty about that letter," Jane tells me, years later. "David had been supportive and good. But I didn't see any way I could see him and not continue having a sexual relationship, and I was terrified of getting pregnant again. The only thing I could see to do was break it off entirely.

"My abortion was the deepest and most intense emotional experience I had ever had up to that point in my life," she recalls. A shadow subdues her lively expression. "I never regretted it, because I knew that going through with that pregnancy would have ruined my life, but I wish it hadn't been necessary. Still, I learned from it. It made me take a good long look at the real purpose and meaning of life, love, sex, and my own strength. Because of it I have had a better sense of myself and my life."

Jane's abortion affected her life in profound and unforeseen ways, both self-destructive and self-discovering. At first she avoided all men. Then she married and took her husband's psychological abuse for years, feeling it was a just punishment for her sin. She attributes her three miscarriages to guilt over her abortion, since no doctor ever found a physical reason for them.

After taking that newspaper job, Jane became obsessed by stories about the deaths of women who aborted themselves with coat hangers and poisons, because they didn't have boyfriends from wealthy families who had access to five hundred dollars in cash. As many tears as Jane shed over the baby that she and David never had, she became more convinced than ever that they had done the right thing and that safe, legal abortion had to be made available to every woman as one option for solving a potentially engulfing problem. She became a social activist and achieved prominence as a political organizer and lecturer crusading for women's rights to birth control, abortion, and other health services.

Jane's story has the kind of storybook ending no novelist would dare to invent. She eventually did bear a healthy daughter, who is now grown—and ardently conscientious about birth control. She found the courage to divorce the husband who had maltreated her. And, just a few months ago, I attended the party she and David threw to celebrate their marriage. After thirty years they had found each other again. Now that Jane was divorced and David widowed, they began to see each other. When they made the exciting discovery that the love they had felt for each other in their youth was flooding back to fill their hearts in midlife, they decided to set out—cautiously—to begin a new life together.

Of course, the two of them never will have a child together. Jane muses today: "Who knows how things might have been different if we had been better prepared at age eighteen?"

With all the obstacles to men's and women's getting together in a climate of trust, it's a tribute to the strength of our drives that we do make contact with each other and that such contact often leads to the most meaningful sexual relationships of our lives. But despite the clouds of romanticizing that billow over the heads of everyone who grows up in this society, true love and good sex do not always go together. The question is: Should they?

According to Tilly Salomon, the answer is "Not necessarily," especially early in one's sexual career. I first met this paradox of a woman through an activist women's organization. Before long, we found our paths crossing at feminist events, sexuality conferences, political discussions, even art exhibits. I'm now fortunate enough to count her as a friend.

Tilly is one of the most sexual people I have ever met in my life, yet no one would accuse her of flaunting her sexuality. By her own description, she is a "gray-haired, grandmotherly-looking suburban matron who limps from an arthritic hip." She makes no pretense of looking younger than her sixty years: she doesn't color her hair, wears no makeup other than soft lipstick or rouge, and dresses in simple skirts and blouses or conservative dresses.

Tilly has influenced countless women through her workshops and lectures, yet she has no letters after her name testifying to an advanced degree or formal credentials as a sex educator. She has enabled many women to overcome the crippling effects of a poor body image or repressed attitudes, yet she has no certification as a sex therapist.

During a conversation Tilly and I have at her home in Great Neck, New York, she talks about the differences in the ways men and women look at sex: "Most women are short-changed because they have been so strongly conditioned to put so much emphasis on love and intimacy and so little on the physicality and raw excitement of sex. With men it's precisely the opposite. I would like to see a healthy trend where we meet a little more in the middle—where women can learn to enjoy sex without emotional involvement and where men can join their emotions to their physical activity.

"We tend to think the emotional and intimate part of sex is good and the physical part is bad. I'd like to see young people do a lot of experimenting and experiencing on the physical level—without guilt—before they ever get their emotions involved. It's just not possible or desirable to engage early sexuality and emotionality together at the same time.

"What would happen," Tilly asks me, "if we learned to be sexual the same way we learn to be musical? When you study music, you first learn lightweight melodies without a lot of emotional freight, like a Chopin mazurka. Then you move on to Beethoven and Bach. No one tells you that music is bad and meaningless and exploitive unless it has emotional or religious content. No one tells you not to play or listen to a Strauss waltz—that it has to be Brahms or nothing. Uncomplicated music has its place. You're entertained by it, you learn from it, and you can use it as a stepping stone to the appreciation of more complex, more demanding themes. I'd like to see that happen with sex. It already has with men, of course. Now I'd like to see that concept accepted by young girls.

"Of course, this analogy isn't perfect," Tilly hastens to add. "You can't hurt anyone through music appreciation. But in sex, responsibility must go hand in hand with liberation—not only with regard to birth control and health, but over valuing the feelings of partners and coping with conflicts over ethics and values.''

Actually, this ''forever problem,'' as Tilly describes the dilemma of bringing the physical and emotional together, is affecting both women and men these days. In his 1983 textbook *Human Sexuality*, sociologist E. R. Mahoney charts the decline of the double standard and the convergence of male and female attitudes and premarital sexual experience. Neither phenomenon is, of course, complete even today—but both are startlingly different from what they were fifty years ago.

''Until perhaps the 1950s, both males and females tended to agree that there were 'bad girls' (those who did) and 'good girls' (those who did not). They also agreed that there were just plain boys (those who did if they had the chance).'' Since more men than women were having premarital intercourse, they were obviously having it with ''bad girls''—girls from lower social classes or different ethnic groups, or girls they wouldn't dream of marrying for some other reason.

A 1959 study found that college men felt guiltier about having intercourse with women they loved than with those they didn't care about—about, as Professor Mahoney says, ''doing 'bad' things with 'good' girls.'' Then the double standard began to erode, and women increasingly accepted the idea of intercourse with a man with whom they were in an affectionate, committed relationship. So the ''good girls'' were doing it more with their boyfriends and the ''bad girls'' were insisting on more commitment before they would do it, and the young men, who held on to the double standard much longer than women did, found themselves in a bind.

Another crucial change occurred as the levels of affection and commitment that women considered necessary for sexual intercourse declined—from marriage, to engagement, to ''steady'' dating with strong affection, to mere affection, and, today for many young people, to strong liking and personal attraction and respect. As a result, men and women have been coming together in bed before marriage at more equal rates.

No, the change has not been total. And yes, women are still more likely than men to invest sex with affection and commitment and to feel guilty about their sexual experiences, whereas men feel affirmed by them. Still, it would be hard to identify by sex many of the statements I read in the sexual autobiographies of those University of Puget Sound students. The following comments were typical:

"I used to be more promiscuous than I am now. It may be because I have matured and realize it is not a little 'game' anymore. I take intercourse as being fairly serious, whereas I used to think of it as the 'thing to do.' I'm glad I have had the experiences I have."

"I have had plenty of close sexual relationships and have always tried never to hurt anybody's feelings. Now I am at the stage in my life where the most erotic thing is to be in love. Sex is a beautiful experience which I cherish and discuss freely with the person I love."

The first of these statements was written by a woman, the second by a man. They illustrate the two common threads of people's feelings about sex at this time of life. First, they value its importance as a way of getting to know themselves, of getting to know other people, of becoming competent at lovemaking, of appreciating sex simply for its own sake. Still, however, almost all young people of both sexes hold out the tantalizing ideal of the total relationship—the one encompassing love and sex, which will bring them as close to ecstasy as possible.

Young adults today seem to have rediscovered love, a topic often shunned in polite society over the past couple of decades. "When I first started teaching undergraduates in the 1960s, you couldn't talk about love," Dr. Samona Sheppard, a professor of human sexuality at New York's Queens College, told me. "The young men especially equated love with being smothered. It's a whole different thing now, and sometimes the young women are surprised to find that men want the same things they do—love and companionship."

This relationship seems to exist for the young married couple we'll call Jack and Jill. As described by Jack, who, like his wife, was a virgin until their marriage, the two of them continue to grow individually as their tie to each other becomes even closer. They had gone together for a year, gradually engaging in more intimate sexual behavior that included hours of petting and eventually oral sex, but stopped short of intercourse because of Jill's desire to remain a virgin until marriage. "That proved to be one of the most difficult decisions I had ever made," writes Jack. "We'd drive out in the country and park for hours at a time talking of all the secrets we had held inside us for so long. It was all new for both of us, as exciting as if we had invented sex ourselves.''

After months of ''sweet torture,'' Jack and Jill were married. The wedding night was thrilling for Jack but a bitter disappointment to Jill, who felt pain and missed the climaxes she had been having regularly from petting and oral sex. During the following week both newlyweds were frustrated and disappointed, until finally Jill felt a powerful orgasm. ''She was so beautiful to me at that moment,'' her young bridegroom writes, ''and I knew we were on the right track at last. I was learning how to please her, how to touch her, how to talk to her, how to excite her. This gave me a new confidence, which seemed to reassure her even more. And sometimes she would surprise me with her outright sexiness.

''I especially like it when she is on top of me during intercourse. She can move her hips in a way I just can't believe and she'll sometimes tease me, threatening to make me climax right away and then stopping just in time. I love to look up at her laughing face, and knowing that she is so in tune with my body really excites me. We have enjoyed many different approaches to lovemaking—dressing up, playing games, doing whatever comes naturally. Nothing is left out if it is good for both of us.

''I enjoy just being free enough in our relationship to be crazy with her, knowing I'll never be laughed at or rejected. I trust my wife in bed and I know that what I do for her will be appreciated and returned for our mutual pleasure. When I am tired or pressured, I appreciate knowing that I don't have to perform. I know I'm a man not because of what I can do with my organs, but because I can think and feel and learn. Sex gives me a way to express all kinds of different emotions and learn about myself at the same time.

''So far I've never had to deal with anything like impotence, but I am sure that should it ever happen I could rely on the foundation of respect and trust we have built. I don't feel threatened that I could lose my manhood at any time or that I will be considered less of a man should my performance slip. The things that make me a man and make sex so special to me are deep inside me. They are trust and self-respect and mostly love. I look forward to the opening of many new sexual doors with my wife, the one woman I love.''

102

Chapter 5

Vales of Venus: The Twenties

In a way it's nice not to feel sexually crazy, not to have that drive that I just have to have sex every other night. I feel as if I've come full circle and I'm a virgin again.

—STEVEN

THE SEXUAL GOALS of early adulthood, which we usually confront in the decade of the twenties, often set the path we tread for the rest of our lives. This is the time when most of us make our decisions on the basic choice of a sexual life style. Do I want to live these years in a carnival atmosphere of casual, recreational sex? If so, what will this mean to me now and in the years ahead? Or do I want to embrace monogamy, married or not? How can I think about settling down with one person for the rest of my life? What kind of person could I even consider as a lifetime partner? Can I "try out" somebody by living together? This will have to be someone I love. But what is love? How can I tell when I love someone enough to marry him or her? How will marriage change my sex life? How will pregnancy and children change my sex life? Am I to express my sexuality as a heterosexual or a homosexual, or will I slide back and forth between the two modes, living a bisexual life? What do I want to do with the rest of my life outside of bed? How does what I do *in* bed affect my professional goals?

* * *

103

In the short space of one generation, we've seen a dizzying change in the sexual life styles of people at all points in the life cycle, with the change most dramatic for people in their twenties. The turbulent 1960s ushered in the "sexual revolution" as young people rebelled against the values and traditions of their parents, their teachers, whoever they saw as authorities. Virginity was a burden to be shed with as little fuss as possible, and if the person who helped rid you of it was not someone you particularly cared about, so much the better, because everybody "knew" that the first time was never much fun anyway. Advances in contraceptive technology made this surge in sexual activity possible, may even have spurred the entire rebellious era by turning at least one oft-repeated maxim on its head, that "bad" girls were sure to get "caught."

Meanwhile, other trends were altering the cultural landscape. A more complex economy dictated a longer span of education across all strata of society: children of parents who'd made it through the eighth grade were now getting associate's degrees from community colleges, offspring of high school graduates were now getting diplomas from four-year colleges, and progeny of college graduates were going on for Ph.D.s, LL.B.s, and M.D.s. The women's movement, with its emphasis on career achievement, influenced many young women to put off their wedding dates and postpone having children. This seemed to fit in fine with the reluctance of many young men to commit themselves "prematurely" to either a profession or a partner. So we saw the emergence of a new social group—singles. People are still flocking to the altar, of course, and the median age for first marriage is still in the early twenties (24.6 years for men, 22.1 for women), but since there are just as many people above this median age as below it, we're talking about a sizable proportion of people who remain single until well into their late twenties, or even later.

Just as it seemed that this life style of busy, sometimes frenetic sexual activity, with its "Why not?" attitude, had become well enough entrenched to make it into the social histories of our times, it looked as if someone had tossed a bitter potion into the punchbowl at the party. Throwing off the shackles of an earlier morality had not been as freeing as the newly liberated and their gurus had hoped.

Sex was still problematic. Everybody was going to singles bars, but nobody seemed to like it—except the owners of the bars. Courses and books proliferated on "How to pick up men," "How to pick up women," "How to overcome shyness." Both men and women were feeling uncomfortable about engaging in one-night stands with people whose names they didn't remember the next morning, or investing time in relationships only if the sex was good—and finding out that often the sex *couldn't* be good, because for so many people, sex is still inextricably bound up with our feelings for the person whose body is entwined around ours.

More and more people have become disillusioned with what *The Washington Post*'s "Miss Manners" calls the "backward courtship"—in which the "ultimate intimacy" comes first and any effort to get to know the other person comes later. This philosophy was straightforwardly expressed by Ken, twenty-four, a University of Puget Sound undergraduate, who in 1980 wrote in his "sexual autobiography" about the twenty-five women he had bedded over the previous year.

"More and more," Ken wrote, "I want to first meet the girl, then go to bed with her. Then if I like her I'll continue the relationship. My main goal isn't to get a girl into bed and then discard her the next day. It's to get her into bed and then be better friends the next day. Since I live a fast-paced life and move around a lot, it's almost impossible for me to have a single-relationship-based love life."

With this approach, of course, the friendship of the next day often doesn't materialize. The man not only doesn't send flowers—he doesn't even telephone. If he does, he may get a brush-off. In either case, the morning after often holds an emotional hangover for both partners, a feeling of "Why did I do it? Was it really worth it?"

As these signs of disillusionment were starting to bubble to the surface, more tangible ones appeared in doctors' offices around the country—a resurgence in gonorrhea and syphilis, both of which were thought to have been virtually wiped out by antibiotics; reports that cervical cancer might be linked to a woman's having become sexually active at an early age and then gone on to have many partners; a rise in genital herpes, which didn't kill anyone but was damned uncomfortable, highly contagious through sexual contact, and resistant to all attempts at cure; an epidemic of the venereal infection chlamydia, which has surpassed gonorrhea as the leading sexually transmitted disease in the country and has left hundreds of thousands of young women infertile; and then AIDS—acquired immune deficiency syndrome—which debilitated and often killed a frightening number of young homosexual men. Moralists talked about the wrath of God visiting the wicked. The over-thirties rejoiced that they had had their fun in a more carefree decade. Virtually everyone agreed that the climate had changed drastically, with sexual activity in some circles plunging to lows that hadn't been seen for twenty years.

Now that it looks as if the party's over, where *are* people in their twenties in the 1980s? What has the sexual revolution meant to them? Are they going through the same kinds of sexual passages as their counterparts of the previous decade? Is their adjustment to what looks like a throwback to earlier eras traumatic—or the kind of relief after excess that fasting can represent after overeating?

A living example of a 1980s person who has ridden the crest of the sexual wave, plunged into its trough, and come up for air, Heather, at twenty-six, is very much a product of her era. She had her obligatory initiation into sex at fifteen with some "hippie type" she hardly knew ("I felt unburdened by having done it. It was a weight off my chest"). She had her time of living with a lover, "playing house" but not taking each other seriously. Tantalized by the fear that she "had been missing out on something because a lot of people I knew seemed to be having more fun—they were very promiscuous," she went to a singles bar, determined to pick up someone that night and go to bed with him. A green-eyed redhead with just enough freckles to make her look innocent and just enough curves to contradict the first impression, she had no trouble attracting someone who took her home with him and left her with a remembrance in the form of a case of gonorrhea, which she unknowingly gave to the man with whom she had an ongoing relationship.

"That was a real turning point for me," Heather tells me. "Getting that disease—and giving it to Roger—turned my head around. I had been floundering, wondering what I wanted. Now I knew I didn't want that kind of experience. It wasn't just the disease itself, although that made me feel dirty. And it wasn't just giving it to Roger, although that made me feel guilty. A lot of it came down to just feeling so vulnerable. I was really naïve. I was under the illusion that people were good and the idea that this guy, who must have know he had it, wouldn't have told me—wouldn't even have called me afterward so I'd know to go to a doctor—blew my mind. Because I didn't even know I had it till Roger developed the symptoms.

"So I decided I didn't want to run the risk of getting involved with any more people like that. Just after that I switched from an IUD to a diaphragm. The IUD had been fine, but I didn't want to feel as if I was always ready for sex at the drop of a pair of pants. I like the idea that I'm giving it some thought before I go to bed with somebody."

The gonorrhea crisis forced Heather and Roger to deal with a subject they had talked about only in the abstract: fidelity. With Heather in Los Angeles trying to break in as a TV writer and Roger in Tucson going for his doctorate in wildlife management, their times together were limited, usually one weekend a month.

"The question of monogamy comes up all the time, and we've always said we have a commitment: We want to be with each other. We're not seeking to replace each other. If we do something here or there, that's our business unless it interferes with the relationship here. Monogamy is not a big issue for me. I've had two or three relationships over the past couple of years that Roger and I have been, well, with each other. But when I'm not seeing anyone else, there are times when I don't have sex for maybe a month or more. It doesn't really bother me. At times I get lonely and frustrated about my future, but it's more that than pure sexual desire.

"I would want a basically monogamous relationship, but I also understand there are times when people need another relationship to fulfill certain things in themselves. I'm not sure if that's something you get out of your system or keeps recurring, and I don't know if that has to stand in the way of making a commitment to someone. I think it's possible to love somebody and sleep with somebody else. I can't imagine having sex with only one person for the rest of my life. That business with the gonorrhea helped me get in touch with my feeling that if I do sleep with anyone else, though, it has to be someone I know and trust.

"So we just had this understanding and neither of us knew just what the other person actually was doing. I guess we both felt if there was something the other should know that we would tell him. This really brought it home for Roger that I was going to bed with other guys, and that was hard for him to take. On the surface, nothing has changed between us. We didn't break up and we didn't swear fidelity. But I think he's still angry at me, and I'm not sure what's going to happen. I'm not even sure what I *want* to happen. I love Roger, but right now I can't see marrying him—or anybody, for that matter. I know that someday I want to get married and I want to have kids, but not yet. First I want to go someplace with my career. I want to feel as if I'm established, not the way I am now, living from one freelance assignment to another.''

Still in the process of choosing her sexual life style, Heather's experiences and attitudes mirror those of many in her age group. The big way she differs seems to be in the way she's managed to keep afloat through the vicissitudes of sexual change, neither engaging in wildly self-destructive behavior nor sinking into deep depression at times of disappointment and crisis. One thing she's expressed relief about is the fact that she learned her lesson through gonorrhea, which can be cured, rather than through genital herpes, a less serious disease but one which still eludes cure.

Steven, now thirty-three, wasn't so lucky. A tall, slender man with straight brown hair and a sandy beard, he has a disconcerting way of keeping constant eye contact with his thick-lashed hazel eyes. Four years ago, a year or so after separating from the wife he'd married when they were both twenty-two, he was living a life style he had fantasized about, maintaining close relationships with three different women. One, Laurie, was seeing another man, who gave her genital herpes, which she passed on to Steven. Steven's life turned somersaults.

"One of the things that herpes is best for," Steven tells me as we sit on a bench in a Chicago park on a balmy June day, "is that it does not allow you to stay in relationships you should not stay in. Would I have gotten out of those relationships anyway, and become celibate the way I am now if it hadn't been for herpes? I don't know. I know I'm a loner, and I know I have trouble with relationships, so it's possible that I'm using the herpes to pull away from sex. As a therapist, I always consider these possibilities for my clients' behavior, so I have to ask myself the same question. I don't know.

"What I do know is that I looked at the other two women I was involved with at the time and made up my mind that I didn't want to carry the responsibility of knowing I had given them something they would have the rest of their lives. So I got out of both relationships. As for Laurie, she's one of my best friends and I love her dearly, but she has certain ways of being selfish in a sexual way, and I can't help wondering whether she knew what she was exposing me to. In any case, once this happened I lost all sexual desire for her, too.''

Steven didn't pull away from sex altogether right away. He continued to see women, taking pains to tell each one about his herpes before they had sex. (In this regard, he seems unusual, since most of the herpes sufferers I've spoken to had not been told ahead of time that they were being exposed to the disease.) To his surprise and pleasure, all the women he saw in that time still were willing to engage in sexual intercourse with him, as long as the disease was not in active eruption.

''Now I understand how women feel about having to be responsible for not getting pregnant. I feel it's *my* responsibility not to give a woman herpes. I would never have sex if I showed anything, but there were a lot of times when I wouldn't feel anything at the time but would break out in the next couple of days and it was nerve-wracking wondering whether I had passed it on. Needless to say, all this interfered with my pleasure in sex.''

It interfered with Steven's enjoyment in another way, too. ''If I had sex for more than twenty minutes, I would break out in two days. Once I realized this, a time bomb would go off in my head after about ten minutes, and I would come immediately no matter what was happening with the woman. So I couldn't have sex the way I wanted to, the way I could feel good about myself sexually. I couldn't enjoy being with the other person, because I was focusing so much on myself that I couldn't concentrate on seeing that she was having a good experience. To me, that's a big part of good sex.

''Finally I did pass it on to someone I cared about.'' Steven's voice drops, and his eyes wander over the path before us. ''I watched her go through the trauma of knowing she had it and I saw her whole sexual persona change. She had always been a very sexual person, lively and flirtatious and seductive in a really nice way, in a way that was part of her professional personality—she's a therapist, too—as well as her personal self. Once she got herpes, she couldn't be like that anymore. She just kind of lost that part of her. I hated to see what I had done to her, and I couldn't stand the idea that I might do this to someone else. It got

109

to the point where sex wasn't worth all the anxiety it caused. I haven't been with a woman sexually in about a year now.''

An airplane flies by overhead, forcing a silence between us.

''Do you miss it?'' I ask.

''I do and I don't. Right now sex to me is like blah, I can take or leave relationships, I can take or leave sex. I'm investing a lot of time and energy in running. I run about eighty or ninety miles a week, and that's one of the real thrills in my life. While I'm training for a marathon and running twenty miles in a pouring rain, I can be feeling quite miserable but still know that this is the thing I want to do. I'd rather be miserable and depressed and know that I'm feeling something—that I'm *alive*—than just go along doing something that on the surface seems like the normal thing to do but just doesn't feel right.

''I'd like to feel alive again with sex. I knew I had died sexually when I met someone I liked who had herpes, too, so I knew I could have sex without worrying about her, but I didn't even try. I'm curious if I'll come back to life. In a way it's nice not to feel sexually crazy, not to have that drive that I just *have* to have sex every other night. I feel as if I've come full circle and I'm a virgin again. It just might be interesting if I meet someone I really want to have a relationship with to come to her as a 'neo-virgin' instead of having been through seventeen sexual relationships in the last year.''

This decade marks another important goal, the beginning of most people's dual dedication of their lives to what Freud maintained were the two most important things in life—*Liebe und Arbeit*, love and work. As choosing a career assumes an overriding importance, people tend to incorporate sexuality into the quest for fulfillment of occupational goals.

In their studies of male development, psychologist Daniel J. Levinson and his colleagues at Yale University point to the way men choose an occupational path, partly to prove and validate themselves as men, partly to define their dreams for the future, partly to support a wife and children, and also, of course, for a variety of other reasons deriving from background, education, and individual abilities. With the selection of a career goes an accompanying life style, and this prescribed life style often dictates the choice of mate.

While these researchers focused their discussion on men, the same type of dynamic occurs with women, especially today when women's career goals are more like those of men than ever before in history. A single woman may well date and have sexual affairs with a variety of men, but when it comes time to settle down, she is most likely to marry not the person who's most exciting in bed but someone whose personality and background fit in with her occupation and its life style and goals. This effectively eliminates a number of people with whom she would interact sexually in very different ways, thus profoundly affecting day-to-day sexual expressiveness.

"The late twenties mark a significant time period for both men and women," New York psychotherapist Tilla Vahanian tells me. "Before this time sexuality has a different quality; it's all kinds of playing around. Then toward the end of this decade—later than in the past, since the whole business of being a child has been prolonged in our society—it becomes more connected with the search for a partner.

"It seems to strike the woman especially at this stage because she has to think about having babies. Today's woman has been able to indulge her youth in a playful spirit for a much longer time than women in past generations, but when she comes close to thirty and listens to the research that says it gets risky to postpone having babies, she starts thinking about building the nest. I'm convinced there's a biological yen in many people that urges them to have a baby—particularly when they have a good memory of their own childhood and want to re-create the childhood situation. While both men and women meet with the biological clock, it ticks more clearly for the woman."

Dr. Vahanian points out another realization common to this age group. "These days both men and women have so much opportunity to have sexual experiences with a variety of partners that they get somewhat jaded. It's not that interesting to go hopping from sack to sack. It becomes much more interesting to have a companion to settle down with in the late twenties."

It's not so easy, of course, to find Mr. or Ms. Right, and the longer people—especially women—wait, the harder it becomes. The period of looking and having more casual sexual encounters during the search stretches out and, says Dr. Vahanian, "for many people it's very sad." By the late twenties, people are likely to have had a couple of long affairs that didn't work out for one reason or another. The more time passes, the harder it is, especially for women, to find someone they can consider living with. They become disillusioned and make less of an effort. It's ironic that one thing that we have to count as a very positive advance in society works against them.

"By this time women realize that they don't need a man to survive," Dr. Vahanian says with a wry smile. "They're very independent. They recognize a man's flaws much faster than they did when they were twenty-one and dewy-eyed, and they're willing to put up with less. By the time a woman is twenty-eight and has been around a bit, she's not so easily enchanted—she knows a line when she hears one. I see many women in therapy in their late twenties and thirties—attractive, bright women who have a hard time meeting partners they can really connect with. In another era these women would have pushed themselves along in a less critical fashion because it was much more important to be married. It's paradoxical that the freedom not to be married backfires in a sense, because if you don't get married while you're still in your twenties it does get harder. There are fewer partners available (at least for women, because the men their age are now seeing younger women), and you're more critical and you look at the possibility in a different way, and you're more aware that you give something up when you marry."

Still, the search goes on, and many people do make their first committed attachments during this decade.

"I'm a great believer in romance instead of sex," Eric, twenty-five, tells me as he describes his relationship with Diana, twenty-eight, with whom he has been living, working, and loving for the past six months. "Not instead of, I guess, but in addition to. The sex is great between us, and I'm sure it's because we love each other. And because we work at loving each other. It's hard work, the kind of trust and commitment where you say to yourself, 'This is worth working on.' You have to have the patience for it. But it's worth it for both of us, because we support each other in so many ways. It goes far beyond just the sex act itself, intercourse. I think people are guilty of putting too much emphasis on just that. Whereas sex between us—it's something special, almost magical."

The magic comes through in Eric's voice as we talk over lunch at one of the trendy little restaurants that have been springing up in Eugene, Oregon, where Eric and Diana went to school and where they now live. Eric fell in love with Diana a year and a half ago. He had walked into a poetry reading at a small coffeehouse in Eugene just as her turn came up to read two of her own poems, one about loneliness and one about spring.

"Something came through to me—in the glow that was on her face and the involvement she was feeling with these poems she had written, and I fell in love with her right then and there." Diana was living with someone else at the time, but over the next year as Eric and Diana discovered the many interests they shared—writing, films, music, love of the outdoors—she found herself spending more and more time with Eric. Their relationship was tumultuous, largely due to the fact that she was just extricating herself from the tie to her lover and was not ready for closeness with someone else.

It was not until Eric went to Italy for three months that Diana broke up with her lover and rented a little house. And not until both Eric and Diana realized that the tremendous transatlantic telephone bills they were running up were due to the "tearing and pain we both experienced from our separation" that they decided to live together. Since then, they've been working together in the business Diana founded, a firm that publishes educational materials for young people, they've been writing a play together, and they've each pursued research and writing projects on their own.

"People warned us about the 'twenty-four-hour syndrome' before I moved in with Diana," Eric says, "about how hard it would be for us to work together all day and live together at night. But it hasn't really struck us, even though we haven't been out of each other's sight for more than a few hours for the past six months. It's like this rubber band around the two of us, and the farther apart it gets the more intense the pain is. So we don't stretch it too far."

Every day Eric and Diana work in their separate offices at the little publishing company and then come home to their little house. "The thing that makes it work is that we each help each other. If one person's energy is lagging, that person will just relax and read, and the other one will go ahead with a project, either one we're involved in together or a separate one, and it's as if both our energies are going into that. It's almost as if we're allowing this energy that has been locked inside of us for the longest time to come out, because each of us helps the other find a way to express it. The same thing is happening with our feelings.

"It's as if both of us can do more things because it's two of us working together. When she does something I consider it something that I've done also, and it's the same for her—it's like she's here with me on this interview, she's part of it, too.

"All of this affects our sexual relationship. Being together alone, as you give yourself over totally to the other person, the rest of the world doesn't exist. You pay a real deep attention to the other person and everything about that person seems important. It's like that story about how people were originally created with male and female in one body and then the gods split them apart because they were too powerful, and so you spend your whole life looking for the other half of you. If you find the right person, there's your other half and whatever they do is as if it's happening to you. So when we make love and I sense her excitement, I get excited too. It's almost as if I can feel with my body what she's feeling with hers. I've never had this with anyone else. This is really my first deep relationship. My sexual relationships have never been love relationships."

One of the major casualties of the sexual revolution has been the divorce between sex and love. For years, religious and other leaders linked the carnal with the caring—especially for women. (Men had always been known to have sexual appetites that could be fed by prostitutes, concubines, chorines, and other available bodies, the enjoyment of which would not sully a man's pure and everlasting love for his Wife, the Mother of his children.) The knowledge that women, too, could enjoy a sexual encounter in the arms of someone other than the Prince Charming she devoted her life to liberated millions of people from the need to lie to themselves, and freed them to enjoy the pleasures of the flesh.

As in so many revolutions, however, the standard-bearers of the new morality denied some truths even as they heralded others. They failed, for example, to recognize that a sexual experience colored by a loving relationship is different from one lacking love. They dismissed as an artifact of Victorian sentimentality the idea that love adds anything to a sexual encounter. And so you won't find the word "love" in the indexes

114

of the milestone books by sexologists like Kinsey, like Masters and Johnson. The word isn't in the indexes because it isn't in the books.

The insistence on looking at human sexual behavior outside of a context of love was essential to free it from the mandatory linkage of sex-and-love, which kept so many women from enjoying the potential of their bodies and drove so many men into the lies inspired by arousal. Now that we've done that, it's time to bring love back into the bedroom. It *can* have an honored place there, as sex therapists are discovering. Research has determined that when sex therapists teach couples with sexual dysfunctions how to show their love for each other, as well as teaching them what to do with their bodies, the couples make much better progress.

Sex and love are not inseparable. You can have one without the other. You can enjoy the transports of the heart and the pleasures of the flesh independently. And sex can be wonderful in many beds with many partners. But as many people discover the first time they experience orgasm with the person they love—or, as more often happens these days, after they fall in love with the person they have orgasms with—sex with someone you love achieves a totally different dimension.

So now, in the 1980s in the United States of America, love is back in style. Two surveys on love and romance by the magazine *Psychology Today* affirm the growing popularity of this pairing. In 1969, only 17 percent of the magazine's male readers who answered the first survey and 29 percent of the women felt that sex without love was either unenjoyable or unacceptable. By 1983, 29 percent of men and 44 percent of women felt that sex had no appeal without love. The trend is clear. A study by sociologist Leonard Cargan of Wright State University in Ohio is also pertinent. When Professor Cargan interviewed four hundred single, divorced, and married people in and around Dayton, Ohio, he found that the degree of sexual satisfaction people experience has little to do with either the frequency with which they engage in sex or the number of people they have sex with. It is, in the words of the social scientists, the "quality of the interpersonal relationship" that counts the most. What most of us call love.

Despite the fact that as many as two out of three couples now live together before they get married and that an even higher proportion have

115

made love before saying "I do," getting married is still a major sexual turning point in the life of virtually everyone who takes this step, as do some 95 percent of the American population.

And despite all the talk these days about premarital, extramarital, and postmarital (after-divorce) sex, marital sex still reigns supreme as the dominant form of sexuality in practically every society around the world. Most people are married most of their adult lives, most people are most sexually active within their marriages, and, by and large, married people are more sexually active than unmarried people. Marital sex is not only approved, it's required by most religious and civil dicta. Given this importance of sex in marriage, it's easy to see why marriage is such a sexual turning point in people's lives.

Even when a couple have lived together before marriage and have established a sexual rhythm between them, getting married often introduces a discordant note. "Too many of today's young marrieds are experiencing a totally unexpected crisis," Samona Sheppard tells me. "The women are not experiencing orgasm, they're not enjoying sex, they're feeling, 'So this is what it's all about?' For many of them, things were much better before they were married.

"When a couple are living together, it's not like marriage. For one thing, there are doors that either one can walk out of, and they both know this and woo each other to stay together. For another, they're not locked into roles. The roles of lovers are not ingrained, because neither partner has a model for that—they can play the roles of lovers by ear. But when they're husband and wife, everything they've learned from the time they were little kids surfaces.

"The husband thinks his wife will do whatever he wants her to, because he's the head of the house. The wife thinks her husband will suddenly turn into a fantastic lover who will give her multiple orgasms every night. Neither one of them has ever learned that there's no such thing as living happily ever after unless you work very hard. It doesn't happen magically."

With living together such a widely accepted, relatively uncomplicated option, why do people get married these days? Aside from the fact that, as Dr. Warren J. Gadpaille says, "heterosexual commitment is the species norm," the rationale for marriage today in the United States is different from what it was in times past and what it still is in

116

many places around the world. It's not the financial benefit it once was; there's no dynastic advantage in two sets of extended families merging their histories and their futures; there isn't the imperative of guaranteeing a staff of workers for the family farm or business. Today, marriage often makes less financial sense than living together would, the bride's and groom's families are usually total strangers, and any offspring are more apt to be seen as an economic liability than an asset.

From the time our country began, Americans have, by and large, married for love. Even though the marriage for money, power, prestige, or convenience is not unheard of, romance has been the ideal of our cultural legacy. Part of "Yankee independence" has been the free choice of mates by young people themselves, as opposed to parent-arranged marriages. We did, however, carry over one Old World standard more appropriate to the pragmatically arranged marriage than the romantic one—that a marriage should last forever. That even when love and romance don't endure, even when "happily ever after" is a sadly accurate antithesis of what has happened to husband and wife, the dictates of convention demand an unbroken bond.

Among the sweeping changes in Americans' views of life and their own place in it, however, has been a rethinking of the marriage ideal. If we marry for love, why stay married after love has died? For many years the economic dependence of women, religious strictures, tradition, provided the answer. Over the past half century, however, a host of societal changes—such as better work opportunities for women, declining levels of religious observance, technological advances in birth control—have led to a different answer, resulting in a steadily increasing divorce rate.

Probably the biggest change in couple relationships that has come about in recognition of the high divorce rate is the tendency for people to delay marriage and to live together, sometimes before and sometimes instead of marriage.

Eric and Diana have talked about getting married, but as Eric told me, "We're not certain about marriage—we're certain about staying together for a long time. But we consider ourselves married even without the document. This was part of the reason that I felt I had to move in with her. If I loved her that deeply, one way of showing it is to say, 'I want to be with this person.' It's a public statement that we're attached, 'Here we are.' As for the legal document—we don't know.''

This trend to cohabitation has been hailed by many as a valuable addition to courtship. Since most people who do live with someone plan to marry someday, this seems to be an ideal way to find out what it's like living with someone else, especially if this is the someone you might be marrying. Despite the eminent logic of this argument, the surprising fact is that people who lived together before marriage don't have more successful marriages than those who don't live together until after their wedding day. In fact, one study found that during the first year of marriage people who had not lived together first got along better than those who had. This may have more to do with the length of time that people are together and the time it takes for problems to surface than with the difference between cohabitation and marriage. Or it may indicate that that legal document is psychologically important after all, that the act of becoming formally married has a deep and very different meaning for people who've already lived together.

As marriage counselor Ned L. Gaylin told me, ''Faith is what makes marriage the ultimate contract. Virtually no one enters into marriage today without the belief that the union is permanent—otherwise they wouldn't marry. When I ask young couples how long they've been married, many of them tend to dismiss the wedding date, explaining that they had been living together for a while before that time. When I repeat the importance of their wedding date and they begin elaborating on their history and the problems that brought them to seek help, they're often surprised at their awareness of the changes that occurred in their relationship following the ceremony.

''The key here is ceremony,'' emphasizes Professor Gaylin, who is director of marriage and family therapy education and training at the University of Maryland. ''Whether sacred or secular, religious or civil, the public commitment to another person in marriage makes it vastly different from living together.'' Marriage still seems to be a crucible for putting relationships to the ultimate test.

Even now, when half of today's first marriages are expected to end in divorce, when any sensible, intelligent young couple would take this step tentatively, realizing that they have only a 50-50 chance of staying married, those who do say their vows generally do so with the expectation and the intention that *their* marriage is forever. Few people walk down the aisle saying, "No need to be nervous—if it doesn't work out, we can always get a divorce."

People still marry for *committed* love and companionship. As Bianca, twenty-four, who had been living with Ben, also twenty-four, for four years, told me, "We love each other and *we* know that, but we want *everyone* to know it. We want to make a public statement of the way we feel about each other. We want to make that commitment that each of us feels as if the other one is the most important person in the whole world. Getting married seems like a good way to do that."

Anybody can fall in love and anybody can find companions, but the biggest advantage of marriage may well be its ability to sustain the Bens and Biancas over the lonely periods when they fall out of love and can't bear each other's company, giving them the time to fall in love with each other all over again. Cohabitation doesn't offer this kind of buttress, which helps explain the fact that when sociologists Pepper Schwartz and Philip Blumstein conducted their eight-year study of contemporary American couples, they finally despaired of finding enough couples who had lived together for more than ten years to base any conclusions on. Apparently, cohabitation is temporary: people either marry within the first few years of living together or they split up.

A major sexual advantage that marriage shares with a living-together arrangement is the luxury of time. Only by living together, morning, noon, and night, day after day, can people take the time to know each other sexually in all sorts of circumstances: to turn to each other upon awakening from an erotic dream, to banish each other's demons that come out in the dark just before dawn, to play the kinds of lighthearted games that help a couple write their own sexual vocabulary, to get to know the rhythms of each other's body—what will arouse him, what will bring her to climax.

This time can be used for the single activity that marriage counselors unanimously agree is the most important for a good relationship— communication. Too often, in sex as in everything else, spouses expect each other to know how they feel without being told ("If you loved me, you'd know what turns me on/turns me off/drives me wild/bores me silly/puts me to sleep"). Furthermore, today, when both husband and wife are likely to have had previous sexual partners, each one needs to consider the feelings, attitudes, and physical needs of the one they're married to, which may be quite different from those of other people they've been intimate with. Problems can spring up around any of these issues while adjustments are being made, and problems with sex may be a symptom of other marital difficulties—or may lead to them.

Considering the impact of marriage on our personality and our sexuality, our extravagant expectations for it, and the lack of preparedness with which most of us go into it, the surprising thing is not how many marriages fail, but how many succeed. As Dr. Gadpaille has written, "Most first marriages are undertaken with a maximum of idealism and a minimum of common sense."

Ben's and Bianca's desire to be the most important persons in the world to each other harks back to an earlier period in their lives, the time when each was the most important person in the world to the one person who was the most important to them, their mother. In fact, Levinson and his colleagues at Yale saw many early marriages as efforts "to seek a dependent relationship with a protective-caring-controlling figure other than a parent." Men and women who marry before achieving the independence of adulthood run the risk of postponing or failing to achieve their own selfhood at all, since they play out with their spouses the struggles they never resolved with their parents. These struggles can doom a sexual relationship, since the taboos of incest are then brought to bear on the spouse who has assumed the role of mother or father and thus cannot be lover as well.

In these days when most people have already been sexually intimate before marriage, there's less likelihood that they'll have problems revolving around sexual incompatibility. The problems revolve around issues of intimacy.

In a marriage ceremony conducted on October 16, 1983, in the Moorish-inspired sanctuary of the oldest synagogue in New York City, Central Synagogue, Rabbi Martin S. Rozenberg speaks to a young bride and groom. "While marriages may be made in heaven, Nelle and Danny," his voice intones sonorously, "the reality is that they still have to be lived here on earth by people who have feet of clay.

"Let me become a little concrete. Our Torah says that the purpose of marriage is the propagation of the human race. Sociology tells us that it is for the purpose of creating a family, which constitutes the basic unit of society. Both statements, of course, have a measure of truth. I would like to suggest to you, however, that when the two of you will be relating as husband and wife, you will not be worrying about the human race or about society. You will be relating as two individuals. And the refinement of that personhood, the holiness that takes place in a relationship that brings out the worth of each individual—*that* takes place in the everyday, mundane interactions of two human beings.

"Character and personhood, believe it or not, is brought out in how you react when the other one fails to put the cap on the toothpaste. It is brought out in how sensitive you will be when the other's mood is low. How decent you will be with one another's mistakes. How understanding you will be of one another's weaknesses. And ultimately, how willing you will be to continue giving—and give some more, even when you will not have received an equal amount in return. It is this kind of interaction that creates a human laboratory that molds character and forges personhood."

And it is, of course, this kind of interaction that makes the first year of marriage such a potentially combustible laboratory and that creates what St. Louis therapist Beverly Hotchner calls "post-honeymoon shock." "The day after the marriage, or several months later—somewhere in that first year—people find out that they have to come to terms with the real person they married, not the fantasy figure they created," she says.

"It's all those little things like how you squeeze the toothpaste, from the top or the bottom, or whether you leave hair in the sink and don't clean it out afterward. When you were just dating, you didn't have to adjust to all these things. You could always back off. You could go to your own separate place or be busy or have appointments so you didn't have to deal with that daily possibility of intimacy. But when you're married or even just living together, this is what you deal with."

The way people solve the puzzles of joining their life with a stranger's is profoundly related to the way they fit their two bodies together, as well. One truth that has emerged from the very few studies we have about marital sex is that sexuality and compatibility are closely linked. The more husband and wife enjoy sex with each other, and the more often they enjoy it, the happier they tend to be. When they lose interest in sex, they also lose interest in doing other things with each other.

Boredom in bed goes hand in hand with boredom out of it. Of course, while many theorize, no one has yet answered the perpetually fascinating riddle: Does wonderful sex create a golden glow in a marriage? Or does a joyously happy bond inspire wonderful sex?

Good sex and good marriage are not, of course, identical. There are couples who make marvelous love together even when their life outside of bed is constant warfare, and there are couples who adore each other but just can't seem to make sex work well between them. But by and large, loving lust seems to go along with laughing about the toothpaste.

We know pathetically little about sex in marriage. As Rutgers University sociologist Cathy Stein Greenblat has said, "This form of sex—the only one that's widely accepted and fully socially legitimate—remains more the topic of jokes than of serious social-scientific investigation." We do know that a couple usually trace the pattern for their sexual relationship very early. The more they reach out in sexual longing and desire for each other the very first year of marriage, the more often they will come together in passion and desire in the years to come. While sex may become more fulfilling in the years to come, it's not likely to be as frequent ever again, even for the most active couples, since, as Dr. Greenblat points out, "From then on almost everything—children, jobs, commuting, housework, financial worries—that happens to a couple conspires to *reduce* the degree of sexual interaction, while almost nothing leads to increasing it."

Still, despite the almost universal decline in frequency over the years, married couples are having more sex more regularly than most people suspected. Blumstein and Schwartz found that even after ten years of marriage, 63 percent of married couples are making love at least once a week and 18 percent are making love three times a week or more. (These figures are down from 83 percent and 45 percent, respectively, for couples married less than two years.)

Couples who resolve this turning point of intimacy early in their marriage, then, are likely to reap sexually fulfilling rewards that will stand them in good stead over the most sexually trying times in a marriage: the first pregnancy and the child-rearing years that follow.

The magical aura around the intentional creation of a new life is a turning point in the lives of most married couples. Given the near universality of the experience and its far-reaching ramifications for both the new mother and father, it's surprising to note how little attention it has received as a significant sexual passage. Fertility is sexy: it implies potency, the ultimate in maleness and femaleness, a sense of the elegant reproductive design in sexual intercourse, the promise of immortality.

Kate, a twenty-nine-year-old mother of three, tells me, "My all-time sexual high came when I was pregnant with my first baby. I felt more aware of myself as a woman and of what was going on in my body, really fortunate to be able to give birth. Of course, it helped a lot that Matt finds pregnant women appealing!"

"I do get turned on by seeing a pregnant woman," Matt says. "I see them walking around with this new life in them, and most of them want the new life, and usually it's come about by two people that love each other. And it just gets to me. The most sexually fulfilling time in *my* life was when Kate and I set out to conceive our second child. We were making love every other night, and I liked the frequency. I also enjoyed knowing we were striving together for a purpose. Before we were married, we'd go to bed together and we'd get that nervous twitch and think, 'Let's be careful—let's not make a mistake.' But now, instead of worrying, we had the completely opposite feeling—that we wanted a pregnancy. It was much more fulfilling—that this was what we were doing and we were doing it together."

As heady as this feeling can be, however, the pregnancy sometimes evokes unexpected reactions that affect a couple's relationship long after the birth of the baby. The emotional static that crackles between Angela and John, for example, as we talk around the kitchen table of the contemporary house they designed and built themselves in a wooded enclave on the outskirts of Pittsfield, Massachusetts, dates back two years, when Angela was pregnant with John, Jr. Until the pregnancy, this had been a story of an exuberant courtship and an ideal sexual relationship, both before and during eight years of marriage.

Johnny was a planned baby. Planned by a mother who loved her work as a fashion executive for a large department store chain but also knew that she wanted with all her being to have John's baby, and who knew that if she didn't have a baby now she'd be so caught up in the travel and overtime her work demanded that the years would go by without ever finding the "right time." And by an athletic father who looked forward to sailing, biking, and playing tennis with his children and, at thirty-five, was worrying about being too old to be the father he wanted to be by the time his children reached their teens. The pregnancy, which occurred immediately, went fine. The sex didn't.

"I never believed that sex was anything you should hold back on to gain something," Angela says. "I always thought sex was a very giving, loving, flowing-back-and-forth thing. I had never in all the time I knew John said no to him when he wanted sex, and I wasn't prepared for the fact that when I was pregnant and was hornier than I've ever been in my life he didn't hesitate to say no to me."

"I'm not sexually attracted to pregnant women," John puts in with a shrug. "If a pregnant woman walks down the street and a normal woman walks down the street, there's a big difference to me. I'm just not turned on by women with big bellies. Besides, I was afraid I'd hurt Angela or the baby."

"I didn't even start to wear maternity clothes until I was six months pregnant," Angela goes on, "and it was just about then that John started to talk about hurting the baby, even though our childbirth teacher had showed us pictures and said that wouldn't be a problem.

"So here I was getting hornier and hornier, and we were just going in opposite directions. John was getting less and less sexually interested in me and I was getting more and more interested in him. I have never had anybody hold out on me. I didn't know what to do. I masturbated a lot. Even toward the end when they said that an orgasm can bring on early labor, I was desperate enough that it didn't matter. I just felt, well, today's the day the baby will come out smiling."

When I ask John, "Did you use any other techniques, like oral or manual sex, to help Angela feel better?" I receive a vigorous nod from him—and just as vigorous a shake of the head from Angela, who says, "I felt that he didn't want me to become sexually aroused because then he wouldn't do what he likes to do best—intercourse. Normally we do all kinds of things, so I felt we had other options if he was afraid of hurting the baby."

"I figured we'd been waiting for this baby and wanting this baby and it was time to concentrate on it. Then we could always go back to sex as usual after the baby was born," John says. "Only it didn't work out that way,'' he adds ruefully. ''After Johnny's birth, Angela wasn't very interested in sex.''

''Before I got pregnant, even if I was very tired, if John was interested in making love, I would. I thought, I'll do it for him, just because. But after spending three months of his not understanding my need for arousal . . .'' Angela's voice trails off.

''I really admired her for never saying no to me. Now that she does, I'm not mad, but I *am* disappointed. I know that other people have the same problem. See, I didn't have that problem before, so that was great. So now I'm right with everybody else. Now she's the old holdout, like a normal wife. Every time I'm interested she says, 'All those months you weren't interested!' She always holds grudges.''

''I don't know if it's holding a grudge, but I just all of a sudden feel as though I don't need to be as giving and open as I was before. It's not as if we never have sex. We probably have intercourse at least three times a week even now, where we used to have it every night. Plenty of times I'm just tired. Or after having Johnny cling to me all day, I'm just not in the mood to have someone else touch my body. I'm not a hold-out by any means, it's just we're not on the same level we used to be. Maybe if John did more with Johnny, I'd have more energy and I'd be more interested. But he practically ignores him unless I specifically ask him to do something.''

John and Angela typify what many couples go through during pregnancy. During a time when each partner needs extra reassurance, all too often lovemaking—one form of communication that could comfort both of them—becomes the lodestone for a bewildering variety of confused feelings. Instead of smoothing out difficulties, sex becomes the most visible magnet for them. Most couples have sexual intercourse less often during pregnancy than they did before and than they will afterward. Sometimes the woman is less interested because of the nausea and fatigue during the early months and the bodily discomforts toward the end. Often, however, the sexual relationship is a casualty of the psychological adjustments both partners need to make.

Expectant mothers receive a fair amount of information, advice, and support to prepare them for the changes in body and soul that occur during pregnancy, but until quite recently very little attention has been paid to what pregnancy means to the expectant father. Yet men seem to

125

report ambivalent feelings longer into the pregnancy than women do, and a man's attitude toward the pregnancy holds important implications for the relationship between the couple. According to psychoanalyst Sue Rosenberg Zalk, associate professor at Hunter College in New York City, who has counseled hundreds of expectant and new fathers and conducted an intensive study of two hundred of them, "Nowhere has this lack of recognition of the man's dynamics during a pregnancy been more evident than in the area of sexual functioning."

The prospect of parenthood dramatically changes a couple's roles from the children of their parents to the parents of their own children, thus marking an end to childhood much more definitively than marriage did. It imposes awesome responsibilities for the care of a being who will be totally and frighteningly dependent upon them for years to come. This responsibility moves marriage still further out of the realm of "playing house," when both partners had obligations only to each other, and it imposes more of a sense of permanence and commitment on the marriage. It also reawakens each partner's own dependency needs: expectant fathers' heightened needs for mothering showed up in one study that found that these young men wrote and phoned their parents more often and wanted to hear stories about their own birth and infancy.

The idea of having one's own child reaches deep into the psyche and calls forth each partner's childhood emotions toward their own parents, often displacing these feelings onto the husband or wife. So the man who as a little boy had incestuous thoughts toward his mother (as all little boys do at some time) now sees his wife in the mother role and resists the idea of being sexual with her. Meanwhile, the woman may look to her husband to take care of her the way she wanted her daddy to when she was little, and feels rejected when he doesn't respond to her the way she wants him to.

John's reluctance to be sexual with Angela is not unusual; men commonly turn away from their wives at this time. Masters and Johnson discovered that a number of men had their first extramarital affair during their wives' first pregnancy. Bittman and Zalk found that some men had a first adult homosexual experience at this time. And a study of battered wives revealed that for one out of four, the first instance of abuse occurred during a pregnancy. Many men experience less interest in sex altogether, becoming asexual, or, in some cases, engaging in such crimes as rape, exhibitionism, or obscene phone calls, acts generally not inspired by sexual motives as much as aggressive ones. Some men repress their sexuality more benignly, expressing affection for their wives through kissing and caresses not directed toward orgasm, but studiously avoiding direct sexual stimulation.

Few men recognize the deep emotional conflicts they're dealing with, the impact of this important phase on their own adult development. They may deny the importance of the pregnancy, saying, ''It's no big deal,'' possibly insisting that their wives accompany them on exhausting outings. Or they may take on pregnancy symptoms themselves, becoming fatigued, nauseated, insomniac, and overweight.

Fortunately, while pregnancy is a stressful time for most couples, many are able to handle its tensions fairly comfortably and are able to meet each other's needs for love in both sexual and nonsexual ways. Some, in fact, experience these months as a time of heightened sexuality. Those who don't, however, usually benefit from recognizing what may be going on between them and from openly acknowledging their anxieties.

Perhaps if Angela could see that John's sexual withdrawal during her pregnancy was not a rejection of her but a reflection of his fears and tensions, her anger might be allayed. If John had openly addressed his anxieties, he might have been less affected by them. Maybe if John and Angela had recognized what was going on between them during her pregnancy, they would have been able to accept the situation as a temporary one—and could have prevented it from seeping into the relationship between them, even after the birth, as it did, contaminating not only their relationship with each other but also John's feelings toward his son.

So often we don't recognize a sexual turning point until long after it has occurred, until it has turned our lives in a certain direction, until it has exerted an influence that may now be impossible to undo. If, however, we can recognize the importance of such pivotal events in our development when they occur, we can sometimes exert powerful leverage over the years to come.

Chapter 6

Fertile Forests:
The Thirties

It's good to hear that the frequency of sex drops for other couples, too, and then rises again, because it helps you realize you haven't lost it forever. Sometimes you think you'll never have the urge again.

—SUSAN

HANK'S THIRTIETH BIRTHDAY was less than six months away the afternoon he sat down for a drink with Wendy, his co-anchor on the television news show they hosted in Pittsburgh—and his lover. He could tell the conversation was going to be serious when she asked the waiter to take them to a quiet table in the corner instead of to her favorite center table where she could be recognized by the fans who frequented the Tahiti Room in the Golden Triangle.

"We've been seeing each other for six months now, right?" Wendy asked.

"Right." Hank looked at her warily.

"And we're pretty good together," she stated. It was not a question.

"Right."

"Then why don't we get married?" Wendy asked, her gaze as direct as it was on-screen when she was posing a tough question to an interviewee.

Hank looked up and said, "Wendy, we've been through this before. You're great. You know I think the world of you. I feel guilty keeping

128

you from finding some guy who would marry you. But I'm not the one.''

"Why not?''

"Well—I like you, I'm crazy about you. But I don't love you. I don't know what's missing, but something is. And I have this crazy idea that people should only marry people they love.''

"Hey, you're going to be thirty years old in five months and fourteen days. I turned thirty last month. Are you in love with anybody else?''

"Nope.''

"Okay. Let me make you a proposition. If you haven't fallen in love with anybody else by the time your birthday rolls around, why don't you marry me? I'd be good for you. I have enough love for both of us. I know once we were married, you would start to love me. Shake on it?''

They shook hands, finished their drinks, and went back to Hank's apartment for the best lovemaking they had ever known. Six months later, two weeks after Hank's thirtieth birthday, they were married in city hall.

"The Age 30 Transition,'' Daniel Levinson and his colleagues at Yale University called it. "Catch-30'' was Gail Sheehy's term in *Passages*. At about the time of the thirtieth birthday, give or take a couple of years, at least one and sometimes several turning points pop up with surprising regularity in people's lives. This is a time when we tend to take a close look at our lives so far.

Some of us slide through this transition of growth and change fairly easily, even as we change our lives in ways that have far-reaching ramifications. Others, however, experience a developmental crisis in which they find their present life structure intolerable—but feel locked into it, unable to form a better one. Or they do something they know is crazy at the time—the way Hank *knew* his marriage to Wendy was crazy, long before he walked into the divorce court to end it—just because they feel an uncontrollable urge to do *something*. To write a new life script. To cast a new group of characters. To leave the old life on the cutting-room floor.

Many of the life crises that loom large at this time have sexual overtones. This is often the time when a bachelor gets married, when a workaholic executive gets pregnant, when a married person's head fills with fantasies of ideal lovers, when a sexual adventurer trades promiscuity for a one true love—or for celibacy.

Sheep and goats wander around the pottery display in the shed by the side of the little Vermont farmhouse. A stocky, apple-cheeked woman wearing a bulky down jacket and a wool cap with the word GOAT knitted into it walks over to me and asks, slightly puzzled, "May I help you?" I explain why I came: "I'm writing this book, and a friend told me you might be willing to talk to me."

She responds warmly. "Sure, I love to tell people about my life. If somebody can learn something from all I've gone through, it makes it worthwhile. Come back later after my friend"—she gestures to the Paul Bunyan look-alike in the corner of the yard—"has finished helping me split my logs."

When I return a few hours later, a gentle, comely woman opens the door for me. She looks prettier this time, more womanly in her long plaid wool skirt and simple blouse.

The free spirit I am meeting is very different from the nun in the cloistered order that Lesley had been from the age of sixteen till she turned thirty-two. She had adjusted easily to the physical demands—going barefoot, shaving her head, sleeping on boards, wearing a wool habit throughout steamy Florida summers, not eating meat, waking up in the middle of every night to pray. She welcomed the regimentation as a way to test her devotion—until passions she had kept harnessed all those years swelled within her, bursting their bonds.

At twenty-four, Lesley fell in love. Although Gavin, a young priest, returned her ardor, their feelings for each other never went beyond one memorable night when they stayed in each other's arms till dawn, kissing and expressing their love for each other. The next morning Gavin went on a mission to Europe. During their night of love, they talked about leaving their religious orders, but neither was ready for such a drastic step. By the time Lesley was ready, just after her thirty-second birthday, she had already known for a couple of years that Gavin had left the priesthood and had married. She was not to flee the convent for his arms.

"It was nothing on the outside that made me want to leave," she tells me now. "I had been throwing pots for about eight or nine years and getting written up all over the state and selling my work in the monastery's gift shop, so I was immersed in work I loved and I wasn't even thinking about going out. I had forced myself to put Gavin out of my mind, even though I still prayed for him. But then after I had accepted a scholarship to leave the monastery for a summer to apprentice to a master potter, and September came and it was time to go back, I just couldn't do it. I didn't know how I would support myself in the outside world, but there was something inside of me that said it's time to move on. I had just had enough.

"The order was good about accepting my decision. They gave me my potting equipment and five hundred dollars, and there was hurting on both sides, but no anger. Now, when things sometimes get rough and I think about going back, the first thing I think is, 'I can't be confined like that anymore.' And then, of course, I could never renounce sex."

"Do you feel guilty about leaving the convent and about having sex with men you're not married to?" I ask.

Lesley throws back her head and laughs lustily. "Lord, no! I have never been plagued with guilt in my adult life. I used to feel guilty as a young girl. In fact, I loved boys so much and loved being kissed so much that I think I entered the convent partly to save myself from a life of sin. But now I know that God doesn't judge you on what you do sexually. What God judges us on is in our kindness and love and respect for people. I know, because I lived with God for sixteen years and I know what He's like the same way I'd know what a husband of sixteen years was like.

"So while I never thought that I'd go to bed with a man without the context of marriage and all that, in the heat of passion at the age of thirty-two, I did. The man was having a hard time handling the fact that he was deflowering an ex-nun, but I was enjoying every minute. I'm a sexy person. I love going to bed with men. I love the feel of a man's flesh next to mine, I love to be kissed, I love the way my body feels while we're making love, I love the emotions of being with someone I care for.

"You know, I've worked with clay for a long time. I've always had a heightened sense of touch. In the monastery I always used to embrace the other sisters as a kiss of peace, not in a sexual way—I'm not at all

131

gay—but just to be close to them. My sexual appetites are an extension of that same urge.

"Imagine, being a virgin at thirty-two! Since then I've had some wonderful experiences with some wonderful men. When I have sex it's always good, because I enjoy it so. I'm attracted to earthy men, take-charge types, men who are in touch with their bodies but can deal with their feelings, too. Not necessarily religious types. I have enough spiritual feelings for both of us."

What does the future hold for Lesley? She supports herself on a subsistence level by selling her pottery, raising her sheep and goats, and occasional substitute teaching. At age thirty-seven, she fervently wants to get married.

"One man has proposed to me, but I'm not attracted to him sexually," she confesses. "My mother says, 'Sex isn't everything,' and I know that. But I want to be one with somebody. I certainly don't want to marry somebody I don't want to go to bed with. I've been celibate too long.

"I've broken up with a couple of men over the past few years and I was devastated, just like a teenager. That's not surprising, since I was in a state of arrested sexual development for so long. But I've been doing a lot of growing up in the last five years, and now I think I'm mature enough so when the right person comes along, I'll be responding to him not out of a teenager's need but from a woman's want."

A woman who met her Age 30 Transition within the walls of a cloistered convent, who responded to her body's sexual needs and her psyche's emotional ones to make the most sweeping life change possible, a woman who looked at the commitment she had made in adolescence and decided that was not the commitment she wanted to make as an adult. A woman who has chosen a hard path to follow, but the one that feels like the only choice for the person she is now.

Some people who have established their identity earlier wait until the thirties to assert it. For many people this decade represents what they see as the final stage of youth before they embark upon the second half of life. When I first met Win a year ago, he looked the very model of the corporate executive in his pin-striped suit. Now, when I see him again, his life has changed radically—again. After having grown up in a succession of tiny Southern towns as the son of a fundamentalist minister, Win vowed to choose a profession and a city where he wouldn't be discriminated against because of his homosexuality. A radio network in Manhattan felt right. Still, as Win was establishing his career he kept a low profile—until he decided that it was time to be true to himself and be publicly gay. This sexual decision had important professional implications, as well as personal ones.

When Win opens the door to his little house on San Francisco's Guerrero Street, I almost don't recognize the man I met a year ago. Gone is the executive in the neat three-piece suit; in front of me is a stranger in a skin-tight, muscle-sleeved black T-shirt and a pair of worn, form-fitting jeans. His head is completely shaven; his chin sports a jet-black Vandyke beard. Win's road toward this transformation in his appearance, as well as his profession, took place in several discrete stages.

First there was his thirtieth birthday, when he went out to lunch with some colleagues. "One of them made a crack about 'faggots' and something sort of snapped in me. Maybe it was the trauma of being out of my twenties. Maybe it was just feeling grown-up enough to assert myself. Anyway, I said, 'Look, for several years we've worked together and I suspect you know I'm gay and I would prefer not to hear any more jokes like that.' There was silence and two or three people said things to gloss over the awkwardness, and then I never heard any more cracks."

A few years later, Win took part in a "Gay Liberation" march for the first time. "This was when Anita Bryant was in her heyday," he says. "It seemed important to me to walk out in public, to show my support for what the gay activists were trying to achieve for all of us, and to extend my statement of who I was even further. It seemed significant at the time, but now it doesn't seem like such a big deal. Maybe because I've marched every year since then."

Win's most momentous change of the decade came just a few weeks after I had met him the year before, when he was faced with an ultimatum—either design a new job for himself or leave the firm.

"I don't think I was fired because I'm gay," he says, leaning forward intensely. "I think it had more to do with the fact that I don't handle pressure well. I felt I was being pushed to keep upping sales beyond what I thought were reasonable expectations, having to justify any expenses, doing a lot of chickenshit stuff that didn't seem worth all the anxiety. I developed an ulcer at about that time. Then I realized that if I left they'd have to pay me severance for my twelve years with the company. At the age of thirty-eight this was the one chance I'd have to come out with a lump sum of money and do something different with my life. It took me about thirty seconds to make up my mind.

"And here I am. I've been freelancing for the past year—writing and editing syndicated radio spots—and while it's been a struggle sometimes, I love the freedom. Part of that freedom is looking the way I do. I didn't set out to do a big physical change, but I thought, 'Why not?' So I got rid of the suits and got rid of what little hair I had left on my head and made up for it by growing some on my chin. And I feel good. I don't know what's going to happen from here on in, but two things I do know. I'll never go back into the closet again, and I'll never go the corporate executive route again. Life is too short and too precious to waste that way."

When the hero of the 1952 play *The Seven Year Itch* stumbled into a brief, guilt-producing adulterous episode, he acted out a fantasy that was so common that the play's title quickly became part of our language. Now, barely three decades later, it seems obsolete.

In 1977, when a group of therapists associated with the Marriage Council of Philadelphia analyzed the council's records of people coming for help, they found that couples in which one or both partners were between the ages of twenty-seven and thirty-two accounted for twice the number of those in any other age range. These couples had been married an average of seven years. The "seven year itch" was alive and concupiscent. More recent surveys have found that this time of disenchantment and restlessness is now peaking at four years after marriage, with a significant drop in fidelity at about this time. This may reflect an added period of living together before marriage, a later age upon reaching the altar, or the increased premarital sexual activity among those who are now feeling this "four year itch." In any case, it still seems to come when one partner is about the age of thirty.

Michael was twenty-nine when he first felt the itch, thirty-one when he first scratched it. He had married at twenty-four, a sexual and emotional naïf. Both he and his twenty-two-year-old bride, Gail, were virgins; both came from families in which emotions were barely acknowledged and rarely discussed; and both brought to their union an overwhelming ignorance of life, love, and their own capabilities for dealing with either one. For about five years they managed to grope along together. Until Michael decided that something was missing in his life. He didn't know what it was, but he knew he wanted it. He knew it had something to do with the fantasies of other women that would crowd his brain and make him faint with longing.

"I used to flirt at parties—my ego liked it that women would find me attractive—but I had never gone beyond that sort of legalized adultery to the real thing," Michael tells me many years later as I talk to this successful fifty-year-old engineer in the conference room of his Philadelphia office.

"Until I met Nicole," Michael adds, looking away from me as he searches his memories of a distant past. A neighbor of Michael's and Gail's on their tree-lined old West Philadelphia block, Nicole, at thirty-four, was three years older than Michael and light-years more intense. He came to know her as they walked their dogs together and then talked by the hour.

"Nicole was the first person I really opened up to. She was the first to awaken in me the capacity to be aware of levels within myself that I had never known existed—and the ability to relate to another person."

One Sunday afternoon when Michael was alone with Nicole in her home, she excused herself for a few minutes and came back wearing a diaphanous red negligee, setting off her Mediterranean coloring and revealing her full breasts and curvaceous hips. That afternoon the two became lovers. Although the affair lasted only a few weeks, it was to change Michael's life forever.

"I was relieved when Nicole ran away with some young English teacher after she asked *me* to and I retreated, scared to death," Michael says, getting up to stretch his long legs. "I was afraid of her intensity, even though even at the time I recognized—and appreciated—the minor miracle she had wrought in taking a totally defended guy like me and making me dimly aware of some buried ability to live and to feel. At least I was able to admit to the appetite for passion and to the possibility that maybe I could have it, it could exist for me."

135

The affair with Nicole was soon followed by another affair, and another, and another. Michael would end each one before it became threateningly intimate. "I would want to be close to someone, but I kept hiding behind my cock. Because I had such a low opinion of myself, I couldn't open up to anybody unless I felt that I had some control over them. My power would lie in my sexual attractiveness."

As each liaison died, Michael would turn to his wife, looking for the kind of vibrancy he always felt at the brink of and furious with her because she was so unlike the women who populated his fantasies. Gail was bewildered by the changes in this man she no longer understood, still in love with the Michael she used to know. By the time I speak to Michael, twenty years after Nicole had fled with her English teacher, he had gone into therapy, found his fiercely passionate union, and has been for some seven years in the most intimate relationship of his life. Not able to marry his lover, he is still wavering about his marriage. At fifty he is still trying to resolve his Age 30 Transition.

Michael's story has a quaintly historical ring to it now. Twenty-four-year-old virgins are rare these days, and today's young married men are less ingenuous. Yet the Age 30 Transition is still powerful, sex is still magical, and the first extramarital affair is still significant—even if it seems to occur more often now, and earlier in a marriage.

Affairs, of course, are nothing new. Back in the nineteenth century Alexandre Dumas noted, "The chains of marriage are so heavy that it takes two to bear them, and sometimes three." In 1948, when Kinsey published his landmark research about men's sexual activities, and again in 1953, when he reported his findings about women, the public was shocked to hear that about half of all men and a quarter of all women reported having had extramarital sex. By 1974, Morton Hunt reported, about the same number of men were saying that they had had sex outside the marriage, but more women were saying the same thing. More recent figures—from a 1980 report of a survey of married female readers of *Cosmopolitan* magazine—run even higher, with seven out of ten women aged thirty-five and older indicating that they had had outside sex.

This is what people have told researchers about what they *do.* And yet when we ask them what they *think,* the answers are surprising. Most people say that extramarital sex is immoral for individuals and dangerous for marriages. Three separate national public opinion polls spanning the years from 1970 to 1977 showed that 75 to 87 percent of people in North America disapprove of married people having sex with people they're not married to. This means, of course, that many people are copulating with their neighbors' wives and husbands and judging themselves as bad. Still, the tidal wave of guilt washing over so many married lovers doesn't prevent them from continuing to immerse themselves in extramarital liaisons.

People have affairs for basically the same reasons they always have; the reasons just seem more compelling these days. According to *Playboy*'s latest survey, in which answers came in from some 40,000 married people, men rank their reasons for extramarital sex in order as: sexual variety, reassurance of their desirability, change of routine, better sex, and sex without commitment. Women's order of reasons runs: reassurance of their desirability, better sex, change of routine, sexual variety, and sex without commitment. Men still have more outside sex than women do, but the women are catching up fast. Almost 45 percent of the currently married men who answered the *Playboy* survey (average age thirty-four) have had an affair, while 34 percent of the wives (average age twenty-nine) have.

At one point the sexologist and marriage counselor Albert Ellis tried to classify "healthy" and "disturbed" motivations for extramarital sex. Among the reasons he saw as healthy were a desire for variety, a desire to add more love to one's life, a drive toward new experiences, a quest for adventure, sexual curiosity, sexual deprivation, and, quite simply, an available opportunity. The disturbed reasons include a low tolerance of marriage, hostility to one's spouse, the need to bolster one's ego, a wish to escape from real life and from marriage, and self-deprecation.

The *Playboy* survey also brought out what previous studies have found—that the earlier people began their sexual careers and the greater number of sexual partners they've had, the more sex they're likely to have outside the marriage. In some cases people have affairs because their marriages are in trouble, and most people still do view an affair as a sign of problems in the marriage. In others, an affair doesn't bespeak disappointment with the marriage itself, only a strain of sexual

137

adventurousness that cannot be contained within the bond of monogamy.

In either case—when the affair sends one or both partners a signal that their relationship needs attention, or when the straying partner is able to reassure the betrayed one that the affair was a meaningless fling—extramarital sex rarely seems to break up marriages. Only 20 percent of *Playboy*'s divorced and remarried respondents think that an affair broke up their marriage.

One of the major changes in American sexual mores over the past couple of decades has been the growing acceptance of extramarital sex. Open marriage, mate-swapping, and the plain old-fashioned, garden-variety affair have all been more openly discussed, not only among the sexual avant-garde, where they were always a staple, but among typical, respectable, relatively conservative middle-class people.

As Martin, a thirty-five-year-old book distributor in Denver, who's been in a happy, monogamous, sexually fulfilling marriage for fifteen years, tells me: "I have no complaints about my wife. We enjoy sex and she's not a wet fish or frigid. I don't think we've ever had a fight about sex. But I read a lot of the magazines and books that I distribute, and I have fantasies of more unconventional sex. I think my marriage is secure enough to handle something like swapping or group sex, an orgy or something like that, but my wife is totally uninterested. I don't want to push her into anything, but if an opportunity for an affair happened to fall into my lap, I think I would do it without any qualms."

Another sign of the times is a new kind of support for people who are doing it—or thinking about doing it—but do have qualms. While the traditional viewpoint among marriage counselors used to be that an extramarital affair signaled a problem in the marriage, and many counselors would refuse to work with a couple in which either wanted to continue his or her involvement in such an affair, a new type of counseling is oriented toward the acceptance of extramarital sex. Psychologist Eleanor D. Macklin of Syracuse, New York, has instituted what she terms "conjoint marital therapy," in which she sees all three members of a triangle together, to help them work through the problems in their complex tangle of relationships.

And now from California comes counseling for married women who are having—or thinking of having—affairs. The typical participant in psychologist Cynthia Silverman's workshops is a well-educated, upper-middle-class woman in her early thirties who's in her second marriage. She comes to the workshop for help in deciding whether her reasons for having an affair are healthy (according to Silverman, "variety" or "romantic adventure" is a healthy reason; "reassurance of desirability" or "relief from a bad marriage" is not), what kind of partner to pick (preferably a married man, who also must be discreet), and how to keep the affair secret from her husband (by covering her absences with uncheckable alibis).

When questioned on the morality of her work, Dr. Silverman answers, "This is not advice on free love. Men and women are both having affairs. The goal is to educate women to make a meaningful decision. Let's see they don't do it moronically or hurt themselves or their families. The bottom line is always that if you have a good marriage, and the affair would harm the marriage, then don't have the affair."

With the birth of their first baby, many couples enter a period that turns out to be the sexual, and often emotional, nadir of their married lives, usually running through the decade of the thirties. Married nine years, Susan, thirty-one, tells me, as we sit in the kitchen of the ramshackle country farmhouse she and Bill share with their three small children, "It's only been within the last year that I got some insight into what's really been going on between Bill and me over the past six years. It hasn't been an easy time, and both of us feel real comfortable about our decision not to have any more babies, to know that that time is behind us."

For the first three years of marriage, Susan and Bill were making love three or four or five times a week. Sex was good, life was fun, and marriage was a state of grace. Moving every six months or so while Bill was in the service lent a honeymoon quality to making love in one new place after another.

"But then when I got out of the army, we settled down, Susan got a job as an operating room nurse in the local hospital, she got pregnant with Rebecca, and then Rachel, and then Josh, and we were in a whole other marriage," Bill says.

Susan, jiggling eighteen-month-old Joshua on her ample lap, adds,

139

"A lot was going on then. Bill was working a night shift in a steel plant, and plenty of times when he wanted sex, I was exhausted from taking care of the baby, so I didn't feel like setting the alarm in the middle of the night to get up with him. As for me, right after all the babies were born, I was content to live like a nun."

Susan demonstrates a paradox of the breastfeeding woman. Lactation is an important phase of female sexuality; when a woman is nursing, as when she is sexually aroused, her breasts become larger, her nipples become erect, her uterus contracts, her body temperature rises, and the hormone oxytocin surges through her system. The nerve pathways from the nipples to the brain are the same whether they're being stimulated by a lover or an infant, and there have been accounts of women who experienced orgasm while nursing. Still, female physiology would seem to discourage sexual activity in the nursing mother: the hormonal changes in her body make the vaginal wall thinner and more sensitive and reduce vaginal lubrication.

What does this mean? That some nursing mothers are sexier than ever and that others, like Susan, would welcome celibacy during this time (which, in fact, is mandated by many cultures around the world). In our society, in which women have a choice, those who love sex are more likely to breastfeed than those who are less sensual, helping to explain why breastfeeding mothers tend to resume sexual relations earlier than women who don't nurse.

At the same time, it's also common for lactation to have the opposite effect on other women. As Susan tells me, "I'm sure that nursing had something to do with my lack of interest in sex. My body was in use all day long. I felt as if somebody was constantly sucking on me and holding me and being held by me, and by the time night came I just wanted to draw an invisible circle around my body and say, 'No trespassing.'"

When Susan and Bill did start to make love again after each birth, they would come together about once every two or three weeks, usually at Bill's insistence and Susan's distracted acquiescence. "We didn't do a lot of talking, of sharing our gut feelings until just about the last year," Susan acknowledges. "I never said to Bill in the early years, 'I really love you but I need some space now for me.' Nor did I tell him about the times I would have liked some hugging and kissing, some quiet time together that didn't end up in intercourse.''

''And I never said anything to her about how deprived and left out I was feeling,'' Bill adds. ''What we did do was fight. I found a lot to criticize in Susan—the house was a mess, the kids were dirty, I didn't have any clean socks.''

Susan took his words as a direct attack on the way she was handling her job as wife, mother, and housekeeper, and she fought back. Today she says, ''Now I realize that it wasn't the socks—it was the sex. Or rather, the lack of it. Now I can let the house go—you can see the way it is now!—and I don't get any of those complaints. As hard as it is, we manage to find time and energy for each other—for talking *and* for sex. It's like being in our *third* marriage to each other.''

Another element that's made their ''third'' marriage so good is the vasectomy Bill had after Joshua's birth. ''This was a great decision for us,'' Susan says. ''As much as I enjoy being with the children and taking care of them, we both feel real good to know that the baby-time is behind us, and we can look forward to focusing attention on each other.''

In one of the few studies of sexuality in marriage, conducted in the late 1970s by Ellen Frank, Carol Anderson, and Debra Rubinstein, the general picture that emerged from the hundred ''normal'' couples (i.e., couples who were not in therapy) surveyed was of frequent, satisfying sex for the first five years, the most troubled for the next fifteen (usually, the child-rearing years), and an improvement again after twenty years together. (Hearing this, Susan said, ''It's good to hear that the frequency of sex drops for other couples, too, and then rises again, because it helps you realize you haven't lost it forever. Sometimes you think you'll never have the urge again.'')

With all the joys that children may bring, a contribution to marital happiness—either in or out of bed—is rarely one of them. As Blumstein and Schwartz reported in their study of American couples, ''Having dependent children in the home has a big impact on marital relationships, a particularly unhappy one on husbands.'' While other studies have found less frequent sex between parents of young children, this one found that *quantity* was not a problem but that *quality* was, especially for men. Women seem to accept the disruptions caused by children

141

much more easily than their husbands. A finding of the 1983 *Playboy* survey that illuminates the all-important role of individual perception is that married people with children do *not* have less intercourse or oral sex than childless couples, but that fathers are less likely to feel satisfied with the frequency of lovemaking than are childless husbands.

Other studies have shown that marital happiness usually diminishes with the birth of the first child and doesn't rise again until the children begin to empty the nest. Within the marital relationship, it's the sexual relationship that suffers most.

Why should this be? Why should the perpetuation of the species often work against the perpetuation of the marriage? The reasons tumble over each other like tots in a sandbox. First come logistical and practical concerns. People waking up every few hours have trouble staying awake, let alone showing interest in each other, and nothing withers an erection or dries up a vagina as quickly as the sound of a toddler opening the bedroom door or an infant squalling to be fed. With everything else that needs to be done, sexual needs often slip down to rank as the couple's lowest priority.

Then there are the physiological barriers, as the biological differences between male and female rise to dominate their life together. The woman's body, which had nine months to prepare for a new life, accommodates itself to the baby's needs by hormonal changes that spur lactation and tend to diminish sexual urgency. Meanwhile, as much as fatherhood may change a man's psyche, it leaves his body unchanged. Typically, the father of a new baby wants sex as much as ever, but he gets less because his wife is so involved, both physically and emotionally, with the infant.

What happens then? He feels frustrated and jealous, rejected and angry. Most new fathers experience what one of them embarrassedly called "spousling rivalry." "I feel like a big baby," Rob told me, "jealous of my own son. I love the baby, sure, but I miss having a wife who cares about me. She goes on and on about him, which I can understand, but occasionally it would be nice if I got the feeling that she cared how I am." If he does express these feelings his wife is likely to throw up her hands, complain about having one more child to take care of, and object that he doesn't appreciate how much she has to do. Now they're both angry. And anger is one of the best birth control devices around.

Beverly Hotchner encourages the young couples she counsels to extend their own sensuousness to include their children, by bringing the father into bed nude while the mother is nursing the baby and following feeding sessions with three-way cuddling, or by taking family baths together. This brings the father into the midst of the family circle and enables sensitive parents to transmit a warm, comforting sensuality without being inappropriately seductive.

A major problem, which persists as children grow older, is the contradiction many people feel between their roles as "parent" and "sexual person." Full enjoyment of sex demands total concentration, the ability to be entirely in the moment with one's partner, without having to think about anything else. Once people have children, they're often unable to shed the parenting role even in bed and thus cannot give themselves over to the total absorption good lovemaking demands. In the 1983 book *Children and Sex: The Parents Speak,* a report by The Study Group of New York of a survey of 225 parents of children between the ages of three and eleven, most of the parents agreed that the quality of their sex lives had changed drastically with the arrival of children.

One reason is this divided focus. Few parents can ignore a child's cry the way they can tune out other distractions. As one father said, "Just when we're getting started, there's a call from the child. My wife runs out and I go limp." Many couples seem to invite this kind of intrusion: about half the parents in this survey said they kept their bedroom doors open while making love, and many vehemently opposed locking the door at any time. The open-door contingent felt—mistakenly, I believe, along with many family relations professionals—that locking their children out would cause deep-seated feelings of rejection and frustration. It's not hard to understand the diminution of sexual satisfaction, for nothing dampens ardor so effectively as the knowledge that a child could wander in at any time. Children *can* understand from an early age that parents have the right to some private time when they are not to be disturbed, and if they know that their parents sometimes make love during this time, so much the better for the youngsters' sex education. What better way is there to learn that the physical expres-

143

sion of love is natural and healthy and the right of everyone to enjoy—even Mommy and Daddy?

Some couples enjoy their best sex when they're away from their children—either by packing them off to Grandma's for the weekend or going off to a motel from time to time themselves. With persistence and imagination, there can be sex—even good sex—after children. Susan and Bill have started a series of "sleep-over dates" in which they take another couple's children for one evening, and the following week the other couple take theirs. "One night every other week may not sound like much to anyone else," Bill says, "but knowing we can look forward to that time alone is like having a hot Saturday night date. Sure, we'll sleep together between times, but with these dates we can plan ahead to take time and do the special kinds of things that we know really turn each other on."

One thing that can hurt a couple's sexual relationship even more than having children is *not* having them if they want them. As much as people may know rationally that they can be fully functioning sexual beings without producing children, the link between sexuality and reproduction is a primal one. That link has a negative corollary as well: Infertility scrapes raw a couple's sexual relationship, and past sexual experiences may well be the cause of difficulty in conceiving.

The unfulfilled longing to be a parent raises troubling questions about maleness and femaleness, leaving would-be parents feeling unsure of their sexual potency, wondering why they can't do what seems to come so easily to everyone else. Then the procedures for diagnosing and treating infertility often strip sex of any pleasure, turning it into a chore for both partners and arousing intense feelings of anger, shame, and embarrassment.

Confronting infertility is often the painful task of people in their thirties. About 15 percent of all couples who want children can't have them, and a recent Yale University study found that while only 10 percent of couples in their twenties don't conceive during the first year they want to, the ratio jumps to 30 percent for those in their thirties. Today, with more women concentrating on career rather than conception during their twenties, with couples tending to postpone marriage and then childbearing, this realization often comes as a shock.

144

"It's in the literature, it's been there for years, but when I asked my doctors for contraception, even though I was thirty-one when I got married, no doctor ever told me, 'If you want to have children, you'd better start trying now, because the older you are the less fertile you are,' " says New York sociologist Joan Liebmann-Smith, whose own difficulties in conceiving inspired her to design a research study to examine the often traumatic relationship between infertility and a couple's sexual functioning.

"Like many of the thirty-five couples in my study group, I didn't find out what a problem it would be for six more years, when my husband and I decided to start a family. And like 95 percent of my sample, I fully expected to conceive the first month. When you don't the first month and the month after that and for what seems forever, there's a lot of anger—at your husband, your doctors, and ultimately yourself."

One reason people turn their anger inward is the suspicion that their sexual activities in the past may have caused sterility in the present. New York Hospital gynecologist Attila Toth points to thirty-two sexually transmitted bacteria that can directly affect fertility in the male or the female. One of these organisms is found more often in men who have had a large number of sexual partners, in infertile men, and in men with a history of such sexually transmitted disorders as nonspecific urethritis and gonorrhea. While other fertility specialists feel the role of these bacteria is overstated, none disputes the fact that they do contribute to the problem. The only question is one of degree.

In years gone by, infertility posed fewer problems of a directly sexual nature. The defect was usually automatically assumed to lie within the woman's body, and, by and large, women have an easier time accepting physical imperfections in themselves than men do. Once a fairly simple round of procedures had been performed, those couples who really wanted a child adopted one, with the luxury of being able to choose the baby's sex, social and religious background, and physical characteristics. Relieved of the need for contraception, sexual relationships sometimes flourished.

As so often happens, however, progress brings its own set of problems. Better means of birth control and the availability of abortion have resulted in a scarcity of adoptable children, forcing childless couples to investigate and try to treat their infertility with all the means available.

145

And research into infertility has produced a host of new procedures, which sometimes solve the problem but, ironically, do massive damage to the sexual and emotional relationship.

Many men cannot deal with the possibility—true in almost half the cases of infertility—that the failure to conceive may be due to some problem in *their* bodies, not their wives', an admission they may not be able to make even to themselves. The difficulty sometimes shows up in a man's reluctance to undergo certain tests. "I've already had two semen analyses. I don't want to go for a third," he may say.

"This is a major area for arguments between husbands and wives," says Liebmann-Smith. "After all, a semen analysis, the most common test, basically requires only one thing—masturbation to orgasm. Meanwhile, the women get hospitalized, cut open, subjected to terribly painful and dangerous procedures. So it's not surprising when women get furious when their husbands balk at being tested."

Typically, for 99 percent of infertile couples, according to Liebmann-Smith, no matter how good or bad a couple's sex life was before they went in for their fertility workups, it falls apart at that point, often never to come back to former levels. The tests proceed. The wife takes her temperature every morning. If she might be ovulating, the couple are instructed to have intercourse every other day to ensure the constant presence of live sperm in the woman's cervix. All non-coital, non-procreative activities are dispensed with. Husband and wife don't go near each other during non-ovulatory phases of her menstrual cycle.

They both become angry. She feels like a malfunctioning machine whose orifices are constantly being probed by physicians. He feels like an instrument whose usefulness is limited to impregnating his wife. Objectified, dehumanized, neither feels sexual desire; neither feels desired by the other. "Sex," says Liebmann-Smith, "becomes making babies, not making love."

The resiliency of human beings, however, shows up in the fact that only three couples out of the thirty-five in this group split up. Possibly because facing infertility forces couples to talk. Says Liebmann-Smith, sociologist and now the mother of one-year-old Rebecca: "This forces you to confront what it is about children that you want, whether it's important to have your own biological children, what it means to adopt, whether you could live with each other without children. Important

146

things that most people don't even think about. While some marriages are very shaky for a while, with separations and getting back together again, I think this kind of talking consolidates a marriage. And I guess that's why so many are as firm as they are.''

''I don't know where all those statistics about the frequency of intercourse between married couples come from.'' Joan Liebmann-Smith shakes her head. ''When I asked the people in my sample—married women in their thirties—I found that sex is just not the main thing in their relationships. They're busy, they and their husbands both work, they both come home tired. What I kept hearing over and over was, 'It seems like other people have intercourse more than we do. Normally, we're only having it once a week, or just on weekends.'

''Then I thought maybe it was just this group that was having trouble conceiving children, and maybe infrequent sex was part of their problem. When I started informally asking friends and acquaintances, though, I found that none of the professional couples I know in their thirties or forties are having sex more often than once a week, usually just on the weekends. The ones with children have it least of all. Everybody's defensive about owning up to it, but they all seem to be saying the same thing.''

Liebmann-Smith's sample seems to be right in the asexual mainstream of today's working couples. Among the 15,000 working couples Caroline Bird reports on in her book *The Two-Paycheck Marriage,* many felt that sex had changed for the worse when the woman went to work and that the tension of professional and business life can cut into sex.

As Tilla Vahanian told me, ''If you're a professional woman, a lawyer, say—as several of my clients are—you have to work very, very hard in a man's world. This means working late, meeting demands much greater than you had anticipated and dealing with the stress of carving out a career. This is something men have had to handle for years, but it's been only recently that significant numbers of women have taken on the same kinds of challenges. These women come home physically debilitated and exhausted, tense about where they are in their careers, and they don't have the emotional or physical energy to be available to their partners.''

Historically, the decade of the thirties has been a period of heavy ca-

147

reer involvement for men, a time when they would set specific goals such as a professorship, a certain level of income, or starting their own business, with a set timetable—often the milestone age of forty. According to Daniel Levinson, who called these years the "settling down" period, this is the time when men work out a life plan. In former decades, a man running his career gears at full tilt usually had help during this period from a wife who kept those gears oiled, while at the same time cushioning a safe haven where he could bask in the enjoyment of a growing family, find release from sexual tensions, and enjoy a companion who listened and counseled and cared.

Today that wife is likely to be running her own career gears at full tilt, and neither she nor her husband has anyone standing by with either an oil can *or* a safe refuge. Both are in pursuit of dreams of success. Or, in the economic climate of this last decade, both are struggling just to stand still. In either case, the demands of work may smother the needs of love. As psychiatrist Jay B. Rohrlich writes in his book *Work and Love: The Crucial Balance,* "Love is the opposite of work in all respects."

Work is doing; love is being. Through work we define our identity; through love we lose it by merging with another. Work uses our aggressive drives; love calls on our sensual ones. Work brings the satisfaction of achievement; love brings the pleasure of sharing. In work we produce; in love we give. Work has goals; love has no agenda. Work thrives in carefully structured time; love grows in joyfully "wasted" time. Balancing these contradictory goals becomes difficult, sometimes impossible.

Tamar, thirty-six, editor-in-chief of a Southern California fashion magazine, tells me, "It's no day at the beach to be married to me. I told Ed—my third husband, the one I'm married to now—what it would be like to be married to a magazine. He didn't realize how difficult it would be and now we're having all kinds of problems. He gets upset because of all the time he doesn't see me. I may be gone for days at a time. I go off and do my thing—the way I told him I would before we ever got married—and he's a homebody, so he sits there taking care of the dog.

"He's threatened divorce about six times now and I finally told him, 'If you say that one more time, just pack your bag.' I've been through this before. I got a divorce from Brad, my second husband, just so we could stay friends. He was my best friend and we always had a wonder-ful time together, so when our careers took us in different directions and we started being ugly to one another, I wanted to protect that friendship. The divorce did it. We've been friends for eighteen years. He's now Ed's friend, too, he has a key to our house, he stores his boat here, and Brad and Ed go fishing together.

"Any problems in my last two marriages have always been caused by my career. Especially as I was getting promoted at the magazine and having more responsibility and becoming more independent about running my own life. Both these men seem to feel emasculated by my success, but I am not about to take orders. I resent getting a thirty-minute lecture on how to park the car, and I can't stand being ques-tioned on when I'll be home. Half the time I don't know and I don't want to have to think about it. I want to be able to concentrate all my energies on getting out the very best book I can. And I can't do that when I have to keep one eye on the clock.

"If this marriage collapses, I won't try it again. I make a better mis-tress than wife, anyway." Tamar laughs, showing white teeth against her tan. When we walk into the restaurant, more than one man's eyes are drawn to Tamar, the "California girl" become a woman. She car-ries herself gracefully, her tall body moving with an easy glide. As she speaks, she touches herself often, flipping behind her shoulders her waist-length hair streaked in colors of taffy and molasses, or lightly touching her hand to her chest to emphasize a point and in the process also emphasizing her voluptuous figure.

Tamar has had a series of sexual turning points. The first was the rape when she was thirteen, which catapulted her into an early sexual initiation. "I never told anybody about it because I thought it was my fault for leaving the dance before I was supposed to. Besides, I was still in one piece, basically unhurt, and I figured my life was too important to let this mess it up. But from then on I just started throwing out all the ways I didn't think I could live with.

"The first was what I had heard from the women around me—that sex wasn't something to be enjoyed, you were just simply doing your duty. I thought there must be more to it than that. Since I wasn't a vir-gin anymore anyway, I figured I might as well see what this was all about." Tamar saw—and realized that despite her youth her sex drive

149

was strong. This realization propelled her into a disastrous early marriage. "Getting married at seventeen was the only way to have sex in the little town I grew up in without getting a terminally bad reputation."

Soon after the collapse of this union, which lasted barely a year, Tamar left the copper-mining town of Ajo, Arizona, got a receptionist's job with a newspaper in San Diego, and met Brad. The sexual bond that had united them initially began to founder, however, when Tamar's job metamorphosed into her career. Her trail of promotions and job changes took her to the editorship of a Los Angeles-based fashion magazine.

"Brad started to resent the fact that I was more involved in my work than he was in his. He had a good job but it didn't mean that much to him. And he thought I cared more about my career than my marriage—and I guess he was right. Maybe because I was so completely self-made and I was loving the idea that I could really go places even though I hadn't been prepared for it, hadn't expected it. Still, here it was. I was getting more responsibility at work and becoming more independent, and that spilled over to our home life."

The divorce from Brad was a major turning point for Tamar, then twenty-six. Like most of the divorced people whose stories are told in the next chapter, this period of being alone made her realize her own strength. "I'd never been on my own before. I didn't know anything. I had never written a check. I had never even filled the car with gas. But I learned, and it was one of the greatest accomplishments of my life to realize that I was totally independent and I didn't need anybody."

Tamar liked the sexual independence, too, that she had in those seven years when she was alone. "I'm a Libra, and I need a lot of romance and excitement in my life—more than I can get with just one person. Sex has always been my favorite sport, but when I married Ed three years ago I intended to give it my best shot and be totally faithful to him. And I was for almost two years. But then things got bad between us. Ed resents my being away so much, so *our* sex life isn't what it used to be, either. You can't be happy in bed when you're miserable and resentful all the time."

At about this time the man who'd been Tamar's lover on an onagain, off-again basis for years turned up again. "I think it works so well with him because it's not a day-in, day-out thing. I'm not cut out to be a wife but I make a terrific mistress. I like having the quality time: when a man is with me he doesn't have to worry about mowing the lawn and I don't have to pick up his dirty underwear.

"I just make sure that I don't wear cologne and that I use the same soap he uses at home, little things like that. And I don't have to answer to him if I want to take a lover when I'm traveling. I know Ed would die if he knew I was going to bed with other men. If this marriage dissolves, I don't want to make this kind of commitment ever again."

While Tamar's career has affected her marital sex life, she feels that her creativity and her sexuality have gone hand in hand in other ways. "I think the features I plan, the writing I do, the photos I oversee are all tied up with my sensuality. That's why I can appreciate all of those sensations that I want to reach my readers with—those colors and tastes and sounds and smells.

"When sex is exciting, I have that joyful feeling like every day is brand-new. I see things differently and produce better. I got a new sense of self-confidence when this special lover came into my life while I was single that carried over to my work and helped me relate better to people. Then I launched a new offshoot of the magazine right after I met Ed. Now, things aren't going well with him and my lover is out of the country, so I'm at a cranky stage when things look gray around the edges and I'm not producing well. But I know that will change."

Work is, of course, only one strand in the intricate network of influences upon our lives. While it seems to have exerted a major influence on Tamar's adult life, it may well be a minor influence compared to a myriad of earlier factors like the rape, her high sex drive, the restless temperament that makes monogamy impossible for her, the stories she heard as a child from her cigar-smoking, whip-carrying grandmother who would go after her husband with a shotgun to the local house of prostitution and who consistently urged Tamar never to become dependent on a man. Still, the work factor *is* there.

Tamar's story is not typical. As no one's story is typical. There are as many ways for work to coexist with sex as there are working sexual beings. Yet this intertwining of the influences of occupational and family factors has been virtually ignored in studies of adult development, an omission slowly being rectified by a number of new studies, includ-

151

ing one which found that women who have good jobs tend to have satisfying sex lives.

Because Jay Rohrlich had always been fascinated by the ways our occupations influence our lives, he decided to seek out some of the most competitive, work-oriented people in the world. So he moved his psychiatric practice from a traditional uptown Manhattan residential location, downtown to the thirty-sixth floor of a Wall Street skyscraper that also houses high-powered international firms in the fields of investment, insurance, and transportation. Dr. Rohrlich believes that for too many of us, the vital balance between work and love is askew, and he tells me about some of the men and women he sees leading unbalanced lives.

There are the goal setters for whom sex becomes something that they're determined to do well also, sometimes making it too much like work, as they set out to achieve the most wonderful orgasm.

Then there's the high achiever who's so insecure that he dare not risk his vulnerability in a real love affair. "Usually the most maniacal achievers are the most insecure people—their insecurity makes them able to achieve so much, and these insecurities usually show up in personal situations. So you find a lot of powerful men, even heads of government, finding their sexual outlets in brothels or with call girls who cater to their neuroses. They want to be loved unreservedly the way a mother does or adored unquestioningly by someone who looks up to them. They can't handle being treated like an equal in a mature, healthy relationship. I don't see this sort of thing with women as much as with men. The women I see usually find a better balance."

There's the successful businessperson whose work is actually a sexual stimulant. Rohrlich gives as an example a securities analyst whose way of proclaiming her femininity is to be intensely sexual. "There's a very healthy quality to the way this woman is conscious of not letting her preoccupation with achievement interfere with the sensual and intimate dimensions of her marriage. It creates its own problems, though, because there's sometimes a drivenness in her sexuality that makes her husband feel he can't satisfy her."

There are the ambitious couples leading parallel lives, in which their work identities become so primary that "sex becomes something you think about when you're on trips or in terms of an office affair. So much of your energy is concentrated on work that you're not even thinking about your husband or wife in a sexual context.''

There are men who don't need sex because their work meets needs that sex often serves. ''Their enjoyment in closing a deal has the lusty physical quality of an orgasm. They're absolutely on fire. The other side of the coin is that when they do have sex, they approach it as if it's another deal. The important thing is winning—making that sale, signing up that prospect, conquest and control. The sex itself is the least important part, and some of the men who are most powerful out in the world are impotent in bed.''

Rohrlich tells the story of two investment bankers who meet at an annual conference and tally up their sexual scores for the year. They allot a certain number of points for having sex above 5,000 feet, for having it with someone under eighteen, for having it with an important client, and so forth. The loser buys the champagne. ''For people like this— almost always men—sex deteriorates into a win-or-lose game rather than what it was designed for, the pure experience of pleasure and intimacy and union with a loved one. But then that's probably the exception rather than the rule for most people.''

Many two-income couples, especially those with children, reject psychological explanations for their impoverished sex lives, citing instead the physical, practical, and logistical barriers to a warm, close, loving sexual relationship. As one retailing executive told me, ''I can handle the job and children fairly well, but I have no time, energy, or creativity left to be a wife. Then we both get so wrapped up in our own schedules that we can't find the time. Plus, he's a night owl, and half the time I fall asleep by nine o'clock. We're out of sync.''

Blumstein and Schwartz found that usually one partner provides the emotional support to take care of the relationship. Traditionally this has been the wife's role, while the husband took care of the family's financial support. In recent years, this equation has changed, and problems arise when both partners become so involved in their work that neither one watches the relationship.

One way to resolve problems may include reducing the amount of time or energy one or both partners put into their jobs. For Mickey and Sheila, an unexpected small inheritance came at just the right time. After ten years of marriage, it was the worst it had ever been. They felt

153

distant from each other, and their once satisfying sexual relationship was now only a memory. He hated his job, and his dissatisfaction poisoned the rest of his life; she had just earned her bachelor's degree and didn't know what she wanted to do with it. So they decided to treat the inheritance as a sign from on high.

Mickey quit his job and Sheila suspended her job hunt. They set aside the next year to concentrate on their relationship and their work goals. "Sexually this was the best year we've ever had," Mickey says as the year draws to a close. "With the kids away at school all day and us at home, we had time like never before. It was the best shot in the arm we could have given ourselves. Now we know that no matter what we decide to do with our jobs, we need to make some time just for us."

Time isn't everything, of course. As Dr. Rohrlich says, "A sexual relationship is a very sensitive barometer of the health of a marriage. Problems with sex usually have more to do with the feelings a couple has for each other than with any outside pressures." A recent survey of married couples concluded, "It's not the hours and the schedule that determine how much time a couple spend with each other; it's how happy they are together." This was confirmed by an account executive with a steel company, who told me, "We try to plan time together, but things sometimes don't happen. We find the time when we're feeling good about one another. When I'm angry I'm not looking to find the time."

Sandra Leiblum, director of the sexual counseling service of Rutgers University's College of Medicine and Dentistry, says, "A lot of couples use time as a rationalization. We need to debunk the myth that you need a lot of time. Not all encounters need a lot of time, with a lot of sensual massage and all of that. They're *nice*—but quickies have their place, too. Also, sometimes having better sex less frequently does the trick. Having five miserable experiences in one week is not as good as having one good one, so I encourage couples to exchange quantity for quality."

Caroline Bird points out that in many two-career marriages, the difference between quality and quantity makes sex "better for her, worse for him. She feels quality is better; he's unhappy because there's less quantity. This seems to have something to do with the fact that she's more likely to have sex only when she wants to, a function of power in the marriage. And women who contribute income have more power in their marriages."

Bird agrees with those professionals who maintain that sex is affected much less by the problems of both partners working than it is by the problems husband and wife are having with each other. As Bird says, "Bad sex is often a function of anger. When couples talk about their marriages, he talks about sex and she talks about help with the housework." This certainly came through in my conversations with John and Angela, the couple introduced in Chapter 5, whose sex life has not been the same since Angela's pregnancy.

Other studies have found that women who contribute a significant proportion of money to family income tend to have satisfying sex lives, and that achievement-oriented, assertive women are more sexually satisfied than more passive, traditionally "feminine" women. This undoubtedly has much to do with the strong relationship between identity and intimacy. People who know who they are can more easily give of themselves in a loving, sexual relationship. And in our society it's easier for a woman to develop a strong sense of self through her job than it is through traditional patterns of homemaking and mothering.

Why, then, is there more divorce among working couples? Why does the rate of divorce rise 2 percent for every additional $1,000 earned by the wife? Mostly because working wives can afford to leave a bad marriage. Another reason is probably the greater intensity of the marriages of working couples. When they're good, they're very, very good; when they're bad, they don't last.

One couple dealing with these issues are Karen, thirty-three, a wiry, energetic newspaper reporter, and Gary, thirty-five, the affable, outgoing sales manager for a network television station. With two young children under eight, one job that involves covering late-night events and meeting tight deadlines, and the other involving travel and evenings out with important clients, sex has become a battleground.

"I'm proud of Karen, I really am," Gary states emphatically. I believe him. "Still, she's not the woman I used to make love to. She comes home from those meetings and she gets into bed and she smells like a man. I don't know what it is—whether it's the smoke clinging to her or the tiredness on her breath or what. All I know is that I'm not about to make love to another guy and I'm turned off."

"You know what *I* think is turning you off," Karen charges. "I think you never counted on my work meaning so much to me. And you're mad that I'm not available at your convenience the way I was when I was covering those little local stories. I can't do as much at home. And you don't like that. You like telling your friends that I have this job, but you don't like what that means in our life. Well, I don't always like it, either, but my work is important to me."

"Rationally," Gary repeats, "I'm very proud of her and what she's doing, that she went and started her own career and is really taking off with it, getting promotions and awards and more exciting assignments. But I can't help worrying about what it means for a relationship when you have two people going in two different directions all the time. With the kinds of jobs we have, neither one of us can give much. Neither one of us can leave everything at the office at five o'clock and come home and be lovers. Our bed has become the place where we catch up on work, not the place where we make love."

Karen says, "He's right. Between the jobs and the kids, I sometimes feel we've turned into problem-solving machines. There's always something—and we always work it out. We're great working partners—but that wasn't what I thought marriage is all about."

Gary, like many men, resents the loss of his "centrality" in his wife's life, a centrality that may have been in the marriage at first—or may have existed only in Gary's expectations, based on what he had seen between his own parents. He feels cheated. Instead of being able to count on her solace when things go wrong for him at work, he often finds her absorbed with her own job troubles. Stanford University sociologist William J. Goode attributes this common feeling of being deserted to the fact that men are more dependent upon women today than they had been in times past when more of them turned to the company of other men. Today, most men will say that their best friend is their wife, while women are more likely to name another woman. When a man's best friend is not there for him, both the emotional and sexual aspects of their relationship suffer.

This, then, is a crucial time, when career-building pressures can add to any other strains in a marriage. The demands of work may not cause the stress, but sometimes they can add just enough weight to make the entire structure collapse. Jay Rohrlich's advice to couples who find themselves with a deteriorating (or deteriorated) sexual or emotional relationship is to ask themselves and each other the kinds of questions that will tell them how much their difficulties have to do with their own individual problems, either in work or in life, and how much with each other. "If there's a good foundation and enough goodwill, people can often see that what they think at first is a marital problem turns out to be an individual problem, a feeling of failure because of lack of work success or a midlife crisis, and they can ride out the crisis.

"Too many people act first and ask questions afterwards," he says. "Sometimes they make the mistake of breaking up—and then realize, too late, that they had a good thing."

Contemporary couples expect more from their marriages than people used to; when they don't get the companionship, the mutual affirmation, the sexual communion that they expect, they can split up—or look for help. After Margie and Bruce, both thirty, had been married for five years, neither one could put a finger on what exactly had gone wrong with their marriage, but neither one could point to what was right with it, either. They signed up for a Marriage Encounter weekend, one of the many "marriage enrichment" programs that have become popular over the past decade in the belief that preventing serious problems is better than trying to treat them and that couples can learn relationship skills to preserve and even enhance the intimacy of the early years.

Bruce describes what happened with them as "crossing the line." "Once you've crossed that line," he says, "you're a different person, and if you came back on any given Tuesday, you could act just the same way you did before—but now you would know you weren't giving your best. It would affect you differently and you would stop. That doesn't mean that Margie and I don't argue anymore, but it means that we're able to communicate to each other the hurts that come about in those arguments, maybe find ways to be more gentle and to stop before getting to the bad hurting points."

It also meant reordering priorities, especially in sex. As Margie tells me, "Marriage is like a cake and sex is the icing. If you eat too much icing you get sick, but the cake without the icing isn't too spiffy. We had a lot of trouble with our icing, so that was the first thing we handled

157

after making our encounter.'' For Bruce this involved confessing a series of casual infidelities to Margie and renouncing all extramarital sex. For Margie it meant confronting her feelings about being ''used'' during sex and making efforts to change her own responses, rather than continuing to blame Bruce for not ''giving'' her orgasms. For both it meant working on the relationship inside and outside the bedroom. The work paid off, so that both of them can now say, fourteen years after their wedding, that this is the most sexually fulfilling time of their lives.

Formal marriage-enrichment programs are not the route for everyone, but all of us can benefit from looking at our marriages from time to time and asking hard questions about where we are and where we're going. Asking the right questions often helps us to find enough answers to strengthen our bonds and avoid the event that for many people is the most traumatic one they will ever face in their entire lives, a divorce.

Chapter 7

Blooming Again:
Sex After Divorce

I used to panic when a relationship ended, but now I know that some people won't like me and I won't like some of them. I know now that even at the age of fifty-two I'm an attractive person and I'm going to find somebody else. And I know I'm going to work through this intimacy problem, just because it's important enough to me.

—ROBERT

"I MISSED THE SUMMER of '42. The summer of '72 was my awakening. That was the year I left my family in the home where we'd lived for more than half of our sixteen years of marriage and took an apartment downtown and was single again."

Robert looks at home in this apartment on the Near North Side of Chicago. I had known him during his marriage and am struck by the difference in his two homes. The suburban colonial he had shared with Sylvia and their two sons had been tastefully furnished in Early American style and what little art had hung on the walls were mostly familiar reproductions. This apartment, overlooking Lake Michigan, is abloom with the plants he always loved but could never keep because of Sylvia's allergies. Its walls are covered with his pen-and-ink sketches of people in public places. The furniture is sleek and contemporary. Certainly there has been a metamorphosis in his environment. I am eager to hear how Robert's life has changed in other ways.

"I was forty-two years old and I was scared. My fear had a lot to do with sexuality, because I really feared I'd be a social misfit. I knew I'd

159

do well job-wise and taking care of myself, but I was convinced I was a failure at establishing an intimate relationship with a woman. I never had a sexual relationship with anyone but Sylvia—she was not a virgin, but I was when I married at twenty-six—and our sexual life was barren and limited. I was a premature ejaculator—had been since my teenage petting years—and Sylvia didn't enjoy sex and resisted a lot of my desires. She wasn't interested in oral sex, either way, and she ridiculed me whenever I'd bring home a book or make any kind of suggestion that we try something new.

"The sex was only part of our problems. We had met in the Communist party, so we shared a lot of ideological values. But then as I became disillusioned with the party, we didn't have this bond anymore, and we didn't seem to have much else. While both of us had trouble showing our feelings, I worked at becoming a feeling, expressing human being. I changed and grew miles more than she did. Then one day I realized that our relationship was really over. There was nothing left. When I left, Sylvia broke down and cried, and I cried myself. I don't recall ever crying before that. I became much more emotional about that time. I knew that before I could get in touch with my joy, I really had to experience my despair."

The month Robert moved out he went to see Cal, a therapist who had been recommended by a colleague in the child guidance clinic where Robert himself did counseling. As he walked into Cal's office, he found himself raising his voice to be heard above the din of barking dogs and meowing cats, which stayed in the office all week until Cal could take them with him to the country on weekends.

Haltingly, Robert told Cal about his premature ejaculation, his worry that at the age of forty-two he would never know sexual happiness. At this point Cal hooted: "Look around this room," he said. "Look at all of these animals jumping on top of each other. They're all doing their sexual thing. And so are people. This is 1972, there are many different ways to fuck. You don't have a problem. I don't consider that a problem, what you're telling me."

On this encouraging note therapy began, opening Robert up in ways he had never dreamed of. Trying to throw off the shackles he felt had bound him tightly all his life, he did the most outrageous things he could think of. At one therapy session, he decided he wanted to work in

160

the nude, asked permission to take off his clothes, and did so, saying in effect to the other members of his therapy group, "Look, this is me. This is my body. Accept me. All of me." And they, who all stayed fully clothed, did. He went to a sexual weekend in an urban commune, knowing ahead of time he'd have to be prepared to go to bed with anyone in the commune, male or female. Despite his fears, he had one sexual experience after another. He picked up women wherever he happened to be.

His first date was a disaster: for the first time in years, Robert felt good about his performance, but the twenty-five-year-old woman who had picked him up on the El and then seduced him with a candlelight dinner told him angrily after their hour-long lovemaking session, "I really like to fuck for about three hours." His next liaison—with a voluptuous woman a few years older than he was who loved sex, could be satisfied in many different ways, and was joyously nonjudgmental—lasted six months and gave him the gift of confidence.

"Through the therapy and the other experiences I've had—I've *forced* myself to have—and through the general climate in society, I've learned a lot. One is that my age was not a factor against me. My problems had nothing to do with age. They had everything to do with me—how I saw myself and what kind of contact I made with other people. These are the things I'm still working on.

"I still have problems with intimacy. Cal pointed out to me my worries about being trapped, being taken over and controlled if I let myself be in an intimate relationship. I see this coming up for me whenever a woman acts too loving—if she buys me too many presents, if she does too many kind acts for me, if she wants to be with me too much. I think I want all of that, but when I get it, I withdraw. And then the relationship ends.

"I used to panic when a relationship ended, but now I know that some people won't like me and I won't like some of them. I know now that even at the age of fifty-two I'm an attractive person and I'm going to find somebody else. And I know I'm going to work through this intimacy problem, just because it's important enough to me."

How does Robert define intimacy? He says yearningly, "Being able to give. Being able to love, to relate to the other person's needs and not just my own. Being aware of who that other person is and loving her as

161

her own person with all the differences between us. First I know I have to love myself and then I can love somebody else and then I can experience the sexuality of myself, and then the other person, and it bounces back and forth. At some level I'm aware of this and at another I'm frightened of it.''

Joan, forty-eight, had been married even longer—twenty-three years—when her husband left her. Now she says, ''I feel a sadness that my marriage ended, a sadness that our family broke up. But in terms of me, me alone, it's the best thing in the world that ever happened to me. My life is a daily adventure. I wake up in the morning and I never know what's going to happen by the end of the day, and at least once a day something adventurous does pop up. I would never be doing the things I'm doing professionally if I were still married to Shelly, and I never would have had this glorious sexual relationship with Richard. And I'm sure I could not have been so creative, feeling stifled as I did in my marriage.''

Joan appears anything but stifled now. Radiating color and warmth, her apartment is full of fresh flowers, impressionistic paintings of children, warm woods of many textures. Most of the furniture and paintings are from the home she shared with her husband, which confirms my view of her as having been the vital force in their relationship, in which he was the passive member just along for the ride.

''During my marriage,'' Joan tells me, ''I used to think, 'Jesus Christ, maybe I'm a nymphomaniac!' We had both been virgins—I was twenty and he was twenty-one—and then after marriage I had such a sex drive, but Shelly didn't. Sometimes we could go for weeks without making love. I would caress him in bed or make an overture, and sometimes he would respond or he would just fall asleep. I would get furious and withdraw and be hostile for days, but we never talked about it.

''Actually we never talked about anything much,'' says this woman from whom words spill out like torrents in a waterfall. ''We never talked when we made love, and even sitting in the living room or out in a restaurant he wasn't very communicative. He was really a passive personality—a sweet man but very constricted. For years I lived with it because I believed marriage was forever.''

This sexual desert of a marriage produced two children. Though parched for passion, we humans can still procreate. Over the years

162

Joan sought fulfillment along avenues other than her marriage. Not in the arms of other men; she never considered having an affair. She devoted herself to her children, took courses, made intellectually stimulating women friends, went back to college. As she changed, so did her relationship with her husband.

"The month I got my bachelor's degree, Shelly began an affair. The day I got my job, he started to talk 'trial separation.' And the week after I got my master's degree, he moved out. He couldn't take my becoming a person in my own right."

For nineteen months after her separation, on the advice of her attorney, Joan remained celibate, not dating, knowing no sexual release other than the kind she could give herself. "I had a need to turn everything around and make a bad thing okay. So I figured, 'Okay, I'll use this time to learn about myself, to monitor my sex drive.' I found out that my sex drive in its pure form—with no external stimulation, no man in my life—was strongest just before my period, and especially in the mornings. I've always loved sex in the morning. Still do. Because that's the most spontaneous."

During the five years since Joan's separation, there has been a happy confluence of the various currents in her life. For the first time ever she has been able to celebrate her sexuality, most especially in the arms of a caring, sensitive lover who, while unavailable as a permanent (or even frequent) partner because of marriage and geography, has given Joan "the most intense, intimate, powerful experiences with a man that I have ever, ever had." Richard, whom Joan had admired while she was married, came back into her life through a professional contact. The three or four times a year she has seen him over the past four years have constituted, for her, "an exquisite relationship on every level."

"I'm not sure I'll ever have this again with another man, intellectually, emotionally, sexually. He has been totally honest with me, describing his marriage as a good friendship that he will never sever. At the same time, he has enabled me to get in touch with a passion, a depth, an intensity that I had never known was possible. And every time gets better for both of us."

While her relationship with Richard has opened the floodgates to Joan's sexuality, three or four nights of ecstasy a year cannot sustain her. Not even in the face of the professional successes she has achieved

163

as she has attained one promotion after another in her field of urban planning. Not even in her awareness that as she has been more open, more giving, more taking sexually, she has poured a new dimension of creativity into her work.

And so Joan sees other men. She has plunged into the singles dating scene, in which there are too many women her age and not enough men; in which, in this marketplace of people searching for other people, even the most attractive, dynamic, sensual forty-eight-year-old woman is apt to be passed over in favor of a woman with fewer years and firmer thighs. She has met men at concerts, art openings, professional conferences, through friends. Along the way she has developed a new way of looking at and classifying these endless variations of the male animal.

"I can go to bed with a man once and tell you all about his personality. I'm lucky—I've never had a really awful experience with a man. But I have known men who hop into bed, are demanding, are very selfish. Then there are men who have to be totally in control, who can give but can't take. It's very rare to find someone who can give as well as take, who can be considerate and sensitive to your needs and yet can freely show you his own pleasure.

"Even so, I feel more alive than I did in my marriage. I'd have to say I'm grateful to Shelly for forcing me out of a marriage that had been keeping me in a tight little box when I didn't have the courage or the strength to break that box myself. Or maybe I did. When I saw that show *I'm Getting My Act Together and Taking It on the Road,* the part that struck home was when Gretchen Cryer said she wanted out of her marriage and so she acted in a way that was sure to make her husband leave her. Who's to say I didn't do that, too?"

Despite the absence of a man in her life, Joan is clearly a sensuous woman, the perfect embodiment of the model described by Beverly Hotchner: "It's a myth that we're not sexual beings unless we're relating to another person. There are lots of ways that single people can be sexual. I'm not talking only about masturbating. You can experience yourself as a sensual, sexual being in so many ways.

"You can enjoy the sensuality of your body when you're showering, when you're bathing. You can enjoy the sensuality of your body in the kinds of clothing you buy, in the way you walk, in the way you talk. I'm not saying it isn't nice to have a partner, but I think we forget that we're sexual beings from the moment we're born to the moment we die, whether we have a partner to express it with or not. We're expressing it all the time.''

It's easy for Beverly Hotchner and me to accept this concept of sensuous singlehood, knowing as we talk that each of us is lucky enough to have a partner ready to share our sensuality. We don't have to face that often asexual loneliness that tortures the newly alone. As Marlene, who divorced at twenty-nine after eight years of marriage, told me, ''I didn't get a divorce to be alone. I got a divorce to find a new relationship in my life.''

Robert Segraves, a University of Chicago psychiatrist, warns that the wounds of divorce may not heal for years. Many of these injuries are sexual. In a 1983 interview with *The New York Times* Dr. Segraves said, ''There's a lot of evidence that divorce is an overwhelming stress for most people, even if they are getting divorced for the right reasons. There's tremendous internal and external reorganization required after a divorce. And the effects are not just short-term. We see a lot of people years later who are having trouble reconnecting with the opposite sex. Men, for instance, often have problems with impotence four or five years later because they're scared to death to be reconnected.''

For those whose aloneness is thrust upon them by their partner's unilateral decision to leave, the pain of loneliness is compounded by rejection. Alan, thirty-nine, who has been separated for only three years, divorced for half that time, has not achieved the equanimity that Joan and Robert have. He tells me, ''When Ginnie kicked me out, I went into shock, then into a depression. I couldn't work, couldn't eat, couldn't stop crying. In a sense I became an infant again, and I had to grow up all over again, only this time I had the awareness to worry about how I would make my way in the world. The thought terrified me.''

By the time Alan's marriage of fifteen years ended, the only strength left in it was the sex; but not even that was strong enough to keep the pair together. Still, Alan would have stayed—even though he knew he wasn't meeting Ginnie's expectations as a provider and, with his interest in public service law, probably never would, and even though they found they had less and less to say to each other. He had married his first girlfriend out of shyness and would have stayed with her out of fear. And out of the attachment he felt toward their two small daughters. But when the Legal Aid lawyers went out on strike and Alan would not consider a more lucrative branch of the law, Ginnie looked into the crystal ball of her future and didn't like what she saw. Ginnie said "Go," and Alan went.

Realizing he was plunging into a frightening abyss, Alan clutched at whatever supports he could hold on to. He went to discussion groups, support groups, group therapy, private therapy. He took a temporary survival job selling shoes, as much to bolster his morale as his bank account. He read every self-help book he could find. And he climbed out of his disabling depression to find a shaky equilibrium on a narrow ledge.

Like so many other divorced people I spoke to, Alan would never have chosen to suffer the pain his divorce caused him. But having come through the worst of it, he *is* stronger and more self-confident now than he had been fifteen years before. "This whole experience shook me so that it opened my eyes to lots of things. I had to examine myself. I had to seek therapy and look at myself, look at other people, try to be more objective and more honest. I'm talking more about my feelings now than I ever did in my whole life, and it's unbelievable. The most incredible part is that I'm finding that the more I tell about myself, the more people like me. Which is just the opposite reaction from what I had expected."

Alan is among those divorcees whom I think of as the "Rip Van Winkles" of the dating game. These people—especially women over thirty-five and men over forty—got married in a world with one set of standards, immersed themselves in the relationship, and then emerged from it fifteen, twenty, twenty-five years later as single persons in a brand-new society. Many of them need to learn the language of a new country. Those who married young often reemerge as the adolescents they had been when they said their vows and need to learn not only new vocabularies and new values but new skills in forming relationships as mature, independent adults. It isn't easy.

The changes in mores that took place while these people were out of the sexual search present a dizzying array of questions for people who were brought up to expect sex to exist only as part of a relationship.

What is a "relationship"? The product of two dates or twenty? Does a relationship imply exclusivity? Can a woman say no to sex without losing a man's interest in her? Can a man say no without losing his self-respect and the respect of the woman he turns down? Can a person be a good parent and a seeker of sex at the same time? How does age affect one's desirability as a sex partner? (Women worry about their looks, men about their potency.)

Some of these newcomers to dating and sexual choices revert to the language of their teenage years. At the age of thirty-nine Alan talks about wanting to be someone's "boyfriend," about a woman friend who isn't his "girlfriend," about his desire to have sex without "going steady." His words have a sweetly anachronistic air, as do his concerns: "If I've been going out with a woman on Saturday nights and I meet someone new, will my first girlfriend feel demoted if I switch her to Friday nights? I don't want to take advantage of a woman—I know most of them would like to be the only girlfriend—but I do like sex. I've always enjoyed it and now that I'm having it with more frequency, it's like—I don't know—it's like, the more you have the more you want."

The toll taken by divorce, more devastating than virtually any other life event, including widowhood, can be seen in the higher rates among divorcees—as compared to the married, never-married, and widowed—for emotional disturbance, accidental death, suicide, admission to psychiatric facilities, medical visits, and death from a variety of causes including heart disease, cancer, and high blood pressure. Most of the emphasis over the past couple of decades, as our divorce rates soared to more than one million a year before leveling out during the past year or two, has been on the effects of divorce on children. Its cataclysmic effects on the adults themselves have rarely been recognized.

One researcher who has studied the effects of divorce on the couple themselves is E. Mavis Hetherington, a prominent psychologist on the faculty of the University of Virginia. Dr. Hetherington and her colleagues spent thousands of hours on detailed interviews with ninety-six families—forty-eight in the process of divorce and a comparison group of forty-eight intact couples and their children. The researchers met with the families at two months, one year, and two years after the legal

167

divorce. What they learned illuminates an often predictable pattern in post-divorce reactions.

The worst time of all for most men and women was one year after the divorce, which may be eighteen months or two or more years after the initial separation. At this time people tend to feel like failures as spouses, parents, workers, and social beings. Women feel helpless and men disorganized. By two years after the divorce, ex-husbands are apt to be in better shape than ex-wives and are more likely to have remarried. David M. Reed, Ph.D., a Philadelphia-area therapist who has counseled and written about divorce as a sexual crisis, maintains that it may take up to two years for a divorced woman to achieve the ability for sexual arousal. "To get over any major change in our lives," he told participants in a recent workshop for the newly single, "usually takes anywhere from eighteen months to two years. Then you can begin to enjoy life. And then it may take another two years to adjust to a new partner."

Dr. Hetherington and other researchers have found that the single most important determinant of a divorced person's state of mind is almost always the presence or absence of a new intimate relationship. If you're in love again, you're happy. If not, you're not. Men have the edge over women here: it's easier for them to meet women (partly because they don't have custody of the children and don't have to get babysitters), and they have a larger pool of women to draw from. Re-pairing with a woman ten or fifteen years younger is so common nobody even remarks on it anymore—except maybe the bitter ex-wife.

It would be surprising if divorced people did *not* suffer from sexual problems since, as Dr. Reed emphasizes, sex and love still go together. "Ninety percent of the sexual dysfunctions people suffer from stem from the separation between sex and love. If you've been hurt in love, you have to accept some sexual dysfunction until you can heal the hurt," he says.

The sexual response after divorce is unpredictable. Some couples continue to have relations even after they've decided to separate. Some maintain a sexual relationship for months, or even years. (The surfacing of anger and the assuming of control are sometimes an aphrodisiac for women who had never been orgasmic before and suddenly find sex exciting.) Some become so depressed they lose all sex drive. Some become obsessed with sex.

In the 1983 *Playboy* report on the sexual behavior and attitudes of more than 100,000 readers, divorced men—as compared to single, married, remarried, and cohabiting men and women, and to divorced women—are the only ones who rate "sex" as more important to personal happiness than "love" or "family life." According to this survey, divorced and remarried men and women do, in fact, have sex often—more often than those in any other category, except for cohabiting partners, who say they have the most frequent and the most satisfying sex of all.

Those divorced people who become very active sexually often do so to help them handle the strong feelings aroused by the divorce. They act out their anger at the other sex (all representatives of whom become extensions of the spouse) by sleeping with everyone they can, without regard for the other person's feelings. They allay their guilt by demonstrating that if they're good in bed, the failure of the marriage can't be all their fault. And they forget their fear and depression by finding solace in the arms and flesh of others.

Women usually suffer more from divorce, both psychologically and sexually. While most divorced women start to have sex within a year of their divorce, they usually want to couple sex with love and affection but often find themselves going to bed with men because they feel they have to, if they're to have any kind of social life at all. They're not enjoying the sex and not feeling good about themselves. Joan found this happening to her as she went from being a neo-adolescent rediscovering herself as a sexual person, who readily went to bed on a first date, on her odyssey to the woman she is now, who demands to be courted and shown respect, who will not add sex to a relationship unless there really *is* a relationship.

On the other hand, some women find the post-divorce years exciting ones, as they seesaw crazily from the highs of sexual self-discovery to the lows of unrequited passions. Marlene had married the only man she had ever gone to bed with, partly, she later realized, in response to his "emotional blackmail"—that if she didn't marry him, he would tell everyone she'd slept with him. She now says, "If the morals of today had prevailed twenty years ago in my circle in Detroit, I think I would not have married him. I was already thinking he was not the best person for me, but I didn't think I could get out of it. I had been attracted to his mind, but I should have bought a set of encyclopedias instead!

"After my divorce, my loneliness became very much wrapped up with sexuality. Not having a man in my life made me feel very needy sexually, and it was hard to separate the two."

For the four years before Marlene remarried, she blossomed sexually, sometimes getting bruised in the process. Then in her early thirties, she felt physical needs for sex as she never had before. She felt desirable to men. She became aware of the sexual vibrations they were sending. When she met someone who seemed to have some potential as a permanent partner, she went to bed with him. She experimented, engaging in oral sex for the first time, feeling for the first time that sex was fun. And when the sex was very good, she fell in love.

She smiles ruefully, "I soon found out that a one-way street doesn't work. I was very naïve and vulnerable at the beginning, and I just couldn't let go of that first man. I couldn't understand how something that seemed so perfect to me could mean so little to him. But I learned how to deal with the casualness and the hardness in the singles world, and I became more cynical. Happily, not so cynical that I wasn't able to fall in love with the man I'm married to now. We've been married for nine years, and our sexual relationship is good when we're getting along well, which we do most of the time.

"Married sex is different, though. It's warm and loving, not that extreme passion at first when we couldn't keep our hands off each other. I'm glad we had that passion—I'm glad I got to the point where I could feel it, and I miss it sometimes, but I wouldn't try to find it with someone else. I wouldn't do anything to jeopardize my marriage, because I love my husband too much."

Peggy found her divorce a different kind of sexual turning point. Judging by some of the changes in her, you might assume that her sexuality had diminished since her separation, a year ago. She dressed provocatively during her marriage, applying makeup generously, combing her bleached hair in cloudlike masses around her face, wearing lacy underwear that shouted "I'm available!" Now, at thirty-five, Peggy looks like the stereotype of the fresh-faced, all-American girl next door: hair short and simple, back to its natural light brown, clothing a nondescript pants suit, underwear undoubtedly no-nonsense cotton. I learn, however, as we sit across a tiny table in the Dallas hotel where we meet for breakfast before she goes off to her office manager's job that she is more sexual than ever. Why?

"Because," she says in the soft voice that's often hard for me to hear, "whenever I had sex it was because I felt I needed to depend on a man. I started to sleep with boys when I was fifteen and I was pretty active till I married a man who was just what I wanted. He was domineering, he told me what to do, and I thought that meant he loved me and would take care of me.

"After we were married, Don started to get us into all kinds of stuff—pornographic magazines, videotapes, all that. Then he wanted me to dress up all the time, wear these tight leather things and see-through teddies and high heels, and even wear them in front of our little boy, even during the day when Don wasn't even around. I didn't think it was right to parade around like that in front of Ryan, so we used to fight about that a lot. For the rest, I feel that's fine on occasion, but it got out of hand. When it gets to be a requirement, the fun goes out of it. Don used to call me frigid. And I guess I got to be. I was never in the mood for sex, not even when we went on a romantic cruise."

Peggy was more concerned about other aspects of their life, about her wishes to go out more with other people, while Don was more reclusive; about her interest in going back to school, which he ridiculed; about her desire for a better job, which he discouraged. As the fights increased, the sex stopped. When Don left Peggy for another woman, Peggy lost sixteen pounds and went into a deep depression at her panic over being on her own. It's painful to imagine what she must have looked like, since now back at her normal weight, she is even slenderer than current fashion dictates. She came out of that tailspin with help from a sensitive counselor who encouraged Peggy's efforts to find the self she had submerged all those years.

"Now I see that I put my husband in a position where he left. I changed and he didn't; as a couple we were in a maze and stuck in the middle of a pocket. He got out of that maze by leaving—and helped me get out of it, too. I'm learning how to be responsible for my own life—to see what I want and to realize that I can't depend on a man to give me my sense of self-worth. I have to do that for myself.''

Peggy is currently seeing two lovers, neither of whom she wants to develop a long-term relationship with. ''Ultimately I'd like to share my life with someone, but I'm not ready for that yet,'' she tells me. ''I have too many things I want to do and I don't feel I can do them in a relationship. I still have to find out who I am. I spent so many years trying to please my husband that I forgot what it was *I* wanted. I need to find out what makes me happy. I've made tremendous strides, but I'm still learning.

''I need to achieve in my work life and my financial situation. I never want to have to depend on someone for my livelihood ever again. I've already enrolled in a computer programming course that should prepare me for a better job with my company. I like being back in school and working toward a goal.''

Peggy's new attitude has paid off sexually, too. ''I feel like I rediscovered sex for its own sake without hang-ups, or movies, or clothes,'' she says. ''It's a nice, comfortable feeling. I've had trouble having orgasms for a long time, but I don't have too much of a problem now. I wasn't communicating what I wanted—because I didn't stop to think what *I* wanted. Now I think about what would please me and I ask for it. From what I hear from my married girlfriends, my sex life is better than theirs. My biggest problem is having sexual relations with Ryan in the house. I try not to let him get involved with my dating life and I don't bring anyone home when he's home, only when he's with his father for the weekend.''

The issue of sex after divorce casts an especially large shadow in the lives of divorced parents whose children live with or visit them. These parents are among the most under-studied group in our population, especially with regard to their sexuality. The good news about the sex lives of these people is that few of them raise issues of sexual dysfunction. Sex itself is rarely a problem. The problems revolve around issues like: What do I tell my children? Do I let my children meet my dates? Do I let people sleep over? If the answer to these latter two questions is ''no,'' the next question is: How can I arrange my schedule to meet my sexual needs without neglecting my children? Of course, the bad news is that so many parents can't get past the logistics, they don't even *know* whether they have a problem.

Torn by the conflict between their own needs for sex and companionship and their children's needs to be protected and reassured, many of these parents deny the ramifications of their sexuality on their children's emotional and sexual development. At a recent meeting of a discussion group for single parents, a church basement shook with the angry accusations hurled by most of the participants at one mother who described the ways she manages to avoid introducing casual dates to her four teenage daughters. "What's the big deal?" one mother asked, articulating the opinion that seemed almost unanimous. *"You're* the sneaky one, creating problems where they don't exist! Wouldn't you want to meet your daughters' dates?"

Still, psychiatrist Stephen L. Zaslow cautions, "Parents have to recognize that there is a real conflict between their needs and their children's. This is a difficult issue to resolve. Right after a marriage breaks up, children need much more of the company of the parent they're living with. If that parent rushes into the dating scene, it can stir up anxieties about abandonment. But parents need time away from children's demands to pursue their own adult lives. This is a dilemma without an easy answer. All that parents can do is make a determined effort to meet everyone's needs."

Even with a determined effort, painful situations often arise, as I learned from Alice, a Tucson, Arizona, mother of six-year-old Sarah. Changed by her grief over her parents' divorce from the lively pigtailed charmer she had been to a quiet, sad little girl, Sarah resisted her mother's early efforts at dating, hoping beyond hope to reconcile her parents. But as the months passed, she accepted the situation and regained much of her old bounciness. Enough so that she completely charmed Alice's lover, Frank, who became a frequent visitor to their home. Childless himself, Frank enjoyed talking to Sarah and spent a great deal of time with her, including time the two spent just by themselves. Then Frank and Alice split up.

"Even if he doesn't like *you* anymore," Sarah asked her mother plaintively, "why doesn't he come back to see *me?*"

"I could kick myself for not having tried to prepare Sarah for Frank's leaving when I realized that he was losing interest in me," Alice tells

173

me. But when Sarah had asked Alice why Frank wasn't coming around so often, it was too painful for Alice to talk about, so she just said, "I don't know."

"Afterward I laid it right out for her. I told her that this is part of life and I can't take responsibility for what someone else does. If she wants to share this part of my life and get close to my friends, she has to be prepared to suffer some losses, too. But since then I've tried to keep her less involved in my dating life. Why should she have to keep getting hurt, too? So I don't encourage anyone to come to the house when she's around unless it's someone I think I'll be having a long-term relationship with. Otherwise, I just tell her I'm going out with a friend, meet my dates away from the house, and don't include her in our dinners and outings."

Alice's new policy would still not have protected Sarah from her sense of having been abandoned by Frank, who had, after all, been in a long-term relationship with Alice. But then, neither single nor married parents can protect their children from all pain. Nor would that necessarily be the best preparation for a life bound to contain some of it.

The way parents handle these issues with their children, especially older children, who often tend to take on a pseudo-parental role, can have implications for the adults' sexuality. As one divorced man told me, "I pay attention to what a woman says to her children as we're going out. If she feels she has to answer to them about where she's going, what she'll be doing, and when she'll be home, a warning signal goes off in my head. This is not an adult woman who can make her own independent decisions, including making up her mind about me. And I don't like the feeling that I have to meet the approval of a woman's children."

So it's a fine line such parents must tread, between being sensitive to children's feelings and still keeping a certain distance from them when making decisions about social life and sexuality. Basically, it involves maintaining boundaries. Parents have to act like adults: they need to protect their children from hurt as well as they can; they need to avoid the temptation of using their children as confidants or parent figures; and they need to, finally, meet their own needs in the ultimate realization that when they are happy, they have more to give to their children.

As family therapist Bob Eakin says, based on his experience in running groups for divorced parents and their children, "After divorce, parents must proceed to work out their lives. The nature of life doesn't necessarily coincide with children's needs. If the issue is handled well, the kids can adjust to dating and sleep-overs. They will learn that this is part of life." With sensitivity and care, both parents and children can cope with this crisis and gain new strength for life and love after the divorce.

Chapter 8

The Amatory Thicket: The Forties

I was forty-three years old and I thought, "It's possible that my whole life is over. My career is over, my marriage is over, my sex life is over, so what's the point of going on?"

—Philip

When I rang the doorbell of the contemporary Long Island home, its owner greeted me warmly. She wore a smile on her face, an azalea in her hair, and a name tag around her neck. And that was all.

Along with seventeen other suburban women, I had come this evening in response to an announcement heralding "A Feminist Body Trip: Sexuality Consciousness-Raising Seminars for Women." For the next five Monday evenings we would be setting out, under the guidance of workshop leaders Tilly Salomon and Flo Walden, to "reclaim our bodies as a source of strength and joy."

At forty-one, I was still going through my "Age 40 Transition," a time that becomes a significant sexual turning point for many people. Some divorce, some embark on affairs, some go into therapy for sexual dysfunction. I had enrolled in a nude workshop. I wasn't sure what I wanted to get from the workshop; I knew only that I wanted to be part of it.

Unlike "pre-orgasmic" workshops that have sprung up around the country in recent years, this one was set up not as a therapeutic, problem-solving vehicle but rather as a variation of consciousness-raising, focusing on sexuality. Not surprisingly, though, just under half the women had been drawn to it because of specific sexual problems. June, thirty, had been inhibited about her body: "I kind of ignored it. I dressed to cover it and it was just something I dragged along with me wherever I went." Lulu, forty-six, had always felt her genitalia were ugly: "Even though I had read books and tried to think of my genitals as being beautiful, I couldn't shake the disgust I felt." Elaine, forty-two, had never had an orgasm. Sonia, thirty-five, had not made love with her husband for five years, since they had conceived their second child.

Though we were all white, suburban, and middle class, we were still a diverse group. We ranged in age from twenty-four to fifty-six; in shape from firm young slenderness to the obesity that left one woman a hundred pounds overweight even after intestinal bypass surgery; in profession from college professor to seamstress to the art teacher at my daughter's school. Our sexual life styles ran the gamut from virginity through celibacy, happy monogamy, unhappy monogamy, adultery, sexually open marriage, sexual experimentation, to proud promiscuity. Only one of us was avowedly bisexual, although in the course of the workshop a few discovered bisexual yearnings or fantasies.

We had all been told ahead of time that the sessions would be held in the nude, but when Flo met me at the door and told me to undress right away, I was still taken aback. Probably 90 percent of prospective workshop members are frightened off by the nudity. Why, then, is this essential? Says Tilly, "Men—even psychotherapists who work with women—are usually astounded to discover that most women are never naked together. Our shame about our bodies is strong, and this is one of those destructive feelings we want to break down." (I realized that I had been nude in a group of women only once before in my life—at a high school party where twenty-five students at Philadelphia's finest public school for girls cavorted like nymphs at the home of one of the girls.)

The nudity in the sessions carried an extra bonus—almost instant intimacy. People who bare their bodies to each other bare their souls more easily, too. Sharing our sexual concerns, expressed in the "go-rounds" that were part of each session, helped to bring us closer to-

177

gether. The initial go-round after our self-introductions gave us a strong common bond, when we were each asked to tell one thing we loved about our bodies. For years we had all been concentrating on all that we *didn't* like—how our breasts were too small or too droopy, how our waistlines were too thick, our thighs too flabby, our everythings too something. Yet most of us found something to love. One, her strength; another, the way her body healed itself after surgery; another, the "juiciness" of her vagina.

We talked about masturbation (Diana: "I masturbate when I'm tense, when I'm unhappy, when I'm bored." Jean: "No wonder you're thin and I'm fat! Those are the times when I eat!"). We talked about fantasies ("I'm in a chair that's a combination of the dentist's chair and the gynecologist's table and all these men are lined up in front of me"). We talked about sources of arousal ("That first scene in *Last Tango in Paris,*" "Mick Jagger in concert," "Seeing my lover undress"). And we talked about beautiful sexual experiences ("The times I went to my husband's apartment before we were married," "The passionate urgency when we made love in a hotel room in Pamplona," "The five days I spent in bed with my new lover").

The sensual peak of the workshop was the group massage at the last session, the part of the curriculum that turned out to be, as Tilly and Flo had promised, "pure pleasure." As the tones of a jazz flute danced about our ears, sandalwood incense filled our nostrils and flames from the fireplace flickered over shadowy naked bodies, we took turns as five of us massaged one of us. That moment when the five givers, who had dipped their hands in scented oil, all placed their hands on the receiver at the same time was for most—both givers and receivers—a mystical experience. During my own massage I felt as if I were floating, and I felt a sense of absolute trust.

Was anything of significance gained from the workshop? After using an electric vibrator, Elaine had her first orgasm after twenty years of marriage. Sonia finally agreed to go to a sex therapist with her husband: "I had known things were bad between us, but now I really wanted to feel what everyone else was feeling." Lulu "loved seeing how many different styles of genitals there are and how normal I am." June gained a sense of wholeness: "It's okay to be the way I am, even if I don't look like a Playboy bunny."

As for me, it extended my boundaries far beyond my expectations, freeing me to look at sex differently, to feel differently about it, to write about it in new ways. I felt better about myself and my body, I changed negative attitudes and affirmed positive ones, and I achieved a new understanding of other women's sexuality.

As Age 40 Transitions go, mine was tame. The sense that at forty we cross over to the shadowy region known as middle age often precipitates the kind of crisis that throws lives into turmoil. The major goals we grapple with during the decade of the forties include coming to terms with the awareness that we have probably passed the midpoint of life, with most of our vigorous years now behind us. We often turn to sexual metaphors to make our peace with this.

"It strikes me funny that a number of men have expressed surprise at the fact that I love sex and that I'm good in bed," Joan had told me. " 'I can't get over a liberated woman like you being so sexy,' they say. As if the two contradict each other. While really it's the other way around. I didn't get so sexy till I became a feminist.

"When I was a passive wimp, letting my husband define my sexuality, *that's* when I was an unsatisfying partner. But now, having a stronger sense of myself as a person helps me to value myself. It also helps me appreciate my sexuality, enter into sex when *I* want to, with a man *I* desire. I can ask for what I want from him and I can enjoy giving him pleasure, and to me all this is the essence of good lovemaking."

Any exploration of turning points in the lives of contemporary women—especially women over the age of forty—has to take into account the tremendous impact of the movement for women's liberation. Women younger than this probably don't see the influence of the women's movement as a turning point, since the points of view expressed and the rights won since the movement's resurgence in the early 1960s have been givens in their lives since childhood or adolescence.

But those women who came of age at a time when they were expected to subvert their desires to those of men, to defer to their wishes in virtually every aspect of life, including the sexual, have to have been affected by the feminist tenet that says that women are equal to men, are just as entitled to be sexual beings, and have just as much of a right to express those feelings. The coin of sexual freedom has two sides: the right to

179

seek sex when you want it and the right to decline it without having to give a reason.

Possibly the biggest contribution the women's movement has made to female sexuality is the way it has encouraged women to develop themselves as individuals. We may need to find our own identity before we can achieve sexual intimacy. And many women have been spurred by the forces of feminism to ask, and answer, the question "Who am I?" Time and time again I heard women in their forties and fifties credit the women's movement with the impetus for major changes in their lives. I heard it from Joan, from Barbara, from woman after woman after woman. And I heard it from researchers documenting the changes in the lives of contemporary women.

For years, women's sexuality was not explored in any systematic sense. Sweeping generalizations, with no real data behind them, were made on the basis of women who sought psychotherapy or on the assumptions of male psychiatrists. Among these assumptions was a devaluing of the role of sexuality in the life of women past the first bloom of youth. As City University of New York professors Samona Sheppard and Sylvia Seidman point out, "Until the advent of the women's movement, our society myopically perceived mature women as heterosexual, married, and monogamous. It also assumed that since they were no longer young, they were neither sexually motivated nor attractive. So powerful were these cultural biases that most researchers ignored the sex lives of midlife or older women."

To obtain some data about contemporary middle-aged women, and about the impact the women's movement has had on them, Sheppard and Seidman divided a sample of 321 women between the ages of forty and sixty into three groups. The "transactional" women were in the process of redefining themselves and renegotiating their relationships. Actively seeking change and willing to take risks, these were the ones most positively influenced by the women's movement. The "transitional" women "want[ed] the best of all possible worlds—a piece of the new action plus the stability associated with traditional values." They wanted excitement and change in their sexuality but were afraid of intimidating their partners, so they trod the middle of the road. And the "traditional" women resisted the changing social values espoused by

180

the women's movement, even though they were apt to be changing more than they realized.

This study found that the transactional and transitional women were enjoying sex more than ever before. As Sheppard says, "If women are enjoying it more, their partners are enjoying it more, too, because there is no way that women enjoy sex if their partners don't. This belies the whole theory that women are making men impotent because we're so pushy and demanding, thanks to 'women's lib.' "

In this sample, which was generally a well-educated, middle-class group of women from around the country, 70 percent were married (86 percent to their first husbands), 24 percent were widowed, separated, or divorced, and 6 percent had never married. Seven percent identified themselves as lesbians. Three-fourths of the married women described their husbands in positive ways, were enjoying sex, but considered the most important thing about marriage to be the companionship. So while changes were taking place—changes that often completely restructured a relationship in the context of a woman's new view of her role in life and love—a surprising amount of stability endured.

One of the issues explored in this study of women at midlife was that of body image. A number of the women I spoke to told me spontaneously about the differences in their sexuality at different times in their lives, depending upon how they looked to themselves. (No man even raised this subject.) Women turn themselves on by their own bodies. When they like the way they look, they're more interested in sex and more responsive. When they cannot look in the mirror and smile, they cannot proudly present themselves to their partners, cannot accept their partners' appreciation of them, and are often, as a result, blocked from expressing their sexuality. It's not surprising that the transactional women in this study were happiest with their bodies and were the most sexually responsive of the three groups. This approval of self depended not on age or any other objective standard, but on self-esteem. The more women value themselves overall, the more they value the way they look.

The importance of body image has special significance for individuals who suffer a physical loss, an all too common crisis of these years. When a trauma occurs to the reproductive organs or some other part of the body specifically associated with sex, the impact on sexual functioning may be defined as clearly and as painfully as an incision.

During the decade of the forties women become statistically more vulnerable to such sexual losses as the removal of the uterus, the ovaries, or one or even both breasts. Ironically, these losses are likely to coincide with other sexual losses—the end of childbearing (either by choice or menopause), the sense of aging that makes women feel less desirable once they hit that fortieth birthday, and the midlife crisis (their own or their partner's, or both), with its reevaluation of one's life, which often precipitates the end of a relationship. Each woman responds uniquely to such losses.

"It was like a nightmare. You wake up and find things gone that you hadn't dreamed of losing and that you didn't even know were gone until somebody told you." Thus does Sharon, a forty-year-old divorced social worker, describe to me her awakening in a hospital bed and being told that after she had gone into the operating room for the removal of an ovarian cyst, the surgeon had taken out both her ovaries and her uterus.

"Once my initial anger was over, I realized it was even worse than I had thought. That hysterectomy, done without my consent, robbed me of one of the most pleasurable aspects of my life—a wonderful sex life. But I'm having a difficult time getting my feelings verified. My doctor says there's no reason why the surgery should affect the way I feel sexually, that it's all in my mind. But *I* know it's different."

Hysterectomy, the removal of the uterus, is the most common major operation performed in the United States. Some estimates predict that more than half of all American women will eventually undergo this surgery. The operation is often accompanied by an ovariectomy, the removal of the ovaries. While the traditional medical wisdom has been to reassure women that hysterectomy will not interfere with sexual functioning, testimony from countless women indicates otherwise.

"I used to think about sex an awful lot," Sharon says. "I'd be with a man I'd just met and these fantasies would crowd into my mind and I'd get physically aroused without even doing anything. Actually, the fantasies sometimes interfered with a relationship or with my work or even with trying to read the morning paper, but I never minded the interference because they were so pleasurable. I got aroused easily. Now I have to really work at becoming aroused: I have to do a lot more thinking, a lot more conscious fantasizing. It doesn't just happen.''

Sharon's experience is not unusual. According to two recent studies, one-third to almost one-half of women say that sex is less satisfying after a hysterectomy. The reasons for such a change are not mysterious. A significant aspect of the orgasmic experience for many women is the rhythmic contraction of the uterus; when there is no uterus this dimension of orgasm is lost. When the ovaries are also removed, there is another loss—the hormones that they had produced, which were largely responsible for stimulating sexual desire and for activating some of the mechanisms of arousal, such as vaginal lubrication. These women are faced with the same kinds of decisions that menopausal women have to deal with, which are discussed in the next chapter.

Fortunately, other women find that sex is better after hysterectomy—because they're not experiencing the pain or the bleeding that the surgery was performed to correct, or because they don't have to worry about getting pregnant. In any case, women need to assume a strong role in exploring their options when a hysterectomy is advised. They need to become informed, they need to obtain a second medical opinion, and they need to carefully weigh the consequences.

Another operation whose necessity is often hotly debated is the removal of a breast. The breast is the leading site of cancer incidence among women, and breast cancer is the prime cause of death for American women between the ages of forty and forty-four. While mastectomy is often the treatment of choice, it isn't the only one. Since this operation, too, holds major implications for survival, self-image, and sexuality, women need to become informed about their medical options. One who regrets not having taken a more active role in the choice of her treatment is Amanda.

Few of the viewers who regularly tune in to the morning TV show that she hosts in a small city in Kansas know, as they watch her interviewing volunteers for the American Cancer Society and other organizations that help women cope with the trauma of breast cancer and the subsequent surgery, that Amanda herself has had two mastectomies. In fact, one of the first things most people notice about this vivacious, stunning redhead is her tall, slim, arresting figure.

''I always thought I would have a mastectomy, first because my

183

mother had had one but also because I was just superstitious enough to think that anything that good wasn't going to last forever. From the time I was first aware of myself as a sexual person, I knew that the best part of me was my breasts. They were what the boys noticed first. They were what I was proudest of the few times when I was with other girls in the locker room, where I could see that mine were firmer and better shaped than anybody's.''

Amanda did her share of necking and petting, allowing two or three special boyfriends to fondle her breasts. When she was seventeen, after a particularly arousing petting session in which her boyfriend had been kissing her breasts, they had intercourse for the first time.

''From that first time,'' Amanda recalls with a rueful smile, ''it was as though the imprint of the way I would enjoy sex was formed in the curves of those breasts. From then on there was one best way for me to have sex. I would be on the top and he—first my boyfriend and then my husband—would be fondling my breasts at the same time. If he wasn't, I seldom came to climax. Penis penetration was important, but it had to be accompanied by breast stimulation.

''My sex life didn't change after the first mastectomy five years ago. At first, like most women, I didn't even think about sex—my first reaction was, 'Am I going to die?' Then after I had grappled with that fear and felt I was going to be all right and was back doing the show and playing tennis and everything else, I had to adjust to the way I looked. I'd wake up in the morning and feel excited about what I was going to do with the day and then I'd get up and see myself in the mirror and get a shock and think, 'Oh, yeah, that's the girl with only one breast.' But eventually I accepted that.

''My husband gets a lot of the credit. He was better in this situation than in any other one I've ever seen him in. He's not a real sensitive man—he can't talk about his feelings and he wants to ignore a lot of things. But he was more tender then, more caring, all the things that I always wanted. It was the first time I really needed him, and I think he wanted to be needed very much. We were closer than we've ever been. And sex was still good between us. I still had all that feeling in the one breast. We were still reaching simultaneous orgasm about ninety percent of the time. We've had a lot of problems in our marriage, but sex had never been one of them.''

184

Amanda's second mastectomy, however, two years after the first when she was forty-three, was a devastating blow to her sexuality.

"I should have fought it, I should have gone for a second opinion. I would do anything now to have that breast back. I know that a lot of women volunteer to have their second breast removed to prevent the recurrence of cancer, but I guess that just shows how different we are. Because for me the loss of that second breast made sex stop being fun and become work instead.

"Without my breasts, I don't get the tension buildup. No matter what position we try or what we do, I just don't complete it. I've tried going to a psychologist, a sex therapist, a hypnotist, and it doesn't make any difference. It's not the way I look, either. It's funny, I liked my looks *better* after the second one was removed—I would look down and feel like a ten-year-old girl and that was okay. And then I finally got breast reconstruction, so now I'm eternally seventeen. I'm better built for my size now than I was—actually my breasts were probably a little too large before and they had started to sag and now they'll always be firm and young-looking. But I still don't feel anything in them."

Both Amanda and Neal feel frustrated at the loss of what had been the most vital element in their marriage. "It's sad because we both enjoyed it. I'd *like* to be able to say that's another part of my life, that's behind me, forget it, but I can't help wanting it back. There's got to be another answer. One that keeps coming up is the possibility of leaving Neal, going to another city, making a new life, maybe meeting someone new. Because if we don't have the sexual excitement between us, we don't have much. He was wonderful when he was afraid I was going to die, but now that I'm better and more independent, we've drifted apart again."

While Amanda's breast-specific sexual responsiveness seems relatively unusual, her sexual problems after mastectomy are not. One British study found that sexual problems troubled half of all mastectomy patients surveyed and as many as 70 percent of those who had undergone both breast removal and chemotherapy. A 1982 study conducted by Dianne Gerard, assistant director of the Family Service Center at the U.S. Naval Station in Honolulu, found that women who had had mastectomies were less sexually responsive than others (both with and without breast cancer) who had both their breasts. Women who had had breast reconstruction surgery were more sexually responsive than other victims of breast cancer, showing the psychological benefits of such plastic surgery.

Nevertheless, once women confront their losses and look at mastectomy as a "sexual disability," according to Stanford University researcher and counselor Regina Kriss, they *can* work through their trauma. "You wouldn't choose it," she says, "but you can make it work for you. A mastectomy is a terrible test, and it has the potential to destroy a person, but it also has the potential to offer the greatest growth." Dr. Gerard concluded, on the basis of her Hawaiian study, that undergoing a mastectomy in midlife is emotionally traumatic but that most women (especially those who've had breast reconstruction) report it as a short-lived trauma. They grieve and then they accept it, without suffering long-term scars on self-concept, sexual functioning, feelings of physical attractiveness and femininity, or relations with their husbands.

"I sometimes think of myself as the oldest 'flower child' of the sixties," Joe, a tall, trim, gray-haired man of fifty-five, tells me with a grin as we sip iced tea by the tennis court of a Puerto Rican resort. His tennis shorts and shirt show off the sturdy muscles from a lifetime of athletics. "I turned forty in 1969, and by then I was ripe to respond to the sexual freedom I was seeing all around me. My response changed me sexually and in other ways as well."

When Joe was thirty-five and had been married about ten years, his closest friend asked him whether he had ever had an extramarital affair. "No," Joe said emphatically. "I know what I have and I'm not about to jeopardize it." What Joe had was a marriage that was still physically satisfying. As he tells me now, after he's been married for thirty years, "I still get turned on by Toby. I liked the way she looked the first time I saw her, and I still do. She's put on a few pounds over the years, and I think it's great—more of her to love." Over these years, he and Toby have also enjoyed a close friendship, a strong shared interest in politics, and a warm family life with their four children.

Still, even with his enduring physical attraction to his wife, Joe found himself sexually attracted to other women, too. "I guess I always had felt some sexual desires for other women, but I had always repressed them,'' he tells me. ''I had imposed certain standards on myself. I felt if I was committed to my marriage, that sexual fidelity was part of that package and if I violated that, I was violating my commitment. But then, with the greater acceptance of sexual freedom in the sixties, I allowed myself to become much more aware of my attraction to other women, and I got up my courage to tell my wife what I was feeling. When I did, I learned that she was feeling some of the same things. We agreed that we'd let ourselves be open to whatever would happen, while at the same time renewing and affirming our love for each other.''

Part of Toby's and Joe's agreement was that, in an effort to minimize feelings of jealousy, they wouldn't tell each other about any outside sexual experiences but that both of them would feel free to have them. It didn't take long for Joe to begin going to bed with other women. His first lover was a divorced fellow attorney whom he had first met through Toby and then became friendly with through their political activities. After one evening meeting followed by a nightcap at her apartment, going to bed together seemed like the most natural thing in the world.

''Soon I was seeking out opportunities for sex with other women, and it was very exciting as I gave life to some of my fantasies. But I wouldn't say that any of these encounters became affairs. They were more like sexual friendships. For years I had had friendships with women—I found it easier to talk to women than to men. Before I knew it, I had a regular 'lunch circuit' of married or divorced women whom I'd see from time to time. Now that I was open to sexual 'vibes' (to use a 'sixties' word), which I had always suppressed, sex became a part of some of these relationships. The sex seemed to deepen the sense of trust we had in each other. Let me explain it this way: If I hadn't acted on the sexual chemistry between me and some of these women, we would have had to dance around it. It was as if going ahead and being sexual with each other—this didn't always mean fucking—broke down barriers and let us really open up to each other.

''This was a great time in my life. I was moving forward in a lot of areas—my law practice, my political work, my sex life with Toby, even my tennis. Sexual awareness permeated my life in other ways, too. When I met people at meetings or work or cocktail parties, I was looking at them in a new way, seeing what kinds of sexual vibes they were

187

giving off. This became part of getting to know them, and I felt I had more of a sense of someone when I was into this aspect of their personalities along with everything else.''

Drunk as he was with sex, Joe still kept a tight rein on his emotions. He never allowed himself to fall in love with any of his other women, never even saw any of them often enough to develop the intimacy that would threaten his marriage. When a couple of them wanted more from him than he was willing to give, he cooled the friendship until he felt the pressure was off.

Since he and Toby had agreed not to discuss their liaisons with each other, to this day Joe has no idea whether she was as sexually active outside the marriage as he was. He chooses to think she was, a belief that relieves the twinges of guilt he still feels at times. While he and Toby went through some stormy times in their marriage, Joe feels there was no connection to the outside sex. He may well be right, because while the marriages of friends, neighbors, relatives, and colleagues collapse like houses of cards all around them, Joe's and Toby's bond is stronger than ever.

"We're in a brand-new place now," he says. "I'm not having any outside sex, and I don't think she is, either. Maybe part of it is the fact that we're both older. That has to have something to do with it. But for me there's something more. I just don't feel as if I have to invest a big part of myself with other women. I'm not into that—I've done it already. I wanted to fulfill some of my fantasies, and once I did, I didn't have to keep doing it. I still have some friendships with other women, fewer than before, but the ones I have are just as deep as when I had sexual involvements. The difference is that I'm not even aware of the sexual chemistry, so it's not something we have to avoid.

"I'm grateful now that Toby was willing to go through that stage with me. I think if I hadn't had that chance to act out my fantasies with her permission, I would have had to do what so many other men do when they get to that point—leave their marriage.''

Taped on the wall over my desk is a yellowed clipping, quoting these words by poet W. H. Auden: "Like everything which is not the result of fleeting emotion but of time and will, any marriage, happy or unhappy, is infinitely more interesting and significant than any romance, however passionate.'' Judging from my difficulties in getting people to talk to me about sex in the context of marriage, however, it seems that not too many people would agree with Auden. The one life style that's been the hardest for me to research has been that of the freely chosen, fulfilling, long-term, monogamous relationship.

The literature says that sex is good in long-term relationships. Women are more orgasmic in marriage and living-together relationships than they are with lovers, committed couples have sex more frequently and in more varied ways, and even people having extramarital affairs tend to rate their married sex as better than their outside sex.

In these days when so many new ways of managing our lives exist, when acceptance is readily given for life styles that used to be scandalous, I wanted to know who the people are who still choose traditional monogamy and why they do it. But most of the people who wanted to talk to me about their sex lives were leading more flamboyant ones. I approached a few people who I believed were faithful to their husbands or wives—and then either found out I had been mistaken or was refused an interview.

''Oh, I wouldn't have anything interesting to say,'' one of them told me. ''I think that true love in a long-term, committed relationship is really interesting,'' I answered. But I still couldn't talk her into it. Finding a faithful husband who would speak openly to me about his choice was even harder. The men I asked seemed to feel it was an embarrassment to have upheld their marriage vows.

And then my friend Mimi told me about Bonnie and Beau, a couple in their early forties whose marriage of twenty years was the wonder of Marin County. They're in business together, running an environmental consultation service; they bicycle and swim and ski together; and neither of them seems interested in having an affair. Bonnie expressed herself often and unequivocally in favor of monogamy and fidelity. And Mimi told me, ''If Bonnie is being faithful to Beau, it's not because she's afraid of or uninterested in sex. Of all the women I knew back in college, Bonnie was the one who loved sex most of all. She was the only friend I could talk to about sex, the only one open about her own sexuality, the one who seemed to me, back then, to be 'more like a man,' because she could go to bed with a date without being in love with him—and without kidding herself that she was.''

189

Bonnie and I meet for lunch on an outdoor terrace of a restaurant in San Francisco's Ghirardelli Square. Tightly wired and lean, she is one of those people in constant motion. I can't imagine her relaxing even in sleep.

I am full of questions: What is her life like now? What is her marriage like? How had one man been enough for a sexy woman like her for so many years?

"I fantasize a lot," she says, with a wry smile. "And I tell Beau that I believe in open marriage. It's silly for two people not to go to bed with anyone else. Sex doesn't have to mean anything more than a good time for two people who aren't exploiting each other.

"Look, I go out to lunch and dinner with clients all the time. I sometimes have some great meals. I go to restaurants that Beau would never set foot in. He's a steak-and-potatoes guy, and I like French and Italian and ethnic and all kinds of exotic spots. I eat food I'd never eat with him. And I have conversations with other men that I could never have with him. And all of that doesn't make any difference in the way I feel about him. I still love him and I'm still his wife and both those things will always be true as long as I live.

"And sometimes I'm sure the same would be true of sex. I went to bed with a lot of guys before I met Beau. I had some wild times. And I loved them. And sometimes I do miss them. Beau's a good lover and I come every time we make love and he'll do anything I ask him to do and even comes up with a new idea himself from time to time. But we *have* been married twenty years. And sometimes I do think it would be fun to get to know somebody else's body.

"But I never have, and I'm not about to. For one thing, I know he'd leave me. He's told me so. He couldn't handle living with me if he knew I was sleeping around. I can't call it unliberated or chauvinist, because fidelity is important to him, in both directions. I would bet on my children's heads that he's been faithful to me all these years. While it doesn't hold as much importance for me, I love him so much that I'm not willing to confront him on it. He's a great guy and I don't want to lose him.

"Beau and I broke up for several months just before we got engaged, and during the time we weren't seeing each other I was in the most pain that I've ever been in in my entire life. I felt as if I had had heaven in my grasp and had let it slide through my fingers. And when we got back together again I swore I would never do that again if I could help it.

"If you're looking for turning points, that was mine. And everything that I've learned since then has confirmed the way I felt. When I was in college, I went to bed with a lot of men, and in my whole life nobody has ever meant as much to me as Beau does. Even my kids. I think part of the problems they've had through life is their feeling that they've been interlopers in our marriage. And you know what, I feel that they *have* been. I think that even when they were babies, I resented them because they took away time that I would have liked to give to Beau.

"People sometimes ask us whether we don't get on each other's nerves, working together all day and then coming home, just the two of us—now that Stacy and Nicky are both at college—to our little house. But I just feel sorry for anyone who asks that. Because what it says to me is that they're married to someone they can't take too much of!

"On another level I don't stay faithful just because of the way Beau feels. It's the way I feel, too. It's funny. I'm practically the only person I know who has never had an extramarital affair. My friends talk about theirs all the time. A lot of these women are nice people. They take good care of their kids, they're good to their parents, they're nice to their husbands. And a lot of them have really nice husbands, too. Whom these friends of mine profess to love. But to me if you can lie to somebody and do something that you know he would hate if he found out, that's not love."

Bonnie's life affirms the "wild oats" philosophy, that promiscuity in youth "gets it out of one's system," enabling the sower to enjoy the contentment of monogamy later on in life. As her story shows, this can and does occur—though it seems to be the exception. By and large, the more sex before marriage, the more outside of it. It's apparently the rare person who, having tasted of the excitement of sexual variety, can give it up, no matter how happy the marriage.

It's noteworthy that there *are* happy monogamous marriages, even though the people in them don't talk about them much. Why the secrecy? As Letty Cottin Pogrebin wrote in *The New York Times*, "Happily married people tend to feel embarrassed about displaying the very condition that is the goal of everyone who has ever gotten married in the first place." They don't want to look silly, they don't want other people to think they're too dependent on their spouses, and they don't want to make their friends jealous.

"I was forty-three years old and I thought, 'It's possible that my whole life is over. My career is over, my marriage is over, my sex life is over, so what's the point of going on?' "

It's hard for me to square that kind of depressed attitude with the aggressive self-confidence of the man sitting tall and straight before me, the fifty-eight-year-old director of a small but successful Chicago advertising agency. But as Philip tells me about what he described as "the worst period in my entire life," I can feel his utter despair at that time, can see why that had been a major sexual turning point for him.

"I had just been fired for the second time in two years. I'd been in New York for five years working for topflight ad agencies, and both times major accounts that I had spearheaded had left my agency and taken their advertising across the street. In the ad game, that's reason enough. I felt totally inadequate, and I hated myself. I felt like I was going backwards—that I'd been given a chance at the big time and I couldn't cut the mustard, and my career was practically out the window. I just wanted to crawl into a corner somewhere and die.

"I had very little sex drive. When I would force myself to try to make love to my wife just to prove I was still alive, I had a lot of trouble getting an erection. I don't know of anything that will take away a hard-on quicker than losing a job. At least that's how it works with me. I feel lousy about myself as a man, and I feel lousy about anyone who's at all close to me. My kids look homely and stupid, my wife looks dull and drab, my friends seem insignificant. I figure that anybody who thinks anything of me has something wrong with them. It's the old Groucho Marx routine about not wanting to be a member of any club that would have him as a member.

"Marsha really tried to be understanding, but every now and then it would get too much for her and she would get tired of being understanding. I guess the thing that was bothering her was, 'Who's going to understand me? I've got my own troubles. Whose shoulder do I cry on?' And I was all wrapped up in my problems and feeling sorry for myself. Everything was getting worse and worse, especially things between us.

192

"I think relations between a man and a woman are colored very profoundly by your sexual relationship. If that's easy and full of fun, then other things are fine. If not, it affects everything else and there's a tension in the air. The tension between us would come out in different ways. She would holler about various things that would irritate her beyond her endurance. And I couldn't stand to look at her a lot of the time."

It was at this bleak time in Philip's life that he had an affair. "Kathy was at this industry bash I went to. Here was this pretty young thing, who had worshiped me when she had been my secretary and still seemed to think I was hot stuff. She kept telling me how crazy my boss had been for firing me. And somewhere in all of this, she invited me back to her place for a nightcap."

As soon as the door of Kathy's apartment closed behind them, she turned to Philip, murmured, "You don't *really* want another drink, do you?" and drew his mouth to hers. Standing there by her front door, they kissed and held tight to each other as she acted out the fantasy she'd carried in her mind for years, and he drew comfort from her ardor as if he were a starving man offered a thick steak.

Philip's problems with getting and keeping an erection disappeared like magic. But his problems didn't. "You know, right after I came, I burst into tears. I hadn't cried like that since I'd been a little kid. I felt guilty as hell. You'll probably be amazed to hear this, but that was the first time in ten years of marriage that I had ever cheated on my wife. I felt like a rat. But then I thought, what the hell, one time, what does it mean."

When Philip got a job in Chicago, his professional life improved, but his sex life with Marsha didn't. So when he came to New York on business, every couple of months, he always managed to see Kathy, who loved his company and loved going to bed with him and accepted the fact that he was not about to leave his wife.

"I knew that this was no solution. I was miserable at home. I *loved* my wife, but I lost all interest in *making* love to her. Sometimes I'd start something because I thought I ought to, but half the time I couldn't follow through. We were having all kinds of lousy sex. If I would wake up with a hard-on, I would try to just jam it right in just because there it was, but it was no fun for either one of us.

"So sex became a vicious circle. You know, the worse it is, the worse it gets. When you don't have an erection the first time, it's not terrible, but it's in the back of your head. If it happens a second time, then you've set up a pattern. If it happens a third time, you're really in trouble because you get so uptight right away and you get so worried that you're not going to make it."

Finally, at Marsha's insistence, the two of them went for marriage counseling. "As much as I hated to go and bare my soul and talk about my problems, that was the smartest thing we could have done because that turned the whole thing around. We were lucky in the person we went to, who was refreshingly candid and down to earth. She ruled out anything physical right away and got down to the heart of things, which was essentially that you have to learn to like yourself and live with yourself."

During the counseling, which went on for almost a year, Marsha continued to refer to what was happening between them as *his* problem. Philip wanted—but was afraid—to tell her, "I *know* it isn't all me," even though the therapist, in private sessions with Philip, urged him to tell her the truth and start over with a clear conscience. "I can't," he protested. "It will break up our marriage." "I don't think it will," the therapist said. "But in any case, you have to take that risk because you'll never get clear with Marsha until you straighten this out with her."

Although Philip could not work up the courage to tell Marsha about his affair, he appreciated other aspects of the counseling. "Some of it was a good, old-fashioned approach—'cut the crap and stop daydreaming and feeling sorry for yourself.' And some of it was solid advice on the mechanics. The big thing she emphasized was not to worry so much about having intercourse, that we didn't have to go 'from A to Z' every time we made love, but that we could 'A' and 'B' a bit—you know, just kiss and fondle and caress and lie around in front of the fire—and if anything happens fine, but if not, well, the other things can be enjoyed for their own sake. This took a lot of the pressure away for me.

"And she emphasized doing more oral sex and stimulating Marsha with my hand. We had always done some of that—but I always figured that was foreplay, not the 'main event.' When I realized that I could make my wife come in these ways, it was like a salvation to me. I figured no matter what, there it is, my wife will not have to suffer because I can't get a hard-on. I also always have my tongue and my fingers.''

The breakthrough came, however, during one counseling session when Philip finally did blurt out to Marsha, ''I know what's going on between us isn't all my fault! How do I know? Because I didn't have any trouble getting it up with another woman!''

''I'll never forget Marsha's reaction,'' Philip says. ''It's funny, it didn't hit her right away. We were in the shrink's office in the afternoon, and she seemed to take it okay. And then we met a couple of hours later—we were supposed to have dinner and then see a show. The minute I saw her at the restaurant, my heart sank. She looked so—so *remote*.

''And then she started to say these phrases right out of the Bible. 'You've deceived me. I'm a betrayed woman. Here I was being a good wife and mother while you're off committing adultery with some other woman.' And so on.

''I cannot tell you how bad I felt. I thought the whole thing was blown and she would leave me and my life would be over. At first I thought I shouldn't have told her. Much later I realized that it would have been worse not to, because my guilt about the affair was one of the things that had been keeping us from getting our relationship back on the track. So at least now it was all out in the open. We never did get to see that show, and we had a rough couple of weeks afterwards. But then the wildest thing happened.''

Philip looks straight at me, his blue eyes seeming to go right through me as his expression takes on the intensity of the memory he is about to relate. ''We had a second honeymoon that was the most exciting sexual experience I have ever had in my entire life—better than the first honeymoon, better than all the catting around I did before I was married, and better than anything my wife and I have had since.

''For about two weeks Marsha and I went at each other day and night. We did things we'd never done before and we did them all the time. She seemed to be a different person. It was as if she had let out a part of her she'd always kept tightly caged until then. And that change stuck. While she had always had a pretty healthy attitude about sex and had seemed to enjoy it, she was usually kind of shy and waited for me to initiate things. After this honeymoon period, things turned around so that then *she* was more often than not the one who started things. I don't think any of this would have happened without the therapy, which got into all kinds of other things in our lives that we had never talked about before—our feelings about our parents, general feelings about sex, the whole self-image routine, things like that.''

Life has been good for Philip and Marsha over the last few years. The move to Chicago was good for both of them. He founded his own agency, and she went back to work for a publisher of educational materials. And, while their "second honeymoon" didn't last forever, sex is again "easy and fun," and the tensions between them have fallen away. From time to time, when problems flare up between them, they go back for "Band-Aid therapy" to the counselor they had seen before.

The events of the fifth decade of Philip's life highlight the close tie between sexuality and all the other threads of our lives: the way his job loss shook his self-confidence and wreaked havoc with his sexual performance, how his sexual anxieties infected his relationship with his wife and drove him into the bed of another woman, the way the affair served as the catalyst to get him into therapy, and then the way the therapy enabled him to salvage his ego, his career, and his marriage.

With that sense of the finiteness of time left to be lived, many people decide in their forties to resolve a dysfunction they have lived with for years, a step that proves to be a major turning point in their sexual development. One such person is Teresa.

A tall woman with a pleasant smile, Teresa surprises me both by her height and her age—forty-five. On the phone her tentative, little-girl voice made her sound very young. Her physical presence is commanding, but her curly brown hair and round brown eyes soften the Scotch-Irish angularity of her face. As we sit in her sparely furnished apartment, she seems comfortable speaking to me, although her words about her sexual development and her difficulty in achieving orgasm come haltingly.

"I only went to Dagmar's workshop because Fred wanted me to," she tells me. "I'd do anything for him because I love him more than I've ever loved anybody in my life—and that includes my first husband, my mother, even my children. It bothers Fred that I don't have orgasms more than it does me. So I told him I'd go, but he'd have to make the phone call. And he did.''

Teresa is the grown-up "good girl" who in many ways is typical of the women who sign up for the workshops that New York sex therapist Dagmar O'Connor runs to help women experience their first orgasm. Like many of them, she signed up ostensibly to please her partner, not herself, a pattern that has run through her life, in which she has constantly sought to please others.

Like 40 percent of O'Connor's women, Teresa grew up in a strict Roman Catholic home. Also typical was her dominating, demanding mother who never spoke to her daughter about sex except to issue grave warnings and to object to every man Teresa expressed interest in. At the age of twenty, when Teresa fell in love with Fred, her mother's objections—"He's common, he's beneath you"—won out. They broke up and a few years later Fred married someone else. Teresa eventually got married, too, to an emotionally troubled man who had problems with drugs and alcohol. Their brief, disastrous union lasted only long enough for the births of a son and a daughter.

Five years after Teresa had left her husband and taken her children to a remote New England village where she found a job teaching first grade, Fred, now divorced, tracked her down. They met for the first time in twenty years, spent the night in a hotel, and even though the sex that night was disappointing, the love they had once felt for each other returned. Despite Teresa's mother's continued objections to Fred, his influence turned out to be stronger, and he and Teresa were married.

Fred's sexual experiences had been limited to fewer than half a dozen women, including the one he had married when both were in their early twenties. Still, at forty-nine, he exudes a lustiness that was born in the years he spent as part of a big, warm, affectionate family that thrived on hugging and kissing. When he fulfills his current mission—to help Teresa achieve orgasm—his life will, he tells me, be perfect.

"Teresa is my dream come true," he says, his voice clear and strong, showing the years of musical training he had before becoming a voice teacher and singer in a small opera company. "She really is the woman I've always dreamed of—in all ways but one. She and I enjoy music together, we love to talk about anything and everything, she's warm and loving and ideal in every respect except the physical. If she only liked sex more!''

Teresa is trying. She's doing her homework, which therapist O'Connor credits for the high success rate of her workshops: "These women want to do well in what they see as a 'course in how to have an orgasm,' so they do their 'homework.' " The homework involves spending one hour every day, in private, on the week's assignment, which may be looking at their nude bodies in the mirror, examining their genitals and striking sexy poses—and then moving on to masturbation with both hand and vibrator. By the end of the ten or twelve sessions, more than 90 percent are achieving orgasm through masturbation.

Teresa has gotten this far, a major achievement for a woman who had never experienced orgasm at all before and one that she considers a turning point in her sexual history, but she's still struggling to make the next leap—to climax regularly with Fred.

"I'm so frustrated," she says, shaking her head. "I do have little orgasms, but they don't satisfy me. I have to build up to this 'big' one. It's almost like climbing a mountain that you're struggling to get over and there's something that's almost pulling you back. I get over that mountain with a vibrator all the time, but I hardly ever do with Fred. The only times I do are if I'm lying on top of him, with his penis inside me and my legs closed, but it takes a long time and it's exhausting for both of us. He says it feels as if I'm using him as a battering ram and his penis actually gets numb. If he didn't want so badly for me to have orgasms, he probably couldn't go through what he does."

Why *does* Fred go through with it? "It's not that I think the orgasm is everything, but it's such an exhilarating thing that I want her to feel this with me," he tells me, clasping and unclasping his broad, strong hands. "When I see her have an orgasm, it really turns me on tremendously and I'm ready to go again. But I'm disappointed that she reaches it almost exclusively with the vibrator. I would like to be the instrument, through my penis, my hand, my tongue, or whatever. We have some good years ahead of us still, and I think our relationship will be better if sex is better."

Teresa's chances for reaching orgasm with Fred are fairly good, according to one follow-up study of twenty-three O'Connor graduates. Two years after therapy the women showed overall improvement in their sex lives, and more than half were experiencing orgasm during lovemaking.

"One reason our success rate is so high is that nobody comes in here without motivation," Dagmar O'Connor tells me. "In most cases people who come in for sex therapy are well motivated to work out their problems. When they say they're just doing this for their partner, I ask them, 'Why are you spending all this money and time and effort? If you don't care, you might as well go home and fake it.' Nobody has quit on that basis yet, which goes to show that they are really here for their own sake. They are very fearful at times of getting over a problem, but once they stick with the program they want results. And they usually get them."

Another reason for success is undoubtedly O'Connor's strong personal involvement in the therapy. She tells the women in her groups about her own experiences with masturbation and orgasms. "I really don't think you should run these groups if you're not fully orgasmic," she tells me, "and by talking about myself, especially toward the end, this is another symbolic way of saying, 'You have now reached the level of being my peer and are not a child anymore and you're ready to go ahead on your own.' "

In the early 1960s, when Masters and Johnson were pioneering with their new, behaviorally oriented techniques for treating sexual dysfunctions, cases were easier to treat. Many people needed nothing more than permission to be sexual, information, or specific suggestions. In those days there were few good books and the social climate was just beginning to be accepting of sexuality as a natural function. Over the past twenty years, however, sex has achieved a new prominence in our society and the people who come for therapy have much more complicated needs. They've read the books, seen the films, accepted their right to be sexual—and are still anxious and in sexual trouble. As William Masters told me, "We don't see the easy cases anymore."

Ironically, in our eroticized society, the most common sexual dysfunction these days—and the hardest to treat, according to psychiatrist Helen Singer Kaplan, founder and director of the Human Sexuality Program at New York Hospital–Cornell Medical Center—is lack of desire. This affects people at all stages of the life cycle—those in midlife who've been married for a long time, but also people in their twenties and thirties. Many sex therapists report "desire dysfunction," or inhibited sexual desire (ISD), as the prime problem for at least half their clients, in contrast with the most common problems in the past, which involved the arousal and orgasmic phases of the sexual response cycle, such as premature ejaculation, impotence, and failure to achieve orgasm.

People suffering from ISD behave, according to Dr. Kaplan, as if their sexual circuits have been "shut down." They're not interested in sex, won't pursue it, and if they do begin to get aroused in spite of themselves, they will "turn off" their sexual feelings. One of the most common ways of doing this is to focus on unattractive features of their partner.

In her book *Disorders of Sexual Desire,* Dr. Kaplan notes some of the common underlying reasons for ISD: "fears of success, pleasure and love; intense performance fears; fears of rejection; neurotic power struggles based on infantile transference towards the partner; anger, mistrust and envy of the partner; fears of intimacy; deep sexual conflicts that have their roots in the patient's early development; and anger caused by poor communication between the couple."

It's not clear whether people are actually experiencing less desire for sex these days or whether more are willing to acknowledge it. It may also be that in our sex-conscious society, in which everyone is assumed to be ready for sex any time it's available, a perfectly normal person with a lower sex drive seems not only eccentric but pathological. Especially if such a person happens to fall in love with a partner whose drive is considerably higher. Jack Sprat and his wife can easily pursue their separate appetites for food, but if their sexual appetites are mismatched, it's harder to lick the platter clean.

When there's a disparity in level of desire between two people, the one with the problem is not necessarily the one who wants sex less, according to sex therapist Sandra R. Lieblum. It may be just as appropriate to ask the enthusiast, "Why do you want so much sex?" as to ask the laggard, "Why are you so uninterested?" Partners need to learn how to deal with differing levels of desire as they deal with other differences.

Beverly Hotchner uses an analogy with food, saying to the less interested partner, "Let's assume that your partner is really enormously hungry and you're not hungry at all. Wouldn't you be willing to sit down and have a cup of coffee just to be sociable? Sometimes when you do this, the food starts to look pretty good and you take a little nibble and your saliva starts flowing, and suddenly you think, 'Hey, I think I'm going to have some.' You don't have to have a whole course—you can have just dessert. It's the same with sex. If you're tired and don't feel aroused, you can masturbate your partner or hold him or her tenderly while he or she masturbates. Or you can take a bath together, which is very sensual.

"What people really hunger for is affection and closeness and warmth and relaxing and fun together. And they have thousands of ways to get that. They don't have to limit themselves to intercourse."

While simple, practical solutions like the above sometimes work wonders, at other times answers remain frustratingly elusive. The questions that people bring to sex therapists—"How much is enough?" "How much is healthy?" "How much is normal?"—are not easy to answer. So much depends on what else is going on in the life of the individual or the relationship.

Many people faced with sexual problems look for solutions not in a therapist's office but in a new bed. And sometimes, despite moral strictures, despite guilt, despite the almost universal yearning among us to find both love and sexual excitement with the person we are committed to, this age-old "therapy" works. A new person, a new body, a new opportunity to discover another's inner self and disclose one's own, is often the ultimate aphrodisiac. This philter is often unbearably tempting to people at midlife, vulnerable as they are to the anxieties aroused by the rippling pages of the calendar.

Chapter 9

Greener Grass: Extramarital Sex at Midlife

When people turn eighteen, they reach their majority. So tell me, does a marriage achieve a majority? Does a person who's been married for eighteen years vault to a new level of independence just like a person who's lived for eighteen years? Do people have to break away a little from their spouses after eighteen years the way eighteen-year-olds have to break away from their parents? Should something be written into the marriage contract providing for that?

—Andrea

When Charles Dickens was forty-four he received a letter from a woman he had not heard from in twenty-four years. He had loved Maria passionately in his youth, but she had rejected him because his "prospects" were too poor. The wildly successful novelist who had been married for nineteen years and had sired ten children immediately fell in love again and wrote several emotional letters to the woman who in his imagination was still the young beauty he had adored so many years before. When these epistolary lovers did arrange a secret meeting, Dickens's reawakened ardor vanished abruptly. Although Maria had warned him in her letters that she was now "toothless, fat, old and ugly," he didn't believe her until he saw her for himself.

While this affair ended before it even began, it kindled in Dickens's mind the possibility that he *could* fall passionately in love again. It was inevitable that he would find someone else to lavish all this unspent fervor upon, someone other than the "sweet, kind, peace-loving" woman he had married. Two years later he found Ellen Ternan, an actress then eighteen, the same age Maria had been when Dickens first fell in love

202

with her. The following year Dickens separated from his wife, forcing her out of their home, away from her children, cut off from the life she had formerly known. He kept up a secret affair with Ellen until his death twelve years later, at the age of fifty-eight.

As Phyllis Rose writes in her book about five Victorian marriages, *Parallel Lives,* the awareness "that the radical dissatisfaction [Dickens] was feeling was in some sense normal . . . could not have offered a solution . . . and might not even have been consoling to a man of Dickens's nature. Perhaps it would have irritated him to think that what he felt could have been felt by others. Probably he would not have believed it."

Anyone consumed by love thinks no one else has ever loved so much; yet midlife upheavals like Dickens's have become commonplace in our time. As I read the research literature of the 1970s and spoke to people in the 1980s, I came upon many accounts of those who had been fairly monogamous most of their lives and then in their middle years had changed—and complicated—their lives with a new relationship.

As I heard these stories of passion and discovery, of guilt and ambivalence, of hurt and rejection, I was struck by the fact that so many affairs spring up within a year or two either side of the milestone birthdays—the fortieth or the fiftieth. What is it about these times in our lives that leads so many of us to change—or add—partners? As psychiatrist Harold I. Lief, director of the Institute for Marital and Sexual Health in Philadelphia, told me recently, "The end of a decade is always a crucial time in a marriage. And when you're talking about the decade of the forties, you tend to run into those situations in which a man turns to a younger woman for reassurance that he's still attractive, he's still vital, he's still sexy. Of course, the same thing happens when a woman turns to a lover for the same kind of reassurance."

Increasingly in recent years, the sauce that spiced up the gander's life is looking better and better to the goose as well. Women are more likely than they used to be—at every stage of life, including the middle years—to enter into an affair themselves. They, too, need reassurance that they're still desirable. But surely this can't be the only reason for the preponderance of midlife affairs. Why *do* middle-aged people, whose lives seem to have been comfortably structured along carefully chosen lines, drift into, fall into, or plunge deeply into affairs? And how do these affairs affect them and the people around them?

Sociologists and psychologists who study such issues find scientific bases for what most of us have already concluded from books and magazines, and from looking around at the people we know. Some affairs are born in the soil of a disappointing marriage, where some vital nutrient is lacking and the marriage has failed to thrive. The missing element may be satisfying sex, a sense of trust, or the intimacy that one partner yearns for and the other is incapable of giving. Other affairs are born in the disturbed personalities of people who use them to avoid intimacy, to pursue unrealistic sexual goals, to act out old angers, or to sabotage a primary relationship. Affairs such as these arise from what marriage counselor Douglas H. Sprenkle and research psychologist David L. Weis call the "traditional script" for sexual behavior. Just like a script for a play, a script for behavior defines a situation, names actors, and plots behavior. The traditional script for extramarital sex transmits these messages: anyone who has an affair, or who wants to, is immoral, immature, or mentally ill; such people are part of a tiny minority of the population; their marriages are already in trouble if they think about having an affair; and the marriage is certain to be doomed if they go ahead with it.

This traditional script simply doesn't apply to all of the extramarital sex that goes on today. A great deal of recent research indicates that a large number of affairs appear to be engaged in by well-adjusted people in basically good marriages, and, contrary to popular wisdom, many of the individuals and their marriages not only suffer no harm but often improve as either a direct or indirect result.

In the same way that every marriage has its own unmistakable fingerprint, unlike any other in the world, so is every extramarital relationship unique. Each one develops from a complex set of motivations etched deeply in the personalities and pasts of at least three or four people—the two in the affair and the one or two spouses on the sidelines. And each affair has the potential to help or to harm all these people.

The affairs that begin in midlife may spring from any of a number of reasons. People who have been married for twenty years or so are likely to be feeling a sense of sameness to their lives, a sense that they keep doing the same things over and over again, that one day is much like the one that went before, that one week is like the last, that this year will duplicate last year. Even though other circumstances in their lives may change, it's still a case of, as one man told me, "waking up in bed next to the same woman morning after morning after morning. Everything else in my life changes except the face on the pillow next to me."

Or as a forty-year-old woman said, when she confided to me her fantasies about calling up an old boyfriend, "I've had four careers over the past eighteen years—first, as assistant to an editor, then full-time homemaker and mother, then freelance editor, and now copywriter in an advertising agency. I've lived in five different apartments or houses in three different cities. I've mothered four children with four different personalities. I've had dozens of different friends and acquaintances. But in my entire life I've only gone to bed with one man. I don't see why I shouldn't have some variety in this part of my life, just as I do everywhere else."

During these years another realization descends. As Bernice L. Neugarten, professor of education and sociology at Northwestern University and one of the nation's leading authorities on adult development, has found, most people undergo a switch in time orientation at some point during the middle years of life. From thinking in terms of the years they've already lived, suddenly they begin to think in terms of the time they have left. With this switch they realize that they can't possibly live to do everything, and they are eager—sometimes desperately so—to make the most of the years they have left. There is often an overwhelming desire to gather those rosebuds before they wither and die on the stem. As one fifty-year-old man said to the wife of his best friend, a woman he had known well, admired, and (secretly) longed for for more than twenty years, "Life is short, and I don't want to die without having made love to you."

While thoughts of their own mortality are churning about in the heads of middle-aged people, they are often faced—right in their own homes—with blatantly exuberant sexuality in the persons of their adolescent children. These coltish young creatures are changing in ways that remind the parents of their younger selves, when they themselves embodied youth and promise. The juices of memory surge forth as the

205

parents see themselves, not in their somewhat lived-in bodies of the present, but in the relatively untried ones of the past.

Furthermore, these teenage reminders of their parents' earlier years are ripening to maturity in a new age, an age free of so many of the constraints that had marked their parents' passage over the threshold of adulthood. The changing sexual mores of the past decade or two remind middle-aged people of all that they missed when they were young and make them feel as if they can replay these years of emerging passion and of new love now, before it's too late. Now, when they have the freedom or the time or the money that they didn't have when they were younger and while they still have the health and vigor and attractiveness that they feel may not be around for many more years.

Sex is not, of course, the only spur to an affair; many people move into sexual liaisons for nonsexual reasons. This seems to be particularly true for men, who, at midlife, are often for the first time in their lives able to acknowledge and express their needs for intimacy—but do not find anyone at home to be intimate with. Their children are by now leading their own lives or may be so imbued with a need for privacy that they rebuff their father's overtures for closeness. The typical middle-aged American man has no close male friends in whom he can confide his deepest fears and anxieties. The relationship he has established with his wife may have been predicated on a comfortable margin of distance between them and would be hard to change now. Even if they are close, he may want to discuss his relationship with her with some third person. "My wife doesn't understand me" is the cliché it is precisely because the feeling behind it has indeed pushed many men into the arms of another woman.

These days, many women are telling other men, "My *husband* doesn't understand me." Because a woman is also experiencing a loss of intimate relationships at this age. At a time when the children with whom she had had such close ties are leaving the nest, she is apt to yearn for the closeness of an additional relationship. Furthermore, in a youth-oriented society she daily sees signs of the flight of her own youth. When a man appears who offers not only intimacy but also reassurance that she's still attractive and sexy, the combination can be irresistible.

Another common reason for the midlife affair arises, according to psychiatrist Jay B. Rohrlich, from the loss of satisfaction that hits many people in their forties and fifties when they realize they've reached the summit of their career ladder. Their work stops giving them the feeling that they're valued and needed. So they turn to sex. Here they can achieve: they can make conquests, they can get the sense of being cared about and looked up to, they can pursue new goals.

Yet many people at this stage of life are not ready to give up half a lifetime of shared experiences with a partner they may feel comfortable with, if not excited by. "I probably would not choose to marry my wife if I were meeting her for the first time now," Michael told me. "But neither am I ready to leave her. We have a history together. We've been through so much with the kids and each other, and everything we've suffered through together or laughed through together has served as one more link between us."

What's left? The midlife affair.

At one time an affair was considered good and sufficient reason for ending a marriage. It was the ultimate betrayal, the sign that love and respect and trust were gone. Or it showed that the errant spouse was acting out his or her needs in a neurotic way. In recent years there has been greater recognition that none of this need be so, that while an affair *may* create anguish for everyone involved, it need not be rooted in pathology of either the individual or the marriage.

In some cases, of course, an extramarital liaison can be the straw that breaks the back of a marriage. The blows from certain betrayals crush so deeply that the injuries they inflict can never heal. This is what happened in one instance I heard about, when, after twenty years of marriage, Barbara learned that Art had been involved with another woman for the past ten. "You've read the same story a million times," Barbara tells me in her soft, mellifluous voice, "but when it happens to you it's absolutely devastating. It all seemed so unfair to me—not that she was able to give him something that I apparently couldn't—but that, having her, he stayed with me.

"I felt he should have told me—and left me—as soon as he began this relationship with this other woman. Our sons were grown and out of the house by then, so he didn't have to stay for their sake. And I could have begun to make a new life for myself a lot sooner than I did. After I found out and he said he would give the other woman up so we could

207

try to save the marriage, I used to have these dreams that I'd be making dinner for someone who was eating somewhere else and he'd come into the kitchen, and I'd say, 'But why did I bother cooking?' And I'd wake up and ask myself why was I bothering to work on a marriage when he was going elsewhere?''

But Barbara did keep working on the marriage. ''I didn't want to divorce him, but I was in such pain all the time. The crazy thing was that now he was ready to give one hundred percent. He was warm and loving. But by this time I felt as if my feelings for him had been totally switched off. I probably would have continued to try to make things work with Art if I hadn't met Howard at about this time. When we became lovers, I knew that this was the kind of sexual and loving relationship I had always yearned for.''

The only problem here, however, was that Howard was married. For the past twelve years Barbara has been the ''other woman,'' a role she has stayed with but still isn't comfortable about. ''Most of the time it's worth it all,'' she tells me. ''For one thing, you can't imagine the enormous sense of freedom I feel now that I'm living alone. But sometimes it's hard. I've told Howard that if I ever leave him it won't be because I don't love him or because there's anything wrong with our sex life—it would be because I wanted to have a date on New Year's Eve.''

It's difficult to evaluate Barbara's sense of freedom. Did Art's affair liberate her from a repressive marriage—or is she rationalizing her way out of a bad situation? What is Art's view of the relationship they had? My impression is that something would have happened eventually to end the marriage. If Art had not precipitated it, the self-knowledge Barbara gained from psychotherapy, her involvement in the women's movement, her growing ability to be assertive, and the generally freer sexual atmosphere in society would have brought a similar result sooner or later.

Some people have always tolerated their spouses' extramarital adventures, because they have felt they have no choice. Many women fear that, lacking skills and experience in the working world, they won't be able to support themselves, and many men fear being alone, without emotional support. But for others, there has been a genuine shift in their attitudes relating to marriage. As psychotherapist Tom McGinnis, former president of the American Association for Marriage and

Family Therapy, told me recently, "People are healthier today. Marriages are getting healthier, and extramarital affairs are healthier, too." In a recent workshop Dr. McGinnis said, "The affair of today is more likely than the one of the past to be a long-term relationship charged with caring, affection, and experimentation. In a society characterized by a lack of intimate friendships, affairs give many people the chance to learn for the first time in their lives how to be intimate with another human being."

The more I've learned about this aspect of people's lives, the more I realize that there are no rules and no sure way to predict results. Still, it seems that the reasons that propelled people into affairs usually affect their outcomes. When the affair stems from a basic problem in the individual or the marriage, both are likely to suffer. But when the outside relationship grows out of a transitional situation or developmental passage in the life of a person whose general ability to cope with life is good, it rarely brings lasting harm. This was apparent in the lives of Philip and Marsha, probably in large part because of the help they got from professional counselors after Philip's affair, which helped Marsha understand her role in their problems, helped soothe her feelings of rejection and hurt, and helped Philip find ways to resolve his problems within his marriage.

Philip's affair had unexpected repercussions in Marsha's life, when she had a brief extramarital fling herself a year or so after their "second honeymoon." Born of equal parts curiosity, retaliation, and equalization of power within the marriage, Marsha's affair did not threaten the marriage the way Philip's had. Even after he found out about it, he didn't become outraged. "I figured I owed her one," he says, with a laugh that makes his blue eyes crinkle and his teeth flash. Still feeling guilty over his misstep, he told Marsha that he actually felt relieved that she had balanced the books, so to speak. "But now that we're even, let's keep it this way," he told her. And tells me that he thinks they have.

"Of course, you never know what's going to happen in the future," he adds as an afterthought, "but somehow I have the feeling that neither Marsha nor I will be interested in ever again going outside the marriage to get what we need. From what I learned about myself, and from what she's told me about herself, I just don't think either of us would have that need to look around. There's something we have now with each other. We know we can have wild sex together. We know we love each other more than we could ever love anybody else. We know we *like* each other. And we both know we never want to go through that kind of unhappiness again. I feel that our marriage is stronger now because we've been tested, and we've come through that test. But there's no need to keep on testing. Why look for trouble?''

Philip's and Marsha's experience is the kind that has led some marriage counselors to rethink the traditional wisdom that said that extramarital sex is always disastrous for a marriage, and, in fact, to actively encourage affairs. Anyone who prescribes extramarital sex for an ailing marriage, however, is recommending a potent medicine that can have unforeseen side effects.

''That is always a risky road to take,'' says psychotherapist Tilla Vahanian. ''The inclination to be involved with someone else always has some impact on the marriage, and you can't predict what that impact is going to be. So much depends on where each person is at the time, what they're looking for and what they find in the other relationship. The one in the affair is always taking a risk that the affair will be corrosive and will eat into the marriage.''

Many people, of course, like Art, don't care about the effect their affairs will have on their marriage. Art may have been among those who go into an affair with the (often unconscious) agenda of finding a new partner to serve as a transition person to hold their hand while they make their way out of the marriage. Others turn to lovers to shore up an otherwise intolerable marriage that they either can't or won't get out of.

In other instances, however, an affair seems to lead to new levels of sexuality and/or intimacy either in or out of the marriage, as in Andrea's experience. Why did Andrea, who had been happily married for eighteen years, embark upon her affair with a fellow real estate broker in the St. Louis suburb where they both own their own homes and sell houses and happiness to other people? She tells me about it as we jog together one Saturday morning around the track at the local high school. Her relish in the entire escapade shows in the expressive mobility of her face, in her expansive gestures, in her roguish smile.

''So there I was, the morning of my fortieth birthday, performing the

210

ultimate masochistic act—standing naked in a sunny room in front of a full-length mirror. I didn't look so terrible for the age I was, but I realized that I'd get more wrinkles and more crow's feet and bigger bags under my eyes and more gray hairs underneath the Miss Clairol and even saggier breasts than I already had. And while I'd had my share of men coming on to me over the years—whom I'd always turned off as the virtuous wife I was—I could see the future and know that one day soon nobody would be dying to take me to bed. And I remembered that 'Life begins at forty.' I was ready for a new beginning.

"Then, too, Paul and I had just celebrated our eighteenth anniversary, another milestone. When people turn eighteen, they reach their majority. So tell me, does a marriage achieve a majority? Does a person who's been married for eighteen years vault to a new level of independence just like a person who's *lived* for eighteen years? Do people have to break away a little from their spouses after eighteen years the way eighteen-year-olds have to break away from their parents? Should something be written into the marriage contract providing for that?"

Andrea's declaration of independence took her into Ron's bed, where the two of them played out their fantasies together. There were no protestations of love or deep emotion on either part. Just raw sex and lots of laughs.

"The crazy thing is that I had never found Ron particularly sexy," Andrea says as we walk back together to her house, her blond-tipped auburn hair damp from perspiration, her lean, ropy body illustrating the fact of modern life that even forty-three-year-olds don't have to look as if they've hit that once-feared birthday that opens up the fifth decade of their lives.

"I had known both Ron and his wife for years and I always found both of them sweet but dull. Even when he came to work at the same real estate agency where I was, I didn't get all whipped up with happy. But then he just happened to do and say the right things at the right time in my life. Whether it was the deep tongue kiss he gave me at the office Christmas party when we were both a little drunk, or his erection that I could feel when we were dancing together at the local charity ball a month or so later, or just the fact that I kept catching him looking at me in a whole new way, I don't know.

"Looking back now, I feel as if I was like Titania in *A Midsummer*

Night's Dream, having drunk that love potion and opening my eyes to see Bottom with the head of a jackass and falling madly in love with him. Well, Ron was my Bottom, and I went wild over him. I thought about him day and night and every time I did I could feel myself get hot and wet as if he were right there with me. The three or four times we did hop into bed were incredibly exciting. Not because of anything he did, but just because—oh, I don't know—because he was somebody new, because I couldn't predict what was going to happen the way I usually can with my husband. I guess what it comes down to is that it was all so exciting just because he *wasn't* my husband.

"I had terrible guilt pangs. The first night after I had been to bed with Ron I woke up every hour all night long. And I would look at Paul and wonder whether he could tell in my eyes that something was different. But I guess he couldn't, because he didn't act differently toward me. And in every other way I was the same good, loving wife I always was. So who was I hurting? In any case, I'm glad I did it, and I can't imagine ever regretting it. The whole experience turned me on so much that it carried over to sex with Paul, which became better than it had been in years. Paul reaped the benefits of all of this as much as Ron and I did. I hope Ron's wife did, too.

"I guess I'm a product of my times, a foot soldier in the sexual revolution," Andrea says. "I don't see anymore why sexual fidelity is considered so important. I didn't always feel this way. I used to look at my parents—married thirty-five, then forty, then forty-five years—and think how beautiful it was that neither of them had ever strayed, that neither of them had ever even wanted anyone else. Now, of course, I wonder about those assumptions. How do I know, *really know,* what they wanted or what they did? I used to thrill to the purity of my feelings about Paul and feel great that *I* never wanted anybody else. When I found out a couple of years ago that Paul had had a brief affair himself, I reacted like your typical outraged wife. All except running to call the divorce lawyer. At least I wasn't that dopey."

For Andrea, as for so many other people, her first extramarital affair was a major turning point in her sexual development—one that she sees as a positive one. I didn't know her before, so I can't draw any comparisons for myself. All I know is that I met a vibrant woman who is radiantly in love—with herself, her work, her husband, her marriage, her sexuality, and with life itself.

Some affairs, like Andrea's, seem to benefit both the individual and a marriage. Some shore up a rocky marital bond but offer nothing more than temporary respite to the lovers. And some, like Michael's, whose Age 30 Transition was described earlier, contribute to the emotional and sexual development of the individual but steal from the marriage. A fifty-year-old engineer, Michael had quit his job with a major New York firm and gone into business for himself in Philadelphia, so he would be able to pick and choose his projects. In both the emotional and the professional spheres of his life, Michael feels a constant tug-of-war between security and freedom. He is unwilling to give up the security he feels within his twenty-six-year marriage but seeks emotional and sexual fulfillment outside it.

Michael exudes a clean-cut, all-American look that would make any woman feel as if she were seducing the local Boy Scout leader or the minister. Over the dozen years that followed his first sally into extramarital sex, he let about a dozen women have that privilege, but none seemed to fill the void he still felt in his life.

"Here I was a professional success, and in everyone else's eyes a personal success—nice wife, nice kids, nice dog, nice cat, nice house in the suburbs, nice everything—and still feeling lousy about myself." So Michael entered therapy. "And that's what really, *really* changed my life. I became so much more aware of my emotions. It's like taking off sunglasses and seeing the true colors of things, or stopping smoking and suddenly getting the real taste of foods for the first time. An unbelievable change."

About six months after he entered the therapy that he would stay with for the next five years, he met another woman, and what started out as just another of Michael's conquests turned into the great love of his life.

"My relationship with Laura has allowed me to open up and experience sex on a totally different level than anything I ever knew before," he tells me, hesitating and pausing as he talks about their sexual relationship, groping for the right words. "I feel safe in saying that she feels the same way—that when we come together, the sex is more than . . . just sex. It's not just making love to a person. It's . . . *sharing* . . .

213

something and somehow melding with them, becoming one with and part of somebody else until we both reach the point where it's more satisfying to give pleasure to each other than to be on the receiving end, because in experiencing the other's pleasure you do feel it in your own body and your own soul. It's a very wild thing and so it just . . . increases.

"For example, when I give Laura oral sex, I bury myself in her and I concentrate on nothing else in the world but giving her pleasure. I have no sense of time—I feel as if I could go on for hours. And when I feel her body writhing in pleasure and I feel her contractions when she comes, I feel as if *I'm* the one having the orgasm. And I get the same feeling from her, that she gets pleasure from giving me pleasure. She'll lick my armpits or suck my toes—both parts of my body that I never thought of before as being erotic—and I get excited by her joy in sensually appreciating my entire body. The orgasms I have with Laura are mind-blowing. They transcend the sexual and move into a state of union that I never knew existed."

"Even now, after we've been seeing each other almost every week for seven years, there's a freshness and an excitement when we come together that I would never have dreamed was possible. I guess that's what people mean by the term 'bliss.' "

"What made the difference—the therapy or the woman?" I ask.

"Both. I don't think Laura would have been attracted to me if she had met me before, before I learned how to feel, nor do I think I could have responded to her in the way that I did. On the other hand, there's no question that it's her realness, her honesty, her lack of inhibitions, the total absence of puritanism in her that have allowed me to feel in this new way. It's such a total joining of love and sex that I can't imagine feeling this deeply about anyone else."

"Not even your wife?"

"Let me put it this way. I feel very warm toward my wife at times and very comfortable, as the good friends we are. At other times I'm very angry with her. If we were not married now, I wouldn't be attracted to her. I wouldn't single her out as the person I would want to live the rest of my life with—even though I *may* live my years out with her, based upon our shared past, our history.

"Compared to Laura, my wife seems wooden, both in the way she

214

touches me and the way she reacts to me. I know she tries, and I know she cares for me, but she has not been able to throw off all the inhibitions she was raised with. I feel lucky that, with the help of Laura and my therapy, I have. So while I wouldn't leave my wife—at least not until our kids are out on their own—I've resigned myself to the fact that things are not going to change much between us.

"Right now I'm trying to resign myself to the fact that Laura will never leave her husband. Her tie to him is stronger than mine to Gail—I don't know whether it's loyalty or love or what. I know I meet a very special need in her life, but I also know—she's told me many times and I believe her—that she won't leave him. I think one of the reasons she has let herself become so close to me is the fact that she perceives me as *safe* because I'm also married and committed to my family. In fact, when I let the depth of my feelings for her show and she could see I was not so safe, she became terrified. Made distance, created anger. All kinds of defenses appeared.

"We've had some very painful times, mostly at times like this when one of us gets scared of where all of this is leading. So the knowledge of this at this point, even though we both try to avoid it, is sort of sitting there between us. It's as if two smoothly polished surfaces that had rubbed together over many years and really were able to fit well kind of have this grain of sand between them now. Sometimes I feel sad about the impossibility of thinking about a life with Laura, and at other times I just feel grateful that we have what we do."

I cannot help wondering whether, in fact, Michael's wife *might* respond to the change in him if he gave her half a chance; whether his joyous liaison with Laura is keeping him from struggling through the barriers between himself and Gail; and whether that bliss that he knows with Laura, whom he sees during the hours each can steal from their other lives, could survive the day-in, day-out, stopped-toilet, colicky-baby, in-law problems that characterize a marriage and are romantically absent from even the most long-lasting affair.

I know that this was one of the big questions that had kept Tony from walking out of his life with Anne and into one with Eileen—at least so far. He was never to find the answer to that question, because Tony and Anne solved their dilemma in a way no one had anticipated. The next time I saw them, it was hard to remember the tears and anguish in their voices as they had relived for me, just scant months before, the most painful time in either of their lives—a time of pain, yes, but also a time of change and growth.

Back in December, Tony and Anne had been in the midst of the greatest crisis of their marriage. During the daily telephone conversations he was having with Eileen, Tony would pour out his feelings for her and his desire to be with her. During the daily marathon talks he had with Anne, which sometimes lasted from early morning until midnight with hardly a break, he plumbed the depths of his feelings for her. Loving both women, he himself regularly dissolved in tears.

Finally, Anne prevailed upon Tony to see a marriage counselor, and their weekly sessions helped both of them put their feelings and their goals, both for their marriage and their lives, into perspective. The counselor, a low-key, pragmatic person, supported Anne's determination to keep her marriage together despite the advice of her friends and family to "throw the bum out." At the same time, he didn't pressure Tony to give up Eileen.

When Tony finally did come to that decision, he did so on his own. As Tony tells me on this hot July day, "Eileen will always be a special person to me, but not special enough to leave Anne for. I thought about how well I know Anne and how the only big problems we've had in over thirty years of marriage have been about Eileen. And then I thought about how little I know Eileen. We've had some great times together, but we've never lived together. I don't know what that would be like. I decided I'd be out of my mind to give up a woman who's been a better wife than any man has the right to ask for.

"It's not out of duty, either." Tony's eyes follow Anne adoringly as she runs in to answer the phone, then turn back to me. "I tell you, this might sound crazy, but I've fallen in love with Anne all over again. I don't know if it was the shock of going through this last thing that really got my head on straight or maybe the fact that I had taken everything for granted—and to think that Anne was doing the things she did for me and for the kids, everything. She's always been my best friend, the person I could talk to about anything, the person who put me before anybody else in the world. It's so clear in my mind how much I love her and who she is—I feel like a newlywed on a honeymoon."

There's something of the newlywed about Anne as well. A mature newlywed with self-assurance. There's something else, too; a sexy aura that she now radiates. Is it in the way she's dressed—the halter that reveals the soft curve of her small breasts when she turns or leans over in certain ways? Or the way she walks, swinging her slender hips in a more pronounced way than I remember?

"Did Tony tell you about our latest activity?" she asks impishly.

And then it comes out. For years Tony had been titillated by the idea of group sex, but Anne always rejected the idea. After Tony had decided to give up Eileen but told Anne that casual sex with other women would still be part of his life, he again brought up the notion of their taking part together in mate-swapping parties. Tony had found the name of a swingers' club about half an hour away from home, sent for the brochures, and showed them to Anne. This time, in an effort to make her marriage Eileen-proof, she reluctantly agreed to go.

"I said I'd go once," Anne tells me. "We've been back half a dozen times." She laughs infectiously. "There I was, a forty-nine-year-old semi-virgin who'd never been to bed with anyone but Tony in my entire life. Now I think nothing of being with four or five men in one night."

Naturally gregarious, Anne was able to cover up her nervousness about going to the motel where the club had its regular monthly get-togethers by pretending she was at a party like any other. She enjoys meeting new people. "Very nice people," she tells me, her warm brown eyes widening. "They're like couples you'd meet anywhere—at a cocktail party or PTA meeting or anything—except that with this group, the difference is that everybody winds up in bed together at the end of the evening."

Anne's memories of the first evening include a dizzying kaleidoscope of male shapes and sizes and ages and approaches. She would feel the weight of a man's body, feel him enter her, and close her eyes. When she opened them, she would see another face and another form. Through it all, she remained remote and unmoved. Not so her husband, whose long-cherished fantasy had finally come true. As Tony saw his wife arousing all the other men, he became more stimulated himself, so that he engaged in intercourse twice at the club, and then went home and made love to Anne. Their sexual relationship with each other, which had remained exciting and constant throughout the troubled times, reached an even higher level. And their emotional bond has become stronger, too.

Faced with such a bewildering variety of female forms and female faces, for the first time in more than thirty years Tony is not going to bed with women other than his wife and their club-mates. "The best part of this," he says, "is that nothing is behind anybody's back. I don't have to lie to Anne anymore, because she knows exactly what I'm doing and who I'm doing it with. And she's doing it, too."

Responding to the skepticism I cannot hide, either as an individual or a journalist, Tony asks me roguishly, "You should see it for yourself. Why don't you and your husband come with us one night? It would be good for your research."

And so my husband and I find ourselves, one Saturday night, in the downtown business district of a small city about an hour outside of Cleveland, slinking through the door of the newly painted storefront that houses the Bel-Air Social Club. We go through the vestibule into the small office where we pay our $15 three-month membership fee and our $25 for this evening's "toga party" to Vince, a soft-spoken, fair-complexioned, tall, slender man celebrating his fortieth birthday tonight. The office is nondescript, although someone—maybe Vince's wife, Doreen, a Junoesque platinum blonde—has made a stab at decorating it by lining up a row of ceramic animals and birds on a shelf.

At just a few minutes after nine, the party is about to get under way. No one is allowed to come in after eleven, even though the party is scheduled to run until six the next morning. When I had spoken to Vince on the phone the week before, he had advised Mark and me to come early, since this was our first time. I hadn't told him I was writing a book and had become interested in swinging mostly to explain what was going on in Tony's and Anne's life, or that my husband and I were not about to take part in the activities. With Tony's and Anne's permission, I introduced us as friends of theirs who might be interested in swinging but weren't sure.

Vince was open and friendly, evangelical about his club and its raison d'être. He offered a half hour's worth of practical advice: "Come in early, make yourself invisible at a table in the corner, look at the people, and when you see somebody you'd like to talk to, go over and say hello. If you don't find anybody you and your husband want to go with, you can just go home. No obligation. Don't do anything you don't want to do. Don't go with anyone you don't want to go with. Just say no and no one's gonna pressure you or make a scene. Because people know that you may say no tonight, but another time you might say yes.''

A former plant foreman, Vince had, over the past six years of running this ''swing club,'' become something of an expert on human relationships, on sexuality, and even on biology. (He had learned, for example, to schedule parties at three-week intervals so that the same women wouldn't be at the same point in their menstrual cycles at every party.) He had to, to keep up a successful operation, for swinging appeals to a very small (but apparently growing) number of Americans. Only between 1 and 5 percent of the population is estimated to have tried swinging at any time in their lives, with those who do it regularly probably totaling no more than 1 to 2 percent. Still, even these tiny percentages represent between 2 and 11 million people openly enjoying sex with someone else's spouse, with their own spouse's permission.

Even if swinging isn't important in its numbers, it symbolizes many basic changes in sexual morality. The fact that such an activity can go on in many small, conservative communities around the country, as well as in the large cities on the liberal coasts, bespeaks a mammoth change in societal attitudes. Furthermore, even though very few people do anything about swinging, many fantasize about it.

So here we are, on this cool September evening with just a hint of fall in the air, walking with Tony and Anne into the lounge behind the office. This is another fairly nondescript room with chairs and couches grouped around small tables, a buffet table laden with an attractive offering of cheeses, crackers, and fresh fruits, and another table holding a large coffee urn. In the kitchen beyond are set-ups and ice, along with a few bottles of liquor that people brought themselves. Vince and Doreen serve no alcohol at the club, and destroy anything left there after a party. Signs in the restrooms warn guests that drugs are forbidden and that anyone either bringing them into the club or showing evidence of having taken them before arriving will be asked to leave and expelled from membership.

As I look around the room, preconceptions fall fast. No one is garishly, or even provocatively, dressed. The men are in ordinary sport shirts and slacks or jeans. The women wear simple dresses, skirts, suits, or an occasional neatly pressed pair of jeans. No elaborate makeup. No heavy perfume. The group is average-looking, with no one outstandingly gorgeous or homely. Apparently you don't have to be young and beautiful to love sex and to be a desirable sex partner. Most of the people seem to be between the ages of thirty-five and fifty-five, with one couple late-twentyish and one early-sixtyish. Conversation is easygoing, and people are less flirtatious than at most of the parties I go to. Practically everyone talks about the easiest topic at hand, the activity they have in common: how they got into swinging, how they heard of this club, how near or far away they live.

Among those present are a long-distance truck driver, an electrical engineer, a few people who run their own small businesses, a private detective, a high school art teacher, a real estate speculator, a nurse, a sales executive, and several homemakers. By and large, swinging is a middle-class phenomenon. This assemblage may have been somewhat below the average in terms of education, occupation, and social class, since the research shows a fairly large proportion of college-educated professionals who swing.

People are very open, freely answering my questions about how they became interested in swinging. "My wife and I had been married for almost twenty years," Rick, the boyish-faced engineer, tells me, pointing to a shapely woman in a simple skirt and blouse in animated conversation with a couple across the room. "She's great and I love her more than ever. But let's face it, sex just isn't the same after all these years. I was getting real depressed because it seemed so sad that the more I loved Ellie, the less she turned me on. I read somewhere that the only aphrodisiac is a new body, and that hit home for me. So I looked for new bodies.

"I started to fool around a little bit, but I got tired of all the bullshit. I'd go to a party and see an attractive woman. I'd try to pick up all the little cues that would tell me whether she liked me, then I'd figure out whether I could call her, what would happen if I did, what we'd have to go through to get together. And I was always worried about Ellie's finding out or else getting caught by some jealous husband. Now, if I see someone I like, I ask her to go to bed. If she doesn't want to, she says so, but there's no beating around the bush and playing games."

Polly, a sweet-faced woman who works with her husband in their sporting goods store, tells me, "We talked about it for a long time before we came. We were real curious. So we started to get some of those magazines, like *Variations*. Month after month, we'd look at them and read the ads. But we never did anything. Then we saw this place written up, so we figured we'd give it a try. It's been really nice. The people are nice and friendly, so we keep coming back."

A typical pattern emerges. A couple marry young, the wife a virgin before their engagement, the husband more experienced. Sex is wonderful at first—until they reach the exhausting years of getting established in occupations and raising children, the years when sex is a low priority. By the time there's more time and energy, sex isn't that exciting. And now comes the realization that there aren't many years of youth and vigor left. The husband has a few affairs. But he loves his wife and hates the secrecy, the lying, the guilt. So he embarks on his campaign to talk his wife into swinging. At first she's repelled by the idea, then she resists it, then she reluctantly goes with him to their first encounter. If that one isn't a disaster, she'll go again. Eventually she's likely to accept the whole idea and may even become more enthusiastic than her husband.

These people seem to pursue few other leisure-time activities; swinging is their chief avocation. When they aren't doing it, they're talking about it, writing or reading ads to meet couples, setting up dates or finding out about clubs like Bel-Air. Otherwise, their lives are like anyone else's. They do their jobs, spend time with their families, vote, bake cookies for the PTA bake sale, watch television.

Kate, a fortyish redhead with laugh lines around her sparkling green eyes, guffaws as she tells me how her four children and the mother who lives with her ask her every Saturday night where she and her husband are going. On the Sunday mornings following Bel-Air nights, the whole family wants to know what time they came home the night before and where in the world they were till so late. "I'm getting great at making up stories," Kate says, with a conspiratorial wink.

Like Kate, many of these swingers strike me as basically "good," conforming people who like having their spouses' permission to be "bad," to flout society's rules, to know that if their relatives and neighbors and business associates knew what they were doing, they would be

221

shocked. They like "going wild" inside a well-defined structure with its own framework of rules and regulations.

Several people make a point of crediting swinging with helping their marriages. It certainly gives couples an interest in common—a new meaning to "togetherness." As a hobby, it seems to have an edge over his going hunting and her going bowling, and as therapy it looks like a lot more fun than sitting in a marriage counselor's office.

A few of the twenty-seven couples here tonight have been swinging for ten or fifteen years. The "regulars" who've turned up in honor of Vince's birthday have become very fond of this ascetic-looking man who quit his job as foreman at a large plastics-manufacturing plant, the firm where Doreen still works as a secretary, to make his living from advancing a way of life he believes in and for which he's willing to take social, financial, and legal risks.

The evening wears on toward midnight, and the crowd in the lounge has thinned out. Tony and Anne disappeared an hour or so ago. Mark and I decide to go where the action is, so we retrieve the sheets we had brought (our togas, if we can master the art of draping them) and carefully negotiate our way down the narrow, carpeted stairs to the basement. The togas have been a source of merriment all along, as mature men and women, feeling silly but willing to go along with the joke, help each other drape, tie, and pin the sheets. Nadine, a Mediterranean-looking woman with a butterfly tattoo on her left breast, had been the first to don hers, twirling around with it up in the lounge.

Then there's Anita, a short, gray-haired woman of about sixty who casually stands nude, unselfconsciously displaying her aging body, while Andrew, the only black at the party, arranges her toga. He looks the best of all of us, the white of his toga stark against his gleaming blue-black skin, its length accentuating his long, athletic body, its folds and drapes turning him from citified young bank teller into noble Masai warrior. Matty, a roundly dimpled art teacher, cheerily helps Mark and me drape ours.

We wander around downstairs, through a lounge that reminds me of the basement "rec rooms" some of my friends' homes boasted during the forties and fifties. Those rooms of my teen years, though, didn't have a dozen people wearing nothing but togas, sitting around on couches fondling each other as they watch the hard-core porno cassettes that run continuously.

Behind the lounge are several curtained rooms constructed of light-weight wood paneling, covered with velvety flecked fabric. The five cubicles with the heavy drapes are the rooms whose privacy is to be inviolable once the curtains are closed. Voyeurs are limited to several spots, like the massage room, behind a curtain of beads, where oil massages can be given on a narrow, waist-high table. (When I look in, the man standing next to the table is not massaging the woman on it, but is being fellated by her. Lying sideways, she easily takes his erect penis into her mouth.)

"Listen," says Stu, the affable trucker whose toga keeps coming apart to reveal his pot belly and small buttocks, "for new guys like you two, the best thing to do would be to go into the mat room. You can be with each other and still see what's going on. Come on over here."

We follow Stu to the room in the corner, about twelve feet square, with four mattresses covering the entire floor. Mark and I settle into the front corner, comfortably away from the tangle of six, or seven, or eight, bodies by the other wall, looking like some exotic sea monster as its innumerable arms and legs reach out and enfold each other in ever-changing positions. We are still uncomfortably close to the couple sitting opposite us, and my eyes meet those of the man fondling the full breasts of the woman astride him. I know that even as a nonparticipant I am allowed, even encouraged, to stare, but the privacy-respecting habits of a lifetime are hard to overcome.

Mark and I nod at each other, clutch our togas closely about us, hoist ourselves to our feet, and leave the mat room, passing by the "Crazy Room," a cubicle lighted by a glowing green light shining over psychedelic-patterned bedsheets. On them a couple moan, writhe, and thrust in rear-entry intercourse. As we turn away, we are again face to face with Stu, who has taken upon himself the role of our mentor. "You gonna fool around tonight?" he asks me. I shake my head. "Well, why don't you two get a private room for yourselves?" "We'd like to," I say. "But they're all taken. Vince should set time limits the way they do at the tennis club—forty-five minutes for singles, an hour and a half for doubles."

We spot a large bare foot, followed by a knee, followed by a toga emerging from one of the private rooms. Tony grins at us, then is closely followed by Doreen, then by Vince, and finally by Anne. They hold the curtains open for us to enter, but we decline. Mark and I say goodbye to Stu. "You're a beautiful couple," he says. "Whenever you want to swing, let me know."

Tonight I am what sociologists call a participant-observer. I'm fascinated. And trying hard to be nonjudgmental of these people who've found a way of life that suits them, at least at this point in their lives, if not forever. For some people, like Tony and Anne, and like Nora, who tells her story in the next chapter, swinging serves as a sexual passage bridging two stages of life.

I realize, of course, that I cannot draw sweeping conclusions based on observations of fifty-four people during one evening at one club in one small town. Still, it's interesting to compare my observations with the findings of some of the research. It's not surprising that my impressions confirm some of it but differ considerably from other reported data, since several of the reports are at odds with one another. Much of this disparity seems to rest in the differences among swingers themselves and in the accident of the particular people a researcher happens upon. Some surveys, for example, have found swingers basically conservative, traditional, and religious people whose swinging is the only nontraditional aspect of their lives. Others have found them unconventional, nontraditional, and irreligious people who espouse liberal, antiestablishment values, are tolerant of drug use and drinking, and of nudity around the house.

Other differences show up with respect to age. The group in one study ranged in age from twenty-six to sixty-three, with an average age in the early forties. Some other surveys show swinging to be an activity engaged in by younger people—in one study, from ages twenty-five to forty-one, and in another from nineteen to sixty, with most under thirty-three.

The disparity is also true with regard to personality characteristics. Eugene Levitt of the department of psychiatry of the School of Medicine of Indiana University and Jane Duckworth of Ball State University have studied the personalities of swingers. While their report is based on such a small sample that it's impossible to generalize from, the results are interesting, especially since this has been the most detailed study of its kind. Levitt and Duckworth administered personality tests to sixteen women and fourteen men who belonged to a swingers' club in a large city. About half were essentially normal, and about half showed varying levels and kinds of personality disturbance. Two basic personality types showed up in the tests: just under half the swingers tended to be traditional, conservative people who regarded themselves as virtuous and moral and tended to view others similarly, and a slightly smaller number showed up as restless and energetic "sensation seekers" who needed a great deal of emotional stimulation.

The sexual histories of one hundred California swingers, compared by sociologist Brian Gilmartin to one hundred non-swingers, conform closely to Tony Rocco's life. Sex per se is generally more important to swingers and has been more important from a very early age. (These findings are somewhat at odds with the sexual histories I heard from the women at Bel-Air, which may indicate that these women are somewhat atypical, or that Gilmartin's findings are not widely applicable, or that the people I talked to still felt the need to cover up.)

The swingers, for example, had had "sweethearts" much earlier, with about a third having had a boyfriend or girlfriend during the years from kindergarten to third grade. They dated earlier and more often, and had dates with more people. They went steady earlier and with more partners (at different times). They had their first sexual inter-course earlier and then proceeded to have premarital sex with more partners. And then they married earlier. Almost 40 percent of swinging husbands married by age twenty, compared to only 12 percent of the non-swinging men; and only 4 percent of swinging wives were twenty-five or older when they married, compared to 20 percent of the non-swinging women. Most of the men had had affairs before they got into swinging, and most felt guilty about them. More of the swinging women were pregnant when they walked down the aisle than were the non-swingers.

So here is Tony Rocco, who first had sexual intercourse at the age of thirteen with a fellow eighth-grader in the clothes closet at school and continued to have "pure and simple sex" with many different girls, until he met Anne, fell in love with her, and, at eighteen, married her. His first affair took place less than a year after their marriage with a girl he met at a bar while Anne was in the hospital having their first child. She was followed by well over a hundred others, most of whose names Tony can't remember now.

For people like Tony, who want a lot of sex with a lot of different partners but with little emotional involvement, swinging seems to fill the bill. For people like Anne, who are not as interested in this kind of impersonal sex but who can accept and go along with their partner's interest, swinging seems to constitute less of a threat than an army of unseen, unknown clandestine sex partners.

Psychologist Bernard I. Murstein, a professor at Connecticut College and past president of the Society for Personality Assessment, believes that there is a biological predisposition to the kind of sexual activity described by Tony and many other swingers. "Not everyone is relationship-oriented," he has written. "There will still be people who will want to limit their intimacy or who will be simply incapable of being intimate. Yet they will sometimes have strong sex drives which demand expression." These are the people likely to be drawn to swinging.

The more I've spoken to people about their sexual inclinations, the more impressed I am with the wide range of people's sexual life styles. And the more accepting I've become of life styles I wouldn't adopt for myself. Some people like to go bowling or play bridge on Saturday nights; I'd rather play tennis or take in a movie. Then there are those who like to have sex with new partners and go home afterward with their spouses; these are the ones who swing. And just as we tennis players run the risks of tennis elbow and sprained ankles and eye injuries, swingers feel that the risks of venereal ailments and unforeseen emotional entanglements are worth playing the game.

"What can I tell you?" Vince had said when I asked him about the risks of contracting herpes. "You're playing with fire." And, as Tony had told me after he and Anne had gone through a tube of Kwell getting rid of "crabs," "If you want to play, you've got to pay."

Bernard Murstein has pored over the literature on swinging and come up with lists of its pluses and minuses. Among its advantages are the fact that swinging is less expensive, less time-consuming, and less emotionally demanding than an affair; it offers sexual variety; it's educational (being with and watching others having sex enables you to pick up a few new fillips of technique); it provides complete satisfaction even

226

when one partner has a much stronger sex drive than the other; it's democratic (no double standard); and it's honest (no stories about "working late at the office"). He sums up by quoting anthropologist Gilbert D. Bartell, who studied more than 280 swingers in the Midwest, Texas, and Los Angeles and characterized swinging as being in the best American tradition: "to be popular, to have friends, to be busy."

Among the drawbacks Murstein cites are the lack of emotional closeness between sexual partners, the "meat market" aura of competition (Is his penis bigger? Her figure curvier?), the cult of youth and surface attractiveness, the embarrassment at rejecting or in being rejected, the persistence of sexual jealousy and guilt, and the fear of venereal disease.

We might compare swinging to hang gliding. Most people have heard of both and have some curiosity about them, but wouldn't dream of doing either. A few people daydream about doing one or the other but decide that the drawbacks outweigh the excitement. And then there are those *very* few who are ready to throw caution to the beckoning winds, whose need for excitement and thrills in the form of flying or sex is so powerful that no risk is great enough to interfere with the overwhelming attraction of the sport. As long as nobody forces me onto a primitive flying machine or into a communal bed, I'm willing to say to any consenting adult, "As long as you look before you leap, the way you spice up your life is your own affair!"

What does all of this say about midlife extramarital sex among Americans in the 1980s? That many of them are engaging in it, yes. That some are being hurt deeply. And that others are being helped. For some people their own affair or their spouse's affair is the turning point that enables them to experience a new level of sexuality. For others, an affair represents a different kind of turning point—the kind that makes people withdraw from their own sexuality and leaves them unable to trust or to love. One affair may enrich a marriage, another may destroy not only the bond but the emotional health of the people in it.

When we look for answers about the effects of extramarital sex, we cannot look to the experts. Even though there's been a swelling of research on this volatile topic, along with the surge in its incidence in our

227

population, we still don't know much more than we know from our own personal experiences. Researchers report that some monogamous people are happily married and others are not; that some who become involved outside their marriages remain happily married and others don't; that some who swing are happy with the activity and each other and others aren't.

The only thing we can say with any certainty is that few people are casual about extramarital sex. They either extol it highly or regret it bitterly. They rarely feel that it doesn't matter—that they would lightly either enter into an affair or stop having one. And everyone remembers the first extramarital foray in as much detail as they remember the first intercourse. Both are significant turning points in a sexual lifetime.

Chapter 10

Bowers in Bloom: The Fifties

I wonder what's going to happen as my sexual powers diminish. I'm not scared. I'm saddened, but I have a sense I'll cope. To put it simply in a corny way, the joy of sexuality is becoming second-place to the joy of loving.

—MICHAEL

PEOPLE IN THEIR FIFTIES continue to deal with the sexual concerns that occupied them during their forties, and those who resolve these crises happily tend to agree with the aphorism "The forties are the old age of youth and the fifties are the youth of old age."

Those who began their midlife transition or crisis during the previous decade are most likely coming out of it now. As a prominent fifty-two-year-old attorney said to me, "I knew I was coming out of my midlife crisis when I went on the beach and the twenty-year-old girls didn't look as good to me as their fortyish mothers. And I knew I had passed it when my wife looked best of all."

Some people, of course, slide imperceptibly from one stage of life to another, never experiencing crisis or even a noticeable bump in the shift from young adulthood into middle age. Still, virtually everyone confronts certain basic issues at this stage of life. Those who didn't acknowledge concerns about health and aging during their forties usually do it now. If they're lucky, this admission is spurred by the illnesses and debilities affecting their contemporaries, or by a realization of the gradual changes they've noticed in themselves. Others face these issues more dramatically when they're the ones suffering the heart attack, the hysterectomy, the mastectomy, the high blood pressure, the diabetes, or whatever.

For women, the most clear-cut signpost of middle age is menopause (the average menopausal age is now fifty-one). The time span of from two to five years during which a woman's body undergoes the various physiological changes that bring it on is known technically as the climacteric. In recent years we've heard a lot of talk about "male menopause," a contradiction in terms since the word "menopause" means the cessation of the menses. This time of a man's life when certain biological changes occur for him is more correctly called the male climacteric. Depending on the particular physiological changes, the psychological orientation, and the life circumstances of every individual, these changes of middle age may or may not be seen as important turning points, and the nature of the turning point may be either positive or negative.

This is the time, too, when the "nest" usually empties, when the children go off on their own (at least physically, if not emotionally or financially). This change often brings its own changes, which may be glorious or devastating.

As people face these events, they forge a new series of turning points at a time of life that many people see as a turning point in itself, as the hopes and dreams of early life assume a new form and a new direction for the years to come.

"I love sex," Marion, fifty-three, told me. "One of the reasons my marriage broke up was because Dick didn't love it as much as I did and we were always fighting about it. The big thing that attracted me to the man I'm married to now was the fact that he *always* wanted sex. But now that I've gone through my menopause, it's different. I don't get those strong genital sensations just from thinking about it, I'm not turned on as much, I don't masturbate as much, and when I do have sex I don't always come. Sex is still enjoyable, but it has a distinctly softer flavor."

While many women seem to glide through the climacteric, barely noticing any change in their lives, including their sexuality, for others this time of life does constitute a sexual turning point. In two recent studies, the largest group of postmenopausal women (44.1 percent in one study, 49 percent in the other) felt that their menopause (either natural or surgically induced through hysterectomy) had no effect at all on their sexuality. The next largest group (38.9 percent and 30 percent, respectively) felt it had had a positive effect, and the smallest number (17 percent and 21 percent) saw a negative effect.

Nora, fifty-nine, is like the women in the second group: "To me it was very freeing to reach this stage of life. I didn't have to worry any more about becoming pregnant and I felt as if I got a new rush of energy. I didn't need as much sleep and I could just go and go and go." For those in the third group, like Marion, menopause may bring a saddening lowering of sex drive, a diminution of bodily sensations that had been exciting, painful intercourse, a sense of advancing age.

A recent upsurge in research on postmenopausal women has confirmed the major hormonal and physiological changes that take place during these years, with important implications for female sexuality. Some of the physical changes linked to the ebbing of the female sex hormone estrogen include a number of changes in the vagina: reduction in depth and diameter, loss of tissue elasticity, decrease in lubrication, and thinning of the vaginal walls. The labia become thinner and the clitoris smaller. For some women these changes result in dyspareunia, pain during intercourse. The commonly experienced "hot flashes" and urinary difficulties caused by tissue shrinkage are also hormone-related. The drop in desire that some women feel at this time may also be due to hormonal changes, since a similar lessening of desire is reported by many younger women who undergo a "surgical menopause" because of hysterectomy (removal of the uterus) and/or ovariectomy (removal of the ovaries).

In one group of forty-two sexually active postmenopausal women, women who were experiencing coital pain (one-third of the group) were compared with women who were not, and significant physical differences showed up in the vagina itself (a shallower canal, a smaller entrance, and less lubrication) among the dyspareunic women. These women had had fewer vaginal deliveries than the other women, and they tended to be thinner. In other areas, however, there were no significant differences between the two groups—in the pleasure they had

231

found in either premarital or marital sex, in menstrual discomfort, sexual guilt or inhibitions, comfort with sexual communication, overall health, or satisfaction with life in general. It seems clear, then, that dyspareunia stems, by and large, not from the mind but from the vagina—that there really are physical changes that change the quality of sex for some women at this time of life.

Happily, this condition responds dramatically to the administration of artificial hormones. The traditional therapy for estrogen deficiency after hysterectomy or menopause, which consisted of estrogen alone, has been implicated as a possible cause of cancer of the endometrium, the lining of the uterus. Recent research, however, seems to indicate that giving women a combination of estrogen and progestin (a synthetic hormone similar to the female hormone progesterone) results in a lower incidence of endometrial cancer than no hormonal treatment at all.

Women suffering hormonally based menopausal difficulties can also opt for more conservative measures, such as the use of a lubricant during intercourse or the substitution of oral or manual stimulation for intercourse.

Many other physiological changes of menopause have been described in the literature—decreases in muscle tension, vaginal expansion and congestion, uterine contractions, skin flush, and a lack of an increase in breast size during sexual stimulation—all physical changes. Yet it's hard to say that it's all in the body, since we know that the sexual link between physical and emotional feelings and responses is a powerful one.

The riddle is complicated by our knowledge that while postmenopausal women ordinarily continue to secrete estrogen until about the age of seventy-three, the amounts of this female hormone in their bodies drop off sharply after they stop menstruating. On the other hand, the levels of testosterone, the major male hormone that is also present in women and that seems to inspire sexual desire in both sexes, are higher in later life. So the picture is far from clear.

Neither is the picture clear of the male situation at this time of life. Despite the fact that men retain the ability to father children into their seventies or eighties, there *are* biological changes in middle age. These include decreased production of testosterone, lower fertility, a delay in attaining erection, a variability in ejaculatory inevitability (the sensa-

232

tion just before ejaculation that nothing can stop it now), lower frequency and shorter time of orgasm, a longer refractory period (the time it takes to achieve an erection again after ejaculation), faster loss of erection after ejaculation, and an increase in impotence.

Some of the physical changes common in middle and old age are not the result of simply growing older, however. Among the physical conditions that can interfere with sexual functioning are diabetes (the most common medical cause of impotence and a frequent cause of ejaculatory problems in men and orgasmic difficulties in women), genital infections, hernias, arthritis, hormonal insufficiencies, scarring from hysterectomy or other internal operations, and prostate surgery. Sometimes it's not the illness itself but the medicine used to treat it that causes the trouble. Drugs commonly prescribed to treat high blood pressure, heart disease, anxiety, allergies, depression, muscle spasms, obesity, ulcers, irritable colon, and prostate cancer have been found to impair sexual function. In some cases the condition can be treated or the medication changed; in others the individual has to adjust to a permanent change in sexual functioning. The good news in all of this is the figure reported by the over-fifty-year-olds who answered a Consumers Union survey. Even among those in fair or poor health, 72 percent of the women and 82 percent of the men continue to be sexually active.

For many people of both sexes, then, physiological changes that begin in midlife do signal significant turning points, which also have important psychological meanings. They differ for men and women, and also for individuals of both sexes.

"Sex has been an important part of my life for the last thirty years, and especially the last few years in my relationship with Laura," Michael tells me as our interview winds to an end. "But now that I'm in my fifties, I'm seeing some physical changes and wondering what's going to happen in the future. I feel arthritis pains here and there, I need an operation on my knee, and my hair is starting to fall out. I see all of this and I get a sense of my finiteness.

"I wonder what's going to happen as my sexual powers diminish." He is silent for a moment. "I'm not scared. I'm saddened, but I have a sense I'll cope. To put it simply in a corny way, the joy of sexuality is becoming second-place to the joy of loving. This is new to me—it used

233

to be so much the other way around. Now, I feel confident that as one ability leaves me, the other ability is growing.''

At fifty-five, Joe has already faced some of the changes that Michael talks about: ''I'm very conscious these days of the aging process. I'm having more difficulty getting turned on, getting an erection, and having an orgasm. I have to work at it more now. If I know I'm going to be having sex, I do more fantasizing beforehand to help me get psyched up and make love better.

''I know this is natural. It just happens. Just like I'm not as fast on the tennis court and don't have as much stamina there as I used to. I do feel it as a loss, but losing is part of aging. And actually some changes in my sex life are not a loss. My wife and I have talked about how our way of making love has changed. We're not thinking about simultaneous orgasm anymore, and we do more oral sex and more manual sex. All this isn't a loss. The loss is that we didn't do more of that before!''

Not all men, of course, accept these changes with the equanimity that Michael and Joe profess. There's Alex, who, after experiencing one incident of impotence at the age of fifty-eight, went to bed with five different women in as many days, to prove to himself that his powers were still intact. There's Zack, who confided to me his one sexual wish at the age of fifty-two: ''Never to be afraid of a 'yes' answer.'' There are the men who withdraw from sex altogether, not wanting to risk failure.

While women, too, feel the pressures of aging, their concern is less often with performance than with being sexually desirable. As Elaine, fifty-two, a divorced woman living with a man she's fond of but doesn't love, confides to me, ''I'm afraid of being lonely. It's hard for a woman my age to find somebody—unless she's incredibly exciting and young-looking. I'm not, and I'm realistic enough to know that my options are limited, so I tell myself I should be happy I have somebody and not be so picky about finding fault with Dave. Sex is still okay between us—not great the way it was when we first came together ten years ago. But I ask myself whether I'd be better off without him, and maybe without any sex—and I stay with him.''

Sexual activity *is* different during the middle years, and some researchers attribute the major differences to the physiological changes in men. One recent study of postmenopausal women (average age fifty-six) found that the major difference between sexually active women (defined as engaging in intercourse at least three times a month) and inactive ones (having intercourse less than ten times a year) was the availability of a healthy, interested partner. The most common reasons the women in the second group gave for inactivity was their partner's illness, loss of sexual interest, or death. Next was their own poor health, and last on the list was their own loss of sexual interest. Both groups of women continued to hold the same ideal levels of sexual activity and both had been equally active before menopause.

Still, men who have been sexually active during their younger years are likely to continue to be sexually active during middle and old age. Masters and Johnson attribute many of the dysfunctions that appear during midlife to a number of factors besides the onslaught of the years—monotony in the relationship, preoccupation with business or money worries, mental or physical fatigue, eating or drinking too much, physical and mental infirmities of either the man (which interfere with his abilities) or the woman (which diminish his desire), or to that psychological saboteur of sex—fear of performance.

Couples who are aware of these potential blocks to sexual fulfillment in middle age and who can design their sex life around them can still find great satisfaction. Michael, for example, has experienced a new, more intense sexual excitement by holding off his orgasm, forcing himself to stay at the brink of ejaculation. He prolongs lovemaking, asking Laura to stop stimulating him while he brings her to orgasm, after which he allows himself to become aroused again.

"The sexual tension and excitement while we're making love is so fantastic that I almost dread my orgasm," he says. "I love to prolong the state of tension because when I have a fast buildup the orgasm is a blinding bang, but it's so fast and instantaneous, such a short burst, it's over so soon. I much prefer the high level of the prolonged sexual excitement, even though the orgasm that follows the slower buildup is not that strong.

"While I'm in that state of tension, the whole outside of my body becomes alive. I read someplace that the main sex organ is our skin. I become very, very much aware of my skin and my nerve endings. Any place on me that is touched or caressed in this state then comes alive. I like spicy food because it makes my whole mouth tingle and I become aware of all the inside surfaces of my mouth, and this is almost the same sensation where I become aware of parts of my body that I never think about. It's a sensual tingle.

"Then after the sex, the relaxation, the peace after the release of the tension, and the holding and the sensuality are also delightful. So this is totally different from the mechanical or just plain sensual sex that I used to have. I know that part of it is because of how I feel about Laura, but another big part is because of changes in me. I've been changing a lot over these past few years and I'm capable now of things I couldn't do or be before. Do you suppose that's what they call maturity?"

Michael and Joe are both among the fortunate men whose partners are knowledgeable and interested enough to provide a great deal of oral and manual stimulation. The women in a Rutgers study reported their sexual repertoire as consisting mostly of intercourse and physical affection, with very little involvement in oral or manual activity and very little masturbation. As Sandra Leiblum, one of the authors of this study and director of sexual counseling at Rutgers Medical School, points out, "At a time when the ability of their male partners to get a prompt, easy, strong erection capable of penetration requires more than the sight of a nude body, these women are saying that they're not interested in helping out by using the range of oral and manual techniques that are available to them. Nor are they interested in maintaining their own sexuality actively through masturbation."

This lack of interest in non-coital sex is undoubtedly due to the sexual values these women were raised with, their sense of what's sexually appropriate. Chances are that when the daughters of these women reach their age, their sexual repertoires will be broader and they will have a very different experience of midlife sexuality.

It's clear, then, that this is another time of life—like adolescence, like pregnancy—when physiology and psychology come together to shape the form of a sexual turning point. With some people, one factor is more important than the other; with others the two meld inseparably to produce a turning point that may either close off possibilities or open up new ones.

For years professional observers of family life have talked about the "empty nest crisis" said to afflict women who had invested themselves heavily in mothering. "The day I came back from driving my oldest

236

daughter to college, I ran into a friend at the library and I burst into tears,'' says Tina, a fifty-seven-year-old college professor. ''I wasn't teaching full-time then, just subbing on a day-to-day basis. And I was too tied up in my children's lives. Their lives had become my life. When she left, this daughter I was closest to, I felt like somebody put a knife in me and left it there. It took me some months to see that a part of my life had ended, that she was going to be a guest in my house, that she would never come home again. And she never did.

''By the time the second one went off to college, I had realized I'd have to live my life for myself and I had invested more of myself in my work. Then when the third one left, I remember this terrible empty feeling that lasted for a day or two. And then I began to appreciate how lovely it was that Ralph and I just had to please each other. Our relationship benefited from the privacy and freedom we hadn't had for years.

''It's funny. The beds always squeak loudly when there are teenagers wandering around the house. It's very inhibiting if they're up when you want to go to bed. When the children are gone, the beds don't squeak anymore. It's true. Any room in the house is suitable for an encounter at any time. It's lovely.''

According to Samona Sheppard, who cites her own and other recent research, ''The empty nest syndrome is a male invention.'' On the contrary, the emptiness of the nest can open up many different possibilities: it can give a woman space to pursue her own concerns, including an enhanced sexuality; it can free an individual or a couple to pursue unconventional sexual behavior, away from the watchful eyes of children (who tolerate less deviance in their parents than their parents accept in them); it can revitalize a marriage that has grown dull and plodding in its orientation around the children's needs; or it can expose a couple, in the glare of their aloneness, to the harsh realization that their bond cannot endure.

The empty nest was a major factor in a momentous turning point for Nora, fifty-nine. Three significant events came together almost simultaneously: her nest emptied, her menstrual periods ended, and she became heavily involved in the women's movement. ''I had three very sweet children when I was in my twenties. I enjoyed them during the years they were growing up. Then I felt a joyous freedom when they were all out of the house and out of town. I was just short of fifty when my youngest left for college.

"The combination of their being away and my involvement in the women's movement opened up the most interesting period of my life. I had been bringing in speakers for a local women's organization, and I realized one day that almost all my speakers had something to say about female sexuality. This interested me greatly. I had an excellent husband and a wonderful marriage, but I had always found monogamy very depriving. I had had your 'all-purpose' secret suburban affair, and I knew that that was not what I wanted. So I went to Carl—my husband—and I told him that I was going to experiment sexually with other men."

Nora was not sent by Central Casting to play the part of a woman with a wild sex life. The day we meet in her modest colonial house on a side street in the Chicago suburb of Highland Park, she is conservatively dressed in loose-fitting pants and a neat, unrevealing shirt. Her almost completely white hair is pulled back from her round face in a tousled, schoolteacherish bun on the back of her neck. Her face, with its plain features and sweet expression, is innocent of makeup. The only indication that she cares at all about her appearance is the exquisite hand-knitted vest she wears over her shirt, a vest she designed and made herself. Her voice is so soft I have to strain to hear her vivid descriptions of her exotic sexual exploits.

Nora had quickly put her plans into effect. Despite Carl's appalled reaction, she took a lover and openly told Carl on which evenings she would be seeing him. Carl's first reaction was hurt, then fear, and then embarrassment at the idea of seeing himself as the kind of man who lets his wife see other men. And then Carl, who had always prided himself on his intellectualism and his disdain for what "they" might think, began to read some of the books Nora recommended. "We've always been bookish people," she says. "Everything we do, we first read a book about it." He hesitatingly accepted Nora's claims that her new activities would not displace him in her affections or damage their marriage, and first "allowed" her her freedom and then joined her wholeheartedly in their new sexually adventurous life style.

Nora and Carl each had affairs in which they fell in love, and when Nora's affair ended and she was grief-stricken, it was Carl who comforted her. "I don't know of another case like that," Nora says, "except for one in literature, by Gogol, I think. Carl had an extraordinary amount of insight and tolerance and understanding and self-confidence. He comforted me the same way he would have if I had lost a sister or a brother. And knowing I would have done the same for him."

During the five or six years that Nora and Carl were living out their fantasies, they spoke openly about them in certain places, including the local Mensa chapter and meetings of various other organizations. They managed, however, to keep their erotic lives secret from anyone at the college where Carl taught, Nora's knit-shop customers, and their own grown children, who were all living far from home. After Carl became ill with the cancer that was to take his life three years later, they both reverted to the monogamy that had for so many years characterized their thirty-six-year marriage.

Another turning point came for Nora when Carl got sick. "I lost interest in what I was doing," she says. "I just wanted to stay home and be with him. I didn't feel I was sacrificing anything. I didn't need all that anymore. It felt like growing up, like I don't need to skip rope anymore. I would not have missed it for the world—I would have felt like a sexual illiterate if my sex life had consisted only of me and my husband. It would be so limited it would be comparable to having read only one author or seen only one artist. I do feel that my life was immeasurably enriched by these experiences.

"Men have always been afraid of female sexuality. I think they always felt that if women were allowed to express their sexuality freely, we would become irresponsible people and screw all day, every day. But this didn't happen with me. I developed my sexuality so it was untrammeled and unrestricted, and I still did my work and fulfilled my obligations and was a good mother and a good wife and a good daughter and a good citizen who worked for the candidates of my choice at election time and kept my house clean and was not a menace to society. I think if all of us allowed our sexuality to flourish to the full we'd still be good people. Perhaps better. Perhaps less neurotic, less conflicted."

Now, six months after Carl's death, Nora has retained friendships with three of the men she met during her swinging days. For her, they are just that—platonic friendships. Even though all three of the men have shown interest in resuming sexual relations with her, she is no longer interested.

"I'm in a peculiar position of being almost sixty with a lot of single men friends, not the usual problem of women in my age group. And I don't bother to stay slim, dye my hair, or look younger. It shows that it's not younger women that men look for, it's available women, women they don't have to take out for weeks and spend a lot of money on before they will finally jump into bed. It bothers me a little that I'm not a sexual being anymore. My latest turning point has been to celibacy. I've closed the sexual chapter of my life, and now I'm more interested in other things. Like being totally on my own for the first time in thirty-six years. Living alone, standing on my own two feet, seeing what that feels like."

Nora and Carl went into their period of sexual experimentation at about the same time of life that Tony and Anne did. Both couples had multiple partners in a dizzying series of encounters that marked a sharp change from their former life styles. It's intriguing to imagine the possibility that the four of them may well have been together at the same orgy. Intriguing, but not likely. Aside from the geographical differences, it's just as difficult to visualize the intellectual professor and feminist philosopher at the Bel-Air Social Club as it is to see Tony and Anne at a Mensa meeting. There are other differences, too, between the couples. Tony and Anne went into swinging, at his urging, in a shaky time in their marriage, and it seems likely that so long as he is interested in bedding other women, Anne will be nearby with other men. Nora and Carl went into experimentation from a stable marriage, out of her curiosity. Once that curiosity was satisfied, the need for acting on it was over.

For both these couples, so very different from each other, their forays into unconventional sexuality seem to have been harmless and possibly beneficial both to their individual development and to their relationships. Still, embracing such a life style is not without risk. While some people strengthen themselves in these waters, others drown in them.

In 1972 the book *Open Marriage,* by Nena O'Neill and the late George O'Neill, suggested the possibility of opening a marriage to outside sexual relationships. In 1984 in a new foreword to a reissued edition, Nena O'Neill noted that almost everything she and her husband had sug-

240

gested to encourage growth in marriage has taken hold—with one notable exception, sexual openness. "Today, a majority of couples still prefer sexual exclusivity. If they fall short of this ideal, and over one-half of marrieds do, they still prefer the hidden affair to any alternative open arrangement." Many of those who tried sexually open marriage ran into trouble with honesty and jealousy. They didn't know how to be honest without being hurtful, and they were unprepared for the powerful surges of jealousy that greeted their experiments. "And so, finally, 'Better an affair,' they said, most preferring not to know about extramarital sex if it occurred."

About a dozen research studies have looked at sexually open marriage to see what happened to couples who tried it. By and large, they have fared no better or worse than comparable married couples who espouse sexual exclusivity. (It's not clear in all cases, however, whether the comparison couples actually practice monogamy or engage in secret affairs. So it's not clear exactly what we're comparing.) The most interesting finding is that certain personality types seem to be attracted to sexually open marriage and to be able to carry if off. Not surprisingly, the successful ones are nonconformist risk takers who are stimulated by complexity and likely to be socially innovative.

After her study of seventy-one people in sexually open marriages, Mary Ann Watson of Metropolitan State College in Denver concluded that "open marriage may best be conceived as a stage, perhaps recurring, in the developmental process of a couple's relationship, rather than as an ongoing lifestyle." This kind of arrangement may be a turning point in the life of a marriage, as it seems to be for Tony and Anne.

Those couples who were handling the openness well had all established ground rules that affirmed the importance of their primary relationship above any others they might make. They told new partners that they were committed to their marriage, set time limits for outside involvements (usually no more than one evening a week), and set their own homes off-limits for sexual encounters. Those who had been in an open relationship and were now separated indicated that they had seen the openness as a way to temporarily leave an unfulfilling marriage. They had been seeing their secondary partners more frequently than the still-married people did (often three or more times a week) and felt that sex was better with these outside partners.

241

When Dr. Watson contacted the study participants in 1980, two years after the original interviews, she found that all the couples who had been in sexually open marriages earlier were still married or living together, but that all but one had returned to monogamous relationships with their spouses. They still believed in the philosophy of opening the marriage at certain times in their lives even though they were not doing so at the moment. All but one of the people who were separated or divorced at the time of the first interview were also in monogamous relationships.

"We were making love. He was in my arms . . . I felt his weight upon me . . . and suddenly his great, big generous heart burst." This was how, on the evening of February 2, 1984, television viewers heard Grace Gardner describe the death of her lover, Sergeant Phil Esterhaus of the popular TV series *Hill Street Blues*. Later during the show they heard some of the police officers talking admiringly about the way their beloved sergeant met his death.

The switchboards of NBC stations around the country lit up with viewers calling to object to the show, the New York station followed its broadcast with an interview with a noted physician, and newspapers called doctors for their reactions. Why all the interest? The cardiologist interviewed on New York's WNBC-TV, Richard A. Stein, M.D., director of the Cardiac Exercise Laboratory at the State University of New York–Downstate Medical Center in Brooklyn, told me, "Dying 'in the saddle' is one of our society's favorite male fantasies. It's become a popular folk myth."

Maybe it helps to reduce the fear of death by cloaking it in the machismo of lovemaking, to couple what for most of us is the worst thing in the world with what to many of us is the best. Maybe it reinforces our culture's puritanical tradition that sex is dangerous. In any case, the belief is strong that sex can kill. Happily, though, according to statistics and modern medical opinion, the risk that sex poses to the heart is minuscule.

Measured heart rates during sexual activity tend to be lower than during many other activities of everyday life, and most people use more energy in the course of their work than they do during sex. "Ah-hah!" counters the careful reader of newspaper medical advice columns. "But

242

what about extramarital sex? I've heard that's the dangerous kind. It's like the fellow said, 'The doctor told me not to get too excited during sex, so I'm just having it with my wife.' ''

A report published in 1963 indicated that 34 Japanese men out of 5,559 who had died suddenly (just over one-half of 1 percent) had died during sexual intercourse, that 17 of these deaths were attributed to heart attacks (about one-third of 1 percent), and that 25 occurred during or after extramarital sex, away from home in hotels or ''sweetheart houses.'' The men were, on average, twenty years older than their partners, and one-third were said to have been drunk at the time.

Over the past twenty years, a mythology has grown up in which doctors and laypersons alike, citing this one report, have issued warnings to recovered heart patients to avoid extramarital sex. (This probably explains why some research finds a drastic drop in extramarital sex after heart problems.) According to a number of experts, however, there's no solid medical basis for this advice.

For one reason, aside from the tiny percentage involved, the Japanese findings have not been replicated in any other study. Second, it's possible that wives underreport the incidence of death during or after intercourse, saying simply that their husbands died in bed. Third, extramarital sex in Japan may have different connotations than extramarital sex in this country. As cardiologist Richard Stein told me, ''No one's ever done a study asking married men who are having affairs to have their heart rates measured while making love with their wives and also with their paramours. So we really don't know whether there's more cardiac expenditure with one or the other, and I don't think there's any medical basis to support the idea that outside sex is more dangerous than marital sex.''

Adelphi University nursing professor Jacqueline R. Hott attributes the wide currency given this belief to the ''puritanical prejudices'' of doctors and nurses who take their own taboos into their professional practices, despite the fact that in such a sensitive realm objectivity is needed more than ever. As Dr. Hott points out, ''For some patients the extramarital partner is the 'usual' sex partner, while activity with the spouse can produce *more* stress.''

A compromise to the dilemma is offered by Holy Cross Hospital in Fort Lauderdale, Florida, which issues to all discharged heart patients

243

a sheet of guidelines. It warns about the possible risk of extramarital sex and urges heart patients thinking about it to discuss the subject with their doctors. Some cardiologists may be startled to find themselves in the unexpected position of advisers in another realm of the heart, but this hospital is to be commended for its moral acceptance of the naturalness of sex and its good intentions in raising the issue at all. While the paper incorporates much of the advice that Dr. Stein claims is gratuitous (like recommending some positions over others and suggesting sex at home rather than in unfamiliar places), it straightforwardly raises the possibility of oral and manual sex, as well as masturbation, as alternatives to intercourse.

For most married heart-attack patients, the most pressing concern is the resumption of sex with their own spouses. This was true of Betty and Al, a couple I met at a meeting of a hospital-affiliated Heart Club. "Before I had my heart attack three years ago, Betty and I were very active sexually. We were making love anywhere from twenty to twenty-four times a month, and we almost always had intercourse more than once in a single session," Al, fifty-eight, says when he and his wife sit down to talk to me. Pleasant-looking, they look more like brother and sister than husband and wife, with similar short, broad features, similar fair coloring and rounded physiques, similar hand gestures, and similar melodious voices.

"Those multiple orgasms were important to us, because Betty usually didn't have hers when I ejaculated the first time, and so she wouldn't be satisfied until we did it the second time," says Al. "Now, not only are we making love less frequently than we used to—about every other night—but multiple orgasms are a thing of the past. Whenever I've asked my doctors about it, I've received a very unsympathetic response.

"My doctors call me a 'sexual athlete,' smirk, or say, 'What are you complaining about? You're way ahead.' Just because most people are less active than we are at our ages and our stage of marriage, they don't see that we're experiencing this change as a loss. Very few doctors are comfortable with the subject of sex, even the endocrinologists and urologists that everyone says you should consult if you have a problem. It isn't part of their training, they've never gotten beyond their own inhibitions and they can't help their patients."

Al's experience with his doctors isn't rare. One research study after another has found that very few physicians talk about sexual matters with their recovering heart patients, and when they do it's usually because the patients themselves initiate the discussion. While doctors give heart patients specific guidelines about diet, exercise, work, and other activities of daily life, information about one common activity—sex—is either ambiguous or not offered at all. (Holy Cross Hospital is apparently a rare gem.) This is one reason why any kind of heart ailment is usually a major sexual turning point in midlife, why most people's sexual activity plummets to 50 or 25 percent of former levels.

Yet according to cardiologist Stein, it needn't. "Sex is not dangerous to the heart," he tells me. "Many daily activities exceed the stress taken on the heart by sex, and most people can resume the same level of sexual activity that they found rewarding before their heart attack or surgery.

"They don't need to change their usual positions, they don't need to change timing, they don't need to do *anything* different—unless they notice any symptoms. If they experience angina, they can prevent that by putting a nitroglycerin tablet under the tongue ahead of time. Some of the symptoms of dysfunction, like lowered libido or problems with erectile function, may be due not to the aftermath of the heart involvement but to the medication the patient is taking. If people tell their doctors they're having these problems, they can usually take a different medicine."

Betty and Al were actually luckier than most couples. Before Al left the hospital, his doctor did tell him that the total energy cost of sexual intercourse is comparable to climbing one or two flights of stairs and that as soon as Al could do that without pain or other symptoms, he'd be able to resume lovemaking. Al reached this point when many people do, about three or four weeks after discharge from the hospital, and Betty and he "tenderly and tentatively" engaged in sex, "both feeling our way," as Al puts it.

At the beginning, both were afraid. As Betty recalls, "The first time or two, you're frightened because you don't know exactly what you dare and dare not do and how quickly it might damage him. It's like when you have a new baby—you have to get over the feeling that he's fragile." Betty would greet Al's early sexual overtures with an onrush

245

of questions: "Are you sure you're feeling up to it? What did you do today? Are you tired? How much work did you do? Can you handle all this stress?" And Al would be annoyed and inhibited by her overprotectiveness. But because sex had always been so important to both of them, they gradually began to engage in it more and more often. With some differences.

"We had some real adjustments to make, because usually I had had my orgasm the second time around," Betty says. "Since Al felt angina pains when he tried having intercourse more than once, we had to develop some new techniques. Al now stimulates me to orgasm manually or orally. Also, I figured out a new position so that I can hold him and stimulate myself at the same time, and this helps. Or else I take matters into my own hands and masturbate.

"I don't have as many orgasms as I used to, but I'm not frustrated and uncomfortable. I think that's partly because since menopause I have slowed down and am not as sexually active as I had been. I don't seem to feel the need for it as much as I used to, so this makes it a little easier.

"I really don't have any complaints about sex. I've never had sex with anyone else but Al in my entire life," Betty goes on, almost with embarrassment. "But I don't feel I missed anything, because it was good right from the beginning and it kept getting better. Al has always considered me an equal. He never tried to put me on a pedestal and keep me in ignorance, nor did I ever feel as if he was looking down on me from a lofty perch. So here we are after thirty-six years and we still care about each other and don't feel blasé and bored. I think we were blessed with having found one another—and we've also worked at it."

They're still working at it. "I think we're closer," Al says, moving over to enfold Betty's hand in his. "I've gotten in the habit of touching Betty more, just holding her, fondling her. For some people whose heart attacks were a lot more severe than mine, it's the only form of lovemaking. If you treasure the human being you're living with, you'll make adjustments to compensate. This may not be as satisfactory as having intercourse, but at least you're making love to someone you care about. You may have to accept some compromise on sexuality, as you do on almost every activity. If you're fortunate enough to have a good relationship in the first place, it will probably bring you closer."

Research backs up Al's statement. When Columbia University psychologist John L. Michela studied forty couples within a year of the husbands' heart attack, he found that both husband and wife were happier in the marriage than they had been before the heart attack, despite the depression and anger that often followed on its heels. The happiness of these marriages may have something to do with these couples' relief at having cheated death. As Betty tells me, "We're closer in the sense that you value what you almost lost. You recognize your own mortality and if you've had a good relationship you treasure every minute of what you have left."

Chapter 11

Perennial Passions: The Sixties

It was phenomenal. I've never met a man that I had so much in common with. Ned and I laughed at the same jokes, liked the same music, enjoyed the same word games. . . . Everything was perfect between us—everything but our ages. I knew from the start that it couldn't possibly work when I was sixty and he was twenty-eight.

—CAROL

MOST DEFINITIONS OF old age (euphemistically known as "late adulthood," "the golden years," "senior citizendom," and a string of other neologisms) pick an arbitrary age of either sixty or sixty-five as its threshold. Yet in today's society men and women in their sixties more often fit the descriptions we phrase for the middle-aged. Most are healthy and vigorous, with those in the first half of the decade likely to be working full-time at the same jobs they've held for years. They don't feel old, don't look old, and don't act old. Fewer than one in four limit any of their major activities because of health. They're politically active, physically active, and generally as active sexually as they have been over the past several decades.

For great numbers of people over sixty (and over seventy and over eighty), sex is a vital and fulfilling part of their lives. Two recent broad-based reports (*The Starr-Weiner Report on Sex and Sexuality in the Mature Years* by Bernard D. Starr and Marcella Bakur Weiner, and *Love, Sex, and Aging: A Consumers Union Report* by Edward M. Brecher and The Editors of Consumer Reports Books) show a rich panorama of sexual ex-

248

perience well into old age, especially for men and women in their sixties, whom some researchers call the "young-old," but who could just as well be considered the "mature middle-aged."

While some observers of adult development talk about the "late adult transition" occurring between the ages of sixty and sixty-five, I get the feeling from Daniel Levinson's rationale, for example, that he's talking about the sixty-year-olds of earlier eras, who really had crossed the threshold into old age. Levinson emphasizes the need to reduce the heavy responsibilities of middle adulthood, to move out of center stage, to renounce positions of formal authority. He describes people of this age as likely to have at least one major illness or impairment, while current statistical reports indicate that 90 percent of people over sixty-five describe their health as fair, good, or excellent. He cites Erikson's final ego stage, "Integrity vs. Despair," the coming to terms with the completion of most or perhaps all of an individual's life work, as beginning at about age sixty. Yet Erikson conceptualized these life stages more than three decades ago, when sixty was still old.

Today, sixty is late middle age, and most people don't consider themselves old till they hit seventy. A recent survey shows that most people in their sixties tend to feel about fifteen years younger than their actual age, and the more money they have and the better educated they are, the younger they feel.

By the end of the sixth decade of life, most people have confronted and dealt with most of the crises of middle age—the empty nest, the menopause, the boredom of the marriage, the sense of the finiteness of time. By this time, they've usually come to terms with those concerns. They've very likely established a sexual pattern, which they continue to maintain, whether it's one of monogamy or infidelity, of the enjoyment of sex or a lack of interest in it. While both men and women experience physiological changes that affect their sexual responses, women who have been having regular orgasms generally continue to experience them with the same intensity. And men's responses now are closely tied to their levels of activity throughout their adult lives.

People in their sixties do face some new crises with sexual implications. A major one is retirement. To many individuals (as well as to some researchers) this is a signpost of old age. Once confronted, however, it often brings unexpected benefits that lead not to disengagement with active life but to a redirection of energies. Goals and activities that had been off-limits in earlier years when a career had to be established and money had to be earned suddenly become possible. The changes in focus, in the use of time, and in the reorganization of a marriage that often follow retirement have sexual implications. As, of course, does a common trauma of this age period—the loss of a spouse. The survivor needs to mourn and then to begin to live and love again, either alone or with someone new. Because of the great preponderance of women over men in this age group and because of cultural standards that encourage men to seek out younger women, most men will find new sexual partners. Most women will not. They must embark on what is likely to become a permanent state, being alone without a regular sexual partner. Resolving these issues are two of the major sexual goals for people at this time of life.

Alex wears the uniform of his profession—impeccably tailored gray flannel suit, paisley tie, and elegantly striped shirt—but in his bulk and manner looks as if he would be more at home in the woods than in the financial canyons of Wall Street. His irregular features—a nose that looks as if it had been broken and never correctly set, perhaps out of a macho pride, a chin that juts out ahead of the rest of his face, a full-lipped mouth—are probably more appealing now at age sixty-five than they were in his youth, before the self-confidence brought by the power of success added its unmistakable stamp.

In stark contrast to the cacophony in the international brokerage firm he founded, Alex's private office is a haven of serenity. Its focus is the huge window with its view of the East River and the tip of Manhattan Island, its only wall decoration a grouping of family photos. A vase with a single lily sits on the glass coffee table in front of the couch where I face Alex in his swivel-base chair. The shoji screen on the wall behind me and the simplicity of the furnishings lend an Oriental spareness to the room.

"I love my wife more than I ever did," he tells me, gesturing toward the photo of a handsome brunette. "When Charlotte and I were first married after a whirlwind wartime courtship, I had a vague feeling that I loved her, but I didn't know then what love was. We were lucky, because we've been happy together for almost forty years.

"Sex has been good, too—Charlotte is a good lover. But if I never made love to her again, I wouldn't miss it. It's sad that as you grow to love someone more, the excitement of the sexual attraction lessens. This has nothing to do with how good a lover the person is, or how beautiful, or how charming. It's just the passage of time. After all, that's why they have so many affairs in Hollywood. They're all beautiful, but even a beautiful body fails to excite when you see it all the time.

"When I came home from the army I went back to college under the G.I. bill and I found myself surrounded by women. I didn't plan to have affairs, they just seemed to happen. And they've been happening ever since. I've been with a lot of women. Only three or four one-night stands, though. Mostly ongoing relationships—one for more than twelve years. And I'm still enjoying sex as much as I ever did. To me sex is so wonderful. Fortunately, my staying power has stayed with me." Alex permits a smile of pride to play across his face.

"I sometimes think everything else in life stems from sex. When I'm with someone new, I'm buoyant, energetic. My work goes better. When I haven't been with anyone for a long time, I get restless. If I couldn't have sex again, that would be cataclysmic. But I'm glad to say I don't see any signs of the end."

He shrugs self-deprecatingly and says, "It may seem funny to say this, but I am a very moral man in a curious way. I have certain rules I've held to over the years. First, I've never gone to bed with anyone I knew socially—anyone my wife knew and whose husband I knew. I wouldn't want to put Charlotte in that situation, and besides, getting to know a woman's husband and kids and personal situation takes away the sexual attraction for me.

"Second, my marriage has always been inviolate. I make that clear to a new woman right from the start. I don't flirt in front of Charlotte, and I take every precaution so she won't find out. I only get involved with women who are in good marriages themselves so they won't make too many demands on me and won't want more than I'm willing to give.

"And I don't want to bring anything home, like herpes, so I won't go to bed with anyone under thirty, even though I have to admit that firm young flesh is what turns me on the most. I don't like this about myself, but if I'm at a party or one of the seminars that I give and I have the choice of speaking to an average young woman who has nothing special about her or to a sparkling, scintillating older woman, I'll pick the younger woman every time. And that's not even with any designs on my part—chances are that it won't go any further than that conversation, that evening. Just the thought of that mild flirtation is titillating.

"Theoretically I don't espouse infidelity," he says. "I read a lot, and if I were to read about a character like me in a novel, I couldn't have much sympathy for him. But I don't consider myself immoral, because I know the context. I know I'm not hurting anyone. One reason I don't feel guilty about going to bed with other women is because my sex drive is much stronger than Charlotte's. She's a good lover—she's interested in everything and I think she has an orgasm every time—but she never initiates sex. I sometimes have the feeling that she wouldn't care if we never made love again.

"I wish Charlotte had known another lover besides me, but I don't think she ever has. At first, even after I had started to make love to other women, the idea that she might have another man enraged me. I used to think I would want to murder her if I found her unfaithful. But then later my ideas changed. Since I really loved Charlotte, I wanted her, too, to know the excitement and the fun and the pleasure of being with someone new.

"Charlotte once said to me, 'I used to think you had affairs with other women. But now I know you don't need that to bolster your security, so I don't think so anymore.' I wanted to say to her, 'Who needs it for security? Why can't you just do it because a good fuck is a good fuck and a good body is exciting and a new woman gives you a thrill? Security, hell!' "

Alex stands up, signaling the end of the interview. "I guess you have a different picture of me now," he says. I do. A picture of a man beset by inconsistencies—one set of standards in his head, another in his groin. A man using his considerable intellect to rationalize actions and attitudes he doesn't like into a portrait of himself as a man he can live with. Maximizing the rest of his life depends heavily on his prowess in bed. For his sake, I hope his sexual powers continue as long as he lives, for he is not the kind of man who can enjoy a softer focused, sensuous kind of sex. Nor the kind who'll be able to settle into a cozy in-front-of-the-fireplace kind of life with the wife he loves but no longer lusts after.

For her sake, I hope he continues to be discreet, so that she can either remain in true ignorance of his infidelities—or can sustain the feigned ignorance that may be keeping this marriage together.

While most marriages roll over at least one adulterous bump, and sometimes many others, the journey often continues only because the other spouse keeps his or her eyes tightly shut. While some extraordinarily close marriages endure, safe in the trust that sexual exploration does not mean the toppling of a primary loyalty, it's still a minority of husbands and wives who can openly acknowledge and allow such sexual freedom to each other. Most married people—and some marriage counselors—concur with Alex's feelings that infidelity is permissible only when hidden.

The Consumers Union survey asked about extramarital sex after the age of fifty. While most respondents reported having been faithful since then, almost one in four married men and one in twelve married women reported having had affairs. Comparing these husbands and wives to those who remained faithful (or whose infidelities had taken place before age fifty), a few differences showed up. For one, adulterers reported a higher enjoyment of sex than did faithful spouses, underscoring my own observations of those who discussed their affairs with me. I often heard straying spouses—like Alex—justifying their wanderings by pointing to their partner's lower sex drive. They may well have been accurate in their assessments. Many people seek outside sex simply because they want more sex than their spouses do. They want it more often or they want it more varied, or both. (Of course, others who experience this same disparity meet their needs through masturbation or sublimation, for reasons that "range from love and honor to timidity and lack of opportunity," according to Consumers Union.)

Another difference between the two kinds of spouses is less related to sex than to ease of movement. Unfaithful spouses are more likely than faithful ones to have annual family incomes of $25,000 or more. Money may not buy happiness, but it can pay the bills for outside sex. Hotel rooms, unexplained absences, and other accompaniments to an extramarital affair are more easily come by when you have discretionary income in your pocket. When we realize that households headed by people aged fifty-five to sixty-five are the most affluent in the nation, with almost twice the discretionary spending power of those under

253

thirty-five, we realize that the relatively low rate of infidelity in this age group is due not to the lack of opportunity but to other reasons.

A third difference is, not surprisingly, the happiness of the marriage. Faithful spouses are more likely to report being happily married, although three-quarters of the adulterers are in happy marriages, too. Alex has much company, including the fifty-seven-year-old wife who describes her marriage to a sixty-year-old man as "loving and wonderful and meaningful to us both" and then goes on to talk about three lovers she has had since age fifty: "The value of extramarital affairs is often the excitement and the novelty. The sex is better—but if the couple were to marry, the same intensity, excitement, etc., would become routine. It is the newness that provides the heightened experience."

Still, there *are* good, sexually fulfilling, monogamous marriages between people in their sixties. Some thrive on the bloom of newness— remarriages between the divorced or widowed. Others, however, continue to blossom after many years of living and loving together. Nearly three-quarters of the wives and two-thirds of the husbands in the Consumers Union survey have been in the same marriage for thirty or more years. An impressive 87 percent of married respondents rated the happiness of their marriage at the high end of the scale. And the older people are, the more likely they are to be happily married. Eighty-four percent of married people in their fifties report being happily married, a proportion that rises to 88 percent in the sixties and 91 percent of those aged seventy and over. This increase in happiness is partly the result of divorce: couples who aren't happy don't stay together. It's also possible that happily married people live longer. And another reason for the increase may be, as some of the respondents in this study point out, "that good marriages, like good wines, improve with age."

According to this report, the single most important factor associated with marital happiness is a high level of communication, and the runner-up is a high level of sexual enjoyment. Marital happiness rarely changes sharply in these years. If people were happy earlier, they're likely to continue to be happy, and the reverse. If they've established an ethos of fidelity, they're apt to continue to live by it, and the reverse. Unless some significant event, such as retirement, illness, or widowhood, disrupts the pattern.

* * *

Hal had always expected to work until he dropped. He had loved the magazine world from the time he first got into it as a reader of unsolicited manuscripts, and he loved it more and more through the string of promotions that eventually landed him in the post of editor-in-chief of a slick sports magazine. The job was a dream come true for a man whose athletic fantasies survived a childhood in which the scrawny and poorly coordinated boy had always been the last chosen for any team. And then "his" magazine was bought out by a conglomerate. And then the conglomerate felt the magazine's profit margins weren't high enough. Nor was its readership. Nor its advertising income. It needed a new image, a new spirit, a new editor. Motivated by guilt toward this man who had been with the magazine for thirty years but who didn't fit the "sports image of the eighties," the conglomerate bought his early retirement with a generous severance settlement and a comfortable pension. Hal, sixty-one, took the money and retired.

When I meet with Hal, he has been retired for just over a year. "The first few months were hard," he tells me. I can see why. Observing the staccato rhythm of his speech, his quick gait, and the restless movements of his hands as we sit and talk, I can't imagine this man sitting still for long.

"By the time the retirement actually took place, my sex life had been almost nonexistent for the preceding few months," Hal says in his hoarse, raspy voice. "When I'm unhappy or pressured, I don't feel very sexy. And I was *very* unhappy. Things had been getting worse and worse at work and I knew what was coming but was trying to fight it. I made some overtures at other magazines, but I couldn't get arrested. I felt washed up, over the hill, ready to be put out to pasture. Every cliché in the book fit me. I was fighting for my life at work and I didn't have any energy left over for home. Fortunately, Ronnie—my wife— understood. She gave me a lot of affection without pressuring me for sex. It was a rough time for her, too, but at the time I couldn't think about anyone but myself."

Hal was worried about more than his feelings of failure. His anxieties were concrete, practical, logistical: What would he do with himself all day? How would he spend his time? He had never developed many outside interests. Oh, sure, he enjoyed an occasional game of golf but not so much that he could see becoming a daily duffer. And he'd always taken umpteen rolls of pictures on vacations and talked about doing more with photography, but he'd seen enough prize-winning photographs in his years in publishing to know what his competition was.

"Along with this, I was quite concerned about how this would affect my relationship with my wife. Ronnie and I used to kid around about 'I married you for better or for worse, but not for lunch,' and here I would be home all the time. And she's been home alone herself for the past twenty-five years or so, since the kids were in school all day, answerable to no one. She can do whatever she wants to do, talk on the phone all day if she wants, have a meeting here—she's the president of one organization and active in a few others and she puts in a lot of time as a volunteer; she takes it seriously. Or maybe she wants to take a nap some afternoon, invite a friend over for a personal talk, whatever.

"And then all of a sudden there's some other character who's around all the time. And even if he's not in the same room with you all the time, he's there. So it's a whole major adjustment.

"It took me a good six months to get acclimated to not working, to ironing out the kinks between Ronnie and me and to make up my mind about what I was going to do." Hal sits up straighter in his chair, his narrative directing his posture, making him grow taller and younger before my eyes. "I did go for the photography and I've been loving it. I built myself a darkroom in a basement room the boys used to use, I got myself all the supplies, and I've been shooting away all over Connecticut. The director of our local library saw a few and asked to exhibit them, so that will be nice. Meanwhile, I'm having a hell of a good time."

He breaks into a smile. "Ronnie and I are having a good time, too. Over the past half year, sex has been better than it had been for years. Not a startling difference, but better. I would attribute it mostly to two things—my emotional frame of mind and to all the time we have now. When I was working I'd come home at night and collapse into a glass or two of whiskey and have dinner and then, frankly, be too tired to do anything more than catch up with competing magazines or watch the tube. And Ronnie's not a morning person. So we mostly made love on the weekends, except for vacations.

"Now we have more availability of different times, and we take advantage of that. Not all the time. Ronnie has her commitments and we work around her schedule. But we'll occasionally roll back to bed after breakfast or get together in the late afternoon or plan an evening around a massage and sex. If I'm interested during the day I sometimes feel I'm pulling her away from something she'd rather be doing, but I figured, what the hell, I may as well ask. After all, if we've been married thirty-five years and I look at her in her tennis dress and I get the hots for her, she'll probably be flattered. I asked her about it and she said, yes, she usually did welcome my advances and when she didn't, she would let me know. I can usually tell how interested she is, anyway. When you've lived together all these years you get to read each other's signals, and while she's not as overt about it as I am, I can usually tell when she's in the mood.

"So while there hasn't been a *great* deal of difference in our sex life, what difference there has been is, now, all on the plus side. We're making love about the same number of times—two or three times a week, but spaced out now, not all on the weekends. There's no radical change in the intensity—when I come it feels as great as it always did. That is, when I'm feeling good. It goes in cycles—there were times in our marriage when I didn't feel much desire for my wife or anyone else, when I couldn't get an erection, or when I did come and didn't feel anything at all. Those were always times when something else was giving me grief—my job, my kids, the stock market, whatever.

"Now I've come into calmer water. I feel I've gone through the rapids and I can float a little bit. My life is freer and easier in general. There's less pressure now. I don't have to prove anything in my business life anymore because I'm out of it.

"And now I appreciate the good aspects of my life. I like not having to work. I like knowing that if I want to play golf occasionally, I can go out on the links, and I do, mostly on Wednesdays with a couple of doctor friends. I'm lucky, of course, that I'm in good health, that I have a wife who loves me, and that the money's there for us. I figure we have some good years ahead."

Hal is typical in the flip-flop his feelings took from his anxiety before retirement to his contentment afterward. People who have already retired are almost twice as likely to have good feelings about it as those who are still working. Health doesn't decline after retirement, nor do

257

self-image and satisfaction with life. Furthermore, retirement doesn't bring about radical changes in either marriage or sex life. The Consumers Union retirees and workers showed just about the same rates of marital happiness, and in the Starr-Weiner study, the majority (about 60 percent) felt that sex was the same after retirement, about a quarter felt it was better, and only about 15 percent thought it wasn't as good. The ones who felt sex was better usually pointed to "the quality of relaxation, the lack of pressure and the flexibility of an uncommitted schedule." As one sixty-six-year-old man said, "We do it when we get the urge."

Psychotherapist Tilla Vahanian affirms another aspect of Hal's experience when she says, "A lot depends on how the self-concept of the man is involved with the retirement. If he looks forward to being away from the stress and having more time for pleasure, it may be very nice sexually, but if he interprets retirement as a loss of virility, it's going to have its impact on the sexual scene." Not until Hal changed his perception of retirement as the thief of his manhood and power to seeing it as the bestower of precious benefits could he enjoy his life or his sexuality.

In the past, retirement was generally more of an issue for men. Couples who could afford it usually lived on the husband's income, while the wife devoted herself to house, family, and volunteer activities, or possibly a part-time job. Even women who worked for many years tended to derive their sense of self more from their involvements with other people than from their work. Now, however, with the burgeoning of career orientation among women, two aspects of retirement have changed.

First, there's the reversal of roles in those marriages in which a wife is still very much involved with her career at a time when her husband is winding down in his. He wants to go on more vacations; she wants to take more business trips. He wants to play; she wants to work. He wants to spend more time with her; she wants to put in more time at the office. He feels abandoned; she feels guilty.

Second, the transition in women's work lives has the potential of becoming more of a crisis for more of them. It need not if they reap the benefits of what retirement counselors working with men have found, that those who are happiest have learned how to *be* as well as *do;* have developed an inner core identity rather than seeing themselves only as the personification of their jobs. As gerontologists Starr and Weiner emphasize, ''No one need ever retire—if living a full life is the job.''

Retirement isn't the only event that reorganizes a marriage later in life. A new change that many long-married couples are dealing with is the one brought by the patter of big feet, as they face one of the most unexpected social phenomena of the 1980s—the presence in the parental home of adult children. Today's under-thirty generation is staying home longer than any generation since the first years after World War II. In 1982 and most of 1983, the rate for establishing new homes was the lowest for young people since the 1950s. Young adults in all sorts of situations are either postponing their departure after high school or college graduation or flocking back to Mama and Papa, mostly for financial reasons. They're single adults in their twenties who can't afford their own apartments; divorcees, either with or without children, who come home for a combination of financial and emotional reasons as they get back on their feet; and even married parents of young children who can't afford to buy their own homes without a temporary financial respite.

Some people see this trend as the embodiment of the extended family of days gone by. In truth it does bespeak a renewed harmony between the generations as both generations get to know each other better as adults, free from the spirit of rebelliousness and alienation that characterized the prototypical young adult of the 1960s and '70s. As one twenty-seven-year-old woman says, ''You get to see your parents in a different light. It really is a wonderful time, a transition period that wasn't available before.''

Still, all is not idyllic. This arrangement usually inhibits the freely expressed sexuality of the young adults, who may be called upon to account for their whereabouts, companions, and activities according to family rules that prevailed when they were teenagers. What the young people don't realize is that their presence puts a crimp in their parents' sex lives, too.

After having been married almost thirty years, one couple came to sex therapist Jacqueline R. Hott because the wife had recently had trouble reaching orgasm. Their sexual relationship had been flowering in the ''empty nest'' as they overcame earlier inhibitions. They enjoyed

259

walking around nude, making love whenever they felt like it, crying out during sex. Then their son and daughter, both in their late twenties, came home. And the petals abruptly fell off the bloom of the parents' newly awakened sexuality.

The mother froze. How could she and her husband make love without inhibitions, with the kids home? She mourned the freedom she'd enjoyed and wept at the loss of her all too brief second honeymoon.

''This family had always had the kind of house where the kids could come into their parents' bedroom at any time,'' explains Dr. Hott. ''So it was a tremendous issue when I suggested putting a lock on the door. 'What would the kids say?' this mother asked. We talked about that, and we role-played and rehearsed what the parents could say. Sure enough, they came back the next week to say that the kids had in fact asked their parents, 'What are you doing in there?' And the parents remembered their lines and said, 'We want some privacy.' And that was it. Once this couple realized that they could be good parents without giving up their own rights, they were on their way to solving this problem.''

It's beautiful to see a situation like this, when a few practical words of advice can work a miracle. Unfortunately, not all problems of later life are so amenable to counseling. One particular one seems almost insoluble to many older women.

''I'll never marry again,'' says Bert, an attractive California widow in her late sixties. ''The only men who have shown any interest in me want either a nurse or a purse. And I'm not willing to be either one.'' Many women her age would envy Bert for the fact that she's had the option of saying no. For the stark fact is that the unmarried older woman is the demographic casualty of our times, the one least likely to reap the benefits of the sexual revolution simply because of the thinned ranks of male revolutionaries. Millions of vital, sexually interested older women are not expressing their sexuality because the men they'd like to express it with are not there. They're either dead, ill, or in the arms of a younger woman—or another man. Thus, while divorce or widowhood constitutes a major sexual turning point for anyone, its impact is particularly severe on the woman in her fifties, sixties, or seventies, young enough to have a healthy interest in sex but too old to easily

260

meet and attract an available man. How bad is this situation and how are women coping?

The situation is very bad. For every unmarried man over fifty in the United States there are 2.7 unmarried women. After age sixty-five the ratio is steeper: 3.3 unmarried women for every unmarried man. About half of all women are widowed before they turn fifty-six, setting middle age as the time women most often have to deal with this loss and old age as the time they integrate their widowed status into day-to-day life. More than four out of ten women aged sixty-five to seventy-four and almost seven out of ten women over seventy-five are widowed, compared to only one in ten men aged sixty-five to seventy-four and two in ten men over seventy-five.

Why this disparity? Because of what we all know but usually don't think about until it affects us personally: women live longer than men, so they outlive men of the same age. To aggravate the problem, they usually marry men a few years older than themselves, thus becoming widows even earlier. Women are less likely than men to remarry after their spouses' deaths, partly because there are fewer men their own age or older and the ones who are available are more likely to seek out younger women, while younger men rarely show interest in older women.

Furthermore, as the Consumers Union report points out: "The official figures seriously understate the problem. They take no account of the fact that more unmarried men than women (57 percent versus 33 percent in our sample) are already involved in an ongoing sexual relationship and are therefore unlikely to be available; nor do they take account of the fact that more unmarried men than women (10 percent versus 1 percent in our sample) consider themselves homosexual. If these percentages from our sample are applied to the official data, the ratio that emerges is *more than five unattached heterosexual women over 50 for every unattached heterosexual man over 50.*" (Italics added.)

How are women coping with this imbalance? According to Consumers Union, of 160 unmarried older women in ongoing sexual relationships, 40 percent have taken married men as lovers, 25 percent have taken lovers who are five or more years older than themselves, 29 percent have lovers five or more years younger, and fewer than 1 percent have female lovers. Elena, a formerly heterosexual woman who drifted into an affair with a woman after having been abandoned, first by her husband and then by her male lover, told me, "I trust her more than I've ever trusted anybody. I also feel good about getting old. I somehow find it more attractive to grow old with somebody who has the same body I do."

Some older women become their own partners, meeting their sexual needs through masturbation. Others do the equivalent of "taking a cold shower"—plunge into a round of activities that keeps them so busy they don't have time to think about sex. Some live on their memories. As Marjorie, a sixty-five-year-old fund raiser for a health organization, who'd had two sexually rich marriages and many affairs, told me, "I have so much of the past to think about that there's enough fulfillment that I don't feel lost. A lot of older women are still searching and I'm not. I find myself very comfortable. When I have some free time, I call up my memories, and it's like watching a wonderful movie that's my own life. So that frees me to go on with the work I'm doing."

And some deliberately choose celibacy. Like Nora, they have other interests in their lives that take priority over sex. "It's ironic," she told me. "When I was a teenager and all those juices were flowing and I was dying to be sexual, I was pressured not to be. Now that I'm in a calmer time of life, I feel that society is telling me I *should* be sexual if I want to consider myself alive. But that's just not as important to me right now as some other things—like being independent, learning how to be self-sufficient."

The particular path a woman takes depends on the individual map she has drawn of her life experiences, her personality, her self-esteem, her current situation. While there are some common patterns, each life is, finally, unique. I was fortunate to be able to speak intimately with several women who confided in me about their late-life experiences.

Ruth is now sixty-nine. She had masturbated from at least the age of four, and then went on to a passionate sex life, including premarital sex with two men from the political and artistic Greenwich Village avant-garde who were her friends during the early 1930s. One was the architect who was to be her husband, with whom she enjoyed a rich, fulfilling sexual life for more than forty years, punctuated by two brief affairs with other men.

Ruth's intense brown eyes crinkle up in a smile as she greets me in the sculpture garden of the museum where she volunteers these days as a docent. "Now my life has come full circle," she says. "My husband is sick and we haven't had sex for about six years, and I'm back to masturbating again. Whenever I feel the need for physical release, I don't have to be frustrated. I get just as good an orgasm as I used to get from sex with a man—the sensation is the same, it really is, it's only the process that's different. Of course, the relationship parts of the experience aren't there. But at my age I'm content. I have no shame. I tell all my friends without husbands they should do it, too, and I've taught a number of them to masturbate. I know that a few of them are doing it but are too ashamed to tell me."

Ruth's turning point from sex with a man to solitary sex came six years ago, the first time her husband was ever impotent. That one failure was enough to discourage him from ever making the effort again. As Ruth puts it, "He retired his penis." From an active sex life that had averaged twice a week, she and her husband had precipitously phased down to three times a month and then once a month before they stopped entirely.

"If I had wanted to, I could have pushed, but I didn't want to. My need became less and less. You want to know why? I fell out of love with my own body. Sex is such a narcissistic thing. You've got to like yourself to enter a sexual relationship and you've got to feel sexy to enjoy it. I always loved the way my body felt when I was making love—I would run my hand over myself even when I was with a man, and I would feel good knowing that he could feel such soft silky skin, such beautiful round breasts. But then when I started getting older and saw things happening all over, with my breasts droopy and my pubic hair mostly fallen out, well, I just turned myself off. When I masturbate I can close my eyes and fantasize that I'm the way I used to be, but I couldn't do that when I was with my husband."

Happily, Ruth is not bound by the taboos against masturbation that prevent many older women from achieving this release from sexual tension. Unhappily, she is in the grip of one of the cruelest stereotypes around, that "old women are repulsive." In an angry essay that appeared in *Saturday Review,* Susan Sontag wrote, "[This] is one of the most profound esthetic and erotic feelings in our culture. Women share

263

it as much as men do. A kind of self-hatred infects most women. Like men, they find old age in women 'uglier' than old age in men.''

What objective criteria are there for beauty and desirability? None, of course. Beauty lies in the eyes of the one who is beheld as much as in those of the beholder. How, then, can we know when we are appealing to others? Often, only by the reflection we look for in another's eyes. Because our culture's standards have decreed that women's looks define their sexual desirability more than men's do and that women's aging destroys their sex appeal more than men's does, too many women pay obsessive attention to the way they are seen—or *think* they are seen—by their men.

As Simone de Beauvoir wrote, ''A woman is usually more narcissistic in love than a man; her narcissism is directed at her body as a whole. She has a delightful awareness of her body as something desirable, and this awareness comes to her through her partner's caresses and his gaze. If he goes on desiring her she easily puts up with her body's ageing. But at the first sign of coldness she feels her ugliness in all its horror, she is disgusted with her image and cannot bear to expose her poor person to others. This lack of assurance strengthens her fear of other people's opinions: she knows how censorious they are towards old women who do not play their proper role of serene and passion-free grandmothers.''

How much better if women as well as men could appreciate each other in maturity for the depth and intensity of their feelings and for the sexual skills and knowledge that come from experience, instead of setting up the kind of physical paradigms for passion that only the immature and inexpert can meet!

''It was phenomenal. I've never met a man that I had so much in common with,'' Carol tells me, her voice leaping out of her in exclamation points. ''Ned and I laughed at the same jokes, liked the same music, enjoyed the same word games. He's the first man who's ever been able to take my competitiveness. At the beginning I kept beating him at tennis and Scrabble, too. One day I said, 'I'd better let you start winning or you're not going to come back.' When he said, 'If you let me start winning I won't come back,' I knew I was a goner.

''Everything was perfect between us—everything but our ages. I knew from the start that it couldn't possibly work when I was sixty and he was twenty-eight. After all, he's normal—he wants to get married, he wants to have children, he wants all the things he couldn't possibly have with me. So when he first started making passes at me almost a year ago, I resisted.''

Carol was sensible. She told Ned, whom she had met through a friend of her son's, ''We're good friends, we really like each other, let's leave it at that. Otherwise, we might ruin something really beautiful.'' But Ned wouldn't stop pressing her. One night after she had sent him home, Carol asked herself, ''Are you going to be the 'good girl' who does what she should do, the way you've been all your life? Or are you finally going to do what you want to do? If you don't do it now, when in the world will you?'' She went to the telephone, Ned came over as soon as he put the receiver down, and that was the beginning of what she considers the only real love affair of her life.

''I don't even think I was in love with my husband,'' she tells me as we sit in the casually disordered kitchen of the Phoenix, Arizona, house that she had shared with that husband for most of their twenty-two-year marriage. ''I was more interested in playing house and having babies and the whole routine I'd been led to expect. Once that part of it had lost its bloom, I realized that I was married to a boring man who had practically no interests, no friends, and nothing to give. I gave it all— and still, when he left me, I was a wreck.

''I had been a virgin when we got married, like a dummy, although I'd had plenty of chances not to be. So when sex was a disappointment, I thought it was me—especially since my husband kept telling me how awful I was in bed. Even after he left and I was hopping in and out of bed like crazy and found that I loved sex and was pretty good at it, I was still lonely, because of all the men I met and dated and bedded over five years, I couldn't find any that I could really fall in love with. Until Ned.

''I wouldn't call this whole experience a 'sexual' turning point, because I've had better physical sex with other men—more oral sex, more skillful techniques on their part, more consistent orgasms on mine. But this was a turning point in my ability to love and be loved, and the sex was an important part of it. I had been afraid that sex would ruin a beautiful friendship, but instead the sex brought us closer together, changed the relationship. If sex doesn't bring you together, what's the point of it?

"This is why it hurts so much now, because if it hadn't been so good, I wouldn't know what I was giving up. There's another part of it, too. Now I'm all alone and my chances for finding another man who'll love me the way Ned did are practically nil. And as heartbroken as he is now, I know that this was just a practice run for him, that he'll get over loving me. As much as it hurts, a part of me feels good knowing he'll be able to love someone close to his own age even more for having loved me so much."

Most older people are afraid of the pitfalls of a relationship with someone so many years younger and don't even fantasize about one. When they describe their ideal lovers, both men and women usually depict someone within fifteen years of their own age, and sometimes someone five to ten years older. Very few specify a young age. As one sixty-two-year-old woman told me, "When I'm so happy with a man that I break into song, I want him to be able to recognize the melody I'm humming!" A man of the same age said, "I have friends who can't understand my interest in mature women, but when I'm with a woman twenty years younger than myself, all I want to do is give her fatherly advice—I can't talk to her as an equal."

Still, May-December sexual relationships have been with us throughout history, and they seem to be on the increase. In 411 B.C., Lysistrata said, "When a man gets back . . . though he be gray, he can wed a young girl in a minute, but the season of a woman is very short." They have almost always been and continue to be mostly between older men and younger women. Carol and Ned are extremely unusual—first, in the simple fact that *she* is the older partner, and second, in the great difference between their ages. She is not only old enough to be her lover's mother, she *is* the mother of people older than Ned.

While the end of this affair brought great pain to both Carol and Ned, both knew that it was inevitable—because they had what one group of sociologists describes as a truly "age-discrepant" relationship, one that involves people who are at different life stages. Carol will be retiring from her government job within the next five years; Ned is just beginning his career as a resident in ophthalmology. Carol is a grandmother; Ned has yet to be a father. As several observers of May-

December marriages have argued, they "have the greatest chance of succeeding if they are based primarily on matching the developmental stages of the couple."

We're likely to see an increase in relationships involving people of widely varying ages—although few, probably, in which the difference is as great as the thirty-two-year gap between Carol and Ned. One factor encouraging them is the high rate of divorce. Second marriages or post-marriage affairs are more commonly age-discrepant, partly because more mature people feel less constrained by cultural "shoulds" and "oughts," freer to seek what they think will make them happy. Sometimes people deliberately seek someone considerably older or younger than the first spouse in an effort to create a different kind of relationship.

Such attachments seem more common in the middle and upper-middle classes, again probably because people at these levels are less bound by societal restrictions. Also, the financial stability of the older partner is often a drawing card for the younger. The stereotype of the beautiful younger person attracted to the wealthy older one has a basis in psychological theory. The "equity theory" of relationships states that people feel most comfortable when there's a fair distribution of rewards and costs and that when two people are not equally matched on one trait (like age or attractiveness), they often balance that by an inequality in the other direction on some other characteristic (like wealth or kindness).

While conventional wisdom judges such relationships as "sick, neurotic, gold-digging and doomed to failure," according to sociologist Felix M. Berardo and his colleagues at the University of Florida, there's no hard, scientific evidence that these characteristics are any truer of these ties than of those in which people are closer in age. In fact, they offer a number of advantages. In the older woman–younger man attachment, she benefits by having a partner closer to her level of vigor and less likely to leave her a widow. He benefits by having a more experienced partner who doesn't depend on him to have enough sexual knowledge for both of them and who's more financially independent.

Another factor encouraging the rise of such unions is the increasing liberalization of age norms in our society. We're no longer as rigid in our expectations of people of various ages. As Bernice L. Neugarten

267

has noted, ''It no longer surprises us to hear of a 22-year-old mayor or a 29-year-old university president—or a 35-year-old grandmother or a retiree of 50. No one blinks at a 70-year-old college student or at the 55-year-old man who becomes a father for the first time—or who starts a second family.'' As today's women, freed by both the sexual revolution and the women's movement, have more self-confidence in their ability to attract younger men, they're likely to generate self-fulfilling prophecies. Especially with a generation of younger men who've been subject to the same kinds of cultural shifts in outlook.

Such changes in attitude have, of course, affected people from one end of the life cycle to the other. This is why we increasingly accept sex in the sixties, or the seventies, or the eighties, as not only appropriate but as desirable and why more people in late life are more openly acknowledging their continued sexuality as one of their great joys.

Chapter 12

Stands of Evergreens: The Seventies and Beyond

I always thought sunsets were more spectacular than sunrises, anyway. Now I'm having some beautiful times in the evening of my life.

—DEXTER

"WE GOT MARRIED two years ago, just before my twenty-first birthday," Dexter tells me. Then he corrects himself: "I mean, my *eighty-*first birthday." In that slip of the tongue this lanky, white-haired retired physician foretells what he'll describe in greater detail over the next couple of hours. This two-year-old second marriage is a new beginning for him, a chance for him to know the easy companionship and fulfilling sex that he didn't have during the sixty years of his first marriage. His excitement at having embarked upon this new life, his eagerness to make the most of every minute, lights up the room. As he looks adoringly at Liz, his new wife, he says to me, "I always thought sunsets were more spectacular than sunrises, anyway. Now I'm having some beautiful times in the evening of my life."

While Dexter nursed his first wife, Bea, through her final illness and mourned his lifelong companion, her death was a sexual turning point in opening up the possibility for him to experience his manhood as he never had before. A naïve youth caught up in his studies, he was a virgin when he married at the age of twenty. The first few years of his mar-

269

riage were happy, despite both Dexter's and Bea's near-total sexual ignorance. After the birth of their second child an abrupt change occurred. Even though Dexter had delivered babies himself, it wasn't until he saw Bea's pain during the difficult breech birth of their son that he determined not to be the agent of such agony ever again.

Bea was content to have no more children, but since she wouldn't use a diaphragm or permit him to use condoms, their only safeguard against conception was Dexter's self-control in withdrawing before ejaculation. A pattern soon developed that would script his sexual behavior for the rest of his married life. He would stimulate Bea orally or manually, enter her briefly, and then go into the bathroom to masturbate to orgasm. Eventually, he could no longer achieve an erection, and so he gave up intercourse altogether. He was still able to reach orgasm from masturbation, which he did regularly.

Why did he accept such an unsatisfying sex life? For one thing, he was offended by what he saw as the crudeness of sex. For all his wide reading, he didn't believe that things could be different for a man of his sensibilities married to a "good" woman. And he couldn't conceive of leaving Bea. In the devout, churchgoing home he grew up in, marriage was forever. If you made a mistake, you lived with it. You did not desert your wife and children. Besides, he and Bea had many interests in common. They both played tennis and bridge, enjoyed the theater and concerts, shared a love of music and art. What they could not *be to* each other, they *did with* each other. And so it wasn't until Bea died that Dexter visited a therapist to learn how to enjoy sex.

Liz had had her own sexual problems in her first marriage. She, however, acted on them far sooner than Dexter did. Though hardly precipitously. Feeling she had to fulfill her obligations to her children, she waited until her youngest child left for college. "So many of us go through life without being fully aware of what it means to have a good sexual life," she tells me in a brisk, cheerful voice that sounds as if it belongs to a much younger woman. I'm astounded to learn that she is seventy-nine. She doesn't sound her age; she doesn't look it; she doesn't act it. Slightly rounded and womanly in her navy slacks and co-ordinated print blouse, she moves quickly and energetically, speaks expressively, laughs infectiously. Nothing about her is old except her years.

"I was married and had had three children and two abortions, and I still didn't know what a good sex life was. But I was sure I could have one if I only made the effort, and I was determined to try." So after twenty-five years with her first husband, who had been a premature ejaculator all his adult life, Liz told him, "I can't live like this anymore," and went into therapy. The marriage didn't survive her newfound strength and self-knowledge. She married again, a union that was satisfying sexually and emotionally for the next twenty-five years until her second husband died.

Two years ago Liz and Dexter met at a folk dance for older adults at a community center in the Kansas City suburb where they were both living. "Why don't you bring your wife to the next dance?" Liz asked him. When he said, "My wife passed away," she stored that knowledge, relieved to know that if she did develop a friendship with him, she wouldn't repeat an experience she'd had several times, when men had expressed interest in her, taken her home, and then shown up later with their wives. Liz and Dexter did meet again, enjoyed lively conversations about books, movies, art, politics, and began to see each other often.

Their encounters soon escalated physically, which presented Liz with some new experiences. "The first time we had any sexual contact, Dexter came to my apartment, we both had a couple of drinks and were a little high. We kissed and hugged and I fondled his penis through his clothes. No one had ever done that for him before, and he called me up the next day to thank me for such a beautiful evening.

"When we started to make love, he manipulated me orally and with his finger, which no one had ever done before for me. I knew about those things, but only as foreplay. I like them, but I prefer regular sex—intercourse—and I couldn't understand why Dexter wasn't interested in that. When he would leave me and go into the bathroom, I'd wonder, 'What in the world is he doing in there for such a long time?' But I didn't let this bother me. Sex has been an important part of my life but not the only part, and we had such a good relationship in other ways that I wasn't complaining."

Dexter had just begun to see a new therapist, since the psychiatrist he had first spoken to had, he felt, brushed off his impotence as an inevitable part of the aging process, a judgment he fortunately refused to ac-

271

cept. When his new therapist asked whether he'd like to invite Liz to come with him and she agreed, they were on their way to a satisfying life together.

"I was sure Dexter didn't have a physical problem, and as it turned out, he doesn't," Liz tells me, smiling as she looks over and catches his eye, eliciting a smile in return. "Sure enough, he achieved penetration for the first time in about forty years. It's had marvelous consequences for him. I'm so happy for him—especially since he told me he's functioning better now at the age of eighty-three than he ever has in his whole life.

"Overall, this is the most well-rounded relationship I've ever had, even in my good second marriage. Dexter and I are intellectual equals—we can talk about anything—and he has a wonderful sense of humor and we have a lot of laughs together. I always say, 'If you can laugh in bed, you're okay, kid.'" She laughs heartily herself, then lowers her voice when Dexter gets up to answer the phone.

"Even though I don't have orgasms most of the time, I'm still happy because we're having such a good time together. When I really feel I need to have an orgasm I use this vibrator that I originally got for my stiff neck. But I don't tell Dexter because I don't want him to feel inadequate. I wouldn't hurt his feelings for anything. I feel we're fortunate that we've reached this point in being able to enjoy our life together, and I think our story shows that it's never too late to find love and sex."

Liz's words—"it's never too late to find love and sex"—should be emblazoned in the minds of every old person, every friend or relative of an old person, every professional person who works with old people. For all too often, stereotypes about old people prevail. Two common ones are that old people *are* sexless and that they *should* be sexless. It has been only fairly recently that researchers studying sexuality in old age have found that sex can be a vital force throughout life. All the surveys of sexuality in old age report that many people continue to be sexually active well into their eighties.

While the testimony mounts that many elderly people are enjoying sex enormously, their experience of it *is* different from what it was earlier in life. By and large, the older people get, the less sexual urgency they feel, the longer it takes them to become aroused, and the less frequently they have intercourse. Some experience a diminution in the intensity of sexual arousal, while for others this intensity endures.

The differences brought by age are particularly evident in men, as changes first noticed in middle age become more marked. As the years go on, it usually takes an even longer time to develop an erection, with direct stimulation of the penis usually required, as opposed to earlier years when the sight of a woman's body or the anticipation of making love could produce a spontaneous erection. Ejaculation is generally delayed even longer, and some older men don't ejaculate at all. Those who do are less conscious of the two stages—the first stage of ejaculatory inevitability and actual ejaculation itself; they tend to blend together into a single sensation. The orgasm is usually briefer and sometimes less intense. The refractory period lengthens, so that it takes a longer time to achieve an erection again after ejaculation. Thus, men who no longer ejaculate can often retain their erections longer than those who do.

Women also experience changes in sexual response. Their breasts don't increase as much in size, their nipples don't become erect as quickly (if at all), the clitoris and labia don't become so engorged, their skin doesn't become so flushed and their vaginas don't become lubricated as quickly or as much and don't expand as much in size. These changes, however, occur in middle age and then remain fairly stable through old age. The elderly of both sexes experience less muscle tension and weaker orgasmic contractions.

Still, most older women and many older men continue to reach orgasm. The female orgasm is remarkably durable throughout the life span, both in frequency and intensity. Women and men who have been sexually active over the years seem to be more active late in life than their peers, affirming the saying "Use it or lose it." While some people report achieving good functioning after long sexual droughts, regular sexual activity tends to be self-perpetuating and an important aid to good sex in old age.

The Consumers Union survey found a decade-by-decade decline in the frequency of male orgasm: 92 percent of men in their fifties reach orgasm every time or almost every time with a partner, as compared to 85 percent of men in their sixties and 70 percent of those aged seventy and older. The figures are comparable for reaching orgasm through

273

masturbation. Still, when we consider that seven out of ten sexually active men over seventy almost always have an orgasm, we can see why so many older men give such glowing reports about their sex lives.

The decade-by-decade changes in female orgasm during sex with a partner are also consistent, showing that the proportion of women who seldom or never experience orgasm with a partner rises from 19 percent of women in their fifties, to 22 percent in the sixties, to 28 percent of women over seventy (put another way, 72 percent of women over seventy with a partner are still orgasmic with that partner). Orgasm during masturbation shows a modest decline—from 83 percent almost every time, to 79 percent, to 74 percent.

Older women's higher rates of orgasm from masturbation may indicate that they may not be experiencing the highest level of sexual ecstasy with partners because they take—or keep—the ones they can get, whether or not they're sexually compatible. It may also reflect the fact that throughout life, many women climax more reliably and more intensely from self-stimulation than from sexual activity with a partner.

Past age seventy, married men and women are at about the same level of sexual activity, but unmarried men are much more active than unmarried women, probably because it's easier for them to find someone to be active with. It's ironic that women, who are likely to remain at almost the same orgasmic level as in earlier years, are blocked off from expressing their sexuality with a partner, while men are doing it more even though they're apt to be enjoying it less than they used to.

By and large, then, the overall sexual activity of old age is neither as intense nor as frequent as it was earlier in life. Still, about three-quarters of the sixty- to ninety-one-year-olds in the Starr and Weiner study said that sex was as good or better now than it ever was, and 95 percent of the happily married fifty- to ninety-three-year-olds in the Consumers Union study reported high enjoyment of sex with their spouses. Why do so many individuals speak in such glowing terms about an activity that by most objective standards should be less satisfying? Apparently because most of these people embrace a broad concept of sexuality.

The man or woman who isn't wedded to the conviction that more is necessarily better and who values quality over quantity will be able to take delight in fewer and better sexual contacts. And the person who doesn't define satisfaction by the vigor of an erection but by the sensuality in a wide range of activities will be able to know sexual rapture as long as she or he lives. The less goal-directed and the more flexible people are, the more they're apt to relish sex. People who think pleasuring is more important than penetration give themselves many more options than those who define sex only as the insertion of penis into vagina.

Many elderly people enjoy being physically close to those they love, even though such closeness does not involve either intercourse or arousal to orgasm. As one seventy-two-year-old husband wrote to Consumers Union, "When actual sex copulation ceases in old age, sexual feelings do not cease. Kissing, fondling, touching are also expressions of sex and there's always the delight and joy of watching the young and admiring beauty. . . . I'm gradually becoming impotent so [intercourse] is not important to me any longer. Like Socrates in the *Republic,* it's a relief to lose the burden of sexuality in its virulent form."

The way a couple deal with the man's impotence is crucial. Many give up sexual activities altogether, like the sixty-seven-year-old woman who wrote, "My husband has been impotent for fifteen years, so we do nothing." Older women become sexually inactive a decade earlier than men do, usually because of partner-related reasons. "Looked at this way, impotence is not only a male problem," write Starr and Weiner. Still, impotence need not signal an end to either male or female sexuality. Many couples who are unable to have intercourse either because the man is impotent or for other reasons still express their sexuality through mutual masturbation or oral sex. Others who don't feel the need for arousal or orgasm continue to enjoy the closeness, tenderness, and warmth that can come from simply kissing, stroking, and cuddling.

When we realize that sex isn't something we do or have but is an intrinsic part of our very natures, we are set free from the notion that we have to express our sexuality in certain circumscribed ways with certain partners in certain circumstances.

The topic of the television show was "Sex and the Elderly." The host: Phil Donahue. The panel: several men and women in their seventies and eighties. The audience: mostly middle-aged women. After the panelists talk about their own sexual experiences, including both short-

and long-term relationships between unmarried people, Donahue asks the audience how they would feel about their own parents becoming involved in such relationships. One middle-aged woman takes the microphone to say vehemently, "I wouldn't give my parents a choice to do something like that. I love them both very much. I wouldn't approve of their having sex if they were unmarried. My mother raised me the right way, so I owe it to her to discourage her from getting into anything like that."

To this, seventy-eight-year-old panelist Cora Cocks says, "In my family I don't give advice. I don't run my kids' lives and they don't run mine. I don't want to be married again for anything. I was very happy in my marriage, but now I'm at a point where I don't want anyone to tell me what to do. The worst thing about being old isn't living with someone you're not married to—the worst thing is being lonely. When you're alone, you know what you miss—you miss getting touched. Nobody touches old people. Instead of telling old people how they should live their lives, touch them when you can. Put your arm around them."

While the righteous moralizing expressed by the middle-aged woman quoted above seemed to be a minority point of view in this Chicago audience, many adult children do put up roadblocks to their elderly parents' sexual involvements. Sometimes because of feelings of loyalty to the dead or divorced other parent, sometimes because of their own emotional conflicts, and sometimes from the mercenary fear that they'll lose some of their inheritance. The way an older person deals with this opposition will have a strong impact on the quality of that person's life.

This issue came up with Dexter and Liz. Liz's children were happy she found someone to care for, and they urged her to accompany Dexter to his Fort Lauderdale apartment when he invited her down for the winter. Dexter's daughter, however, aged fifty-eight, warned him against predatory women and, as he says, "was teaching me as to how my conduct should be."

"She was apprehensive," he says, with the gravelly edge to his voice that often comes with old age, "and sparks and sharp words flew between Liz and my daughter. So I told my daughter, 'Flossie, don't get me involved in this. I am too happy. Liz has made life beautiful for me and I'm not going to let anything disturb this life. I will not take sides, and I will not hurt my relationship with her. Whatever displeasures you have between you, you will have to iron it out yourselves.' ''

"I like the fact that he didn't try to defend me, because I feel capable of defending myself, but that he did stand up to his daughter when he felt she might be hurting his life," says Liz. "Flossie said a lot of hurtful things—that there was a power struggle between the two of us over her father and that I was trying to manipulate both of them. I'm the last person to try to manipulate anybody. But I understand that that girl really has a problem, not wanting to let go of her father, especially since her own marriage fell apart, and I can live with the situation now. I know Dexter isn't going to give up what he wants just because she tells him to. I think the way he handled this situation had a very good effect on our relationship, and I felt proud of him for it."

As I spoke with people over the age of forty, I was impressed by the number of stories I heard of people seeking out and getting back together with lovers of bygone years. Such a reunion was always a significant turning point in both people's lives. Despite the common-sense mathematics that states there's no one perfect match for any one person, apparently a sizable number of people found something so special in a previous lover that they were impelled to go back and seek out that person, to rekindle the spark that had ignited a flame so many years before. So I wasn't surprised when the Consumer Reports researchers found the same pattern cropping up often enough among their respondents to remark upon it—and to offer it as practical advice to the older woman looking for a new sexual partner.

This worked in reverse for Donald and Mae. According to Donald, seventy-two, a stocky man of medium height with short, spiky gray hair, who pounds the coffee table in the living room of his modest row house to emphasize his points, "Mae and I are having a helluva good time. It's goddamned lucky. *[pound]* As far as my sex life, I can't complain worth a nickel. It's the book of records. *[pound]* Now there aren't many women of seventy-seven who enjoy a man—and there aren't too many women of seventy-seven who can get a man. So that works to both our advantages. *[pound]* In the meantime, our sex life is unbelievable. It's better than it ever was when she was twenty-five and I was twenty and lost my virginity to her." *[pound]*

Fifty-two years ago Donald and Mae met in the college town where he was a student and she was a secretary. Although she had been to bed with one man before him, she loved only Donald. Still, neither thought about marrying the other. After having been sexually molested as a little girl by her grandfather (as described in Chapter 2), Mae went through life feeling contaminated, unworthy of marriage. Donald did want to get married, but not to Mae. He saw too many differences between them. He was a brilliant student preparing for a career as a physicist; she shared few of his interests and could not keep up with his quick mind. He did everything rapidly; she would not be hurried. His quick temper frightened her; her placidity irritated him.

Mae's heart broke when Donald told her he was going to marry someone else. "I never thought he'd get married," she tells me, when we speak the day after my meeting with Donald. She shakes her head at the memory. "That idea never entered my mind. I thought we'd continue as we were the rest of our lives. I should have known better. I went into a terrible state. I used to walk across the street and not look, so a car would hit me. How I managed to stay alive I'll never know."

Mae did stay alive. She worked as office manager of a small manufacturing plant in the Pennsylvania coal town where she moved back to live with her widowed mother. She never married. She took only one other lover, and after his death in an industrial accident she remained celibate. Until Donald came back on the scene. In 1965, after thirty years of a close but quarrelsome marriage, Donald's wife died. She died on a Thursday; on Saturday Mae received the news in a letter from Donald. She phoned him, he came to visit, and they picked up sexually where they had left off thirty years earlier. Until he told her again he was going to marry someone else. On the morning of Mae's birthday in 1973, Donald called to tell her that, after six years of marriage, his second wife had died. Again, they picked up where they had left off. And have been seeing each other regularly ever since.

"I'm not looking to get married again," Donald tells me. "I think I'm too goddamned old to look. Mae thinks it's a wonderful arrangement the way it is. I go out to Pennsylvania to see her for a few days, or else she comes down here to Baltimore and stays with me for a week or two. Then we're apart for a couple of weeks or so and then we get back together again. That's perfect, because we're always battling. I have very little tolerance for fools and she does some pretty stupid things. So

278

I lose my temper and she says, 'I'm never going to see you again. Don't call me.' But then that blows over. When we're in bed we never fight. I never criticize her there about what she's doing because she does everything right. She wrote the book.

"We're having more fun than we ever had. My kids are out of the house, so we have it all to ourselves. We had to go in a car when we were young, and we had to be home at a certain time. Now we can get up any time we feel like it, go to bed any time. There are advantages at our extreme old age. She's got no responsibilities, we're both retired. We both have enough money to go where we want. We take trips. We have nobody to tie us down. I tell her she's better than a girl of seventeen. She's multi-orgasmic. I call her 'Two-a-Minute McGuire.' Which is what it is. Last week during one forty-five minute session, she had 103 orgasms. Now *that's* unusual. *[pound]*

"We just use the missionary position. She has arthritis and isn't agile anymore, so that's the only thing she can do. It doesn't bother me at all. I keep a little calendar just for the hell of it, because after a while I realized this was really running up a terrific record."

Donald reaches into the hip pocket of his trousers and pulls out a small notebook. He flips through till he finds the page he's seeking and reports a total of forty sexual encounters and an astounding total of 2,073 orgasms for Mae during a recent month-long trip. I remember what the noted interviewer for the Kinsey reports, Dr. Wardell B. Pomeroy, told me was the key to interviewing people about their sexuality: "Never appear surprised. Never seem shocked." And so even though Donald's count seems impossibly inflated to me, I don't question him. If Mae perceives each of these moments as an orgasm, who am I to dispute her word? I quietly go on to ask Donald about his own orgasms.

"I don't have them anymore," he says matter-of-factly. "It stopped about a year ago. That's why I can keep up for forty-five minutes and have intercourse two to five times a day when Mae is with me. When you think about it, there's two sides to it.

"I'm perfectly happy because I can feel her orgasms and I know she's enjoying it. I enjoy the closeness. I always touch her. I'm always touching people—I like a lot of physical affection, and she gives it to me. She also gives me instant feedback. The best thing is whatever I do, she says, 'Oh, that's *nice.*' Now some people won't say 'Boo!' They might *think* it's nice, but they wouldn't think it was ladylike to say so. Well, she's not that way at all. And I think that's great.''

Donald's delight in Mae's expressions of pleasure was a theme I heard often from people of every age, especially when I asked for a description of an ideal sexual partner. In bed, as in so many other avenues of life, we need feedback, we thrive on responsiveness. When we know that our partner loves being with us, we feel powerful. When we know that our partner loves what we do, we are inspired to do it more often and better.

The tendency of old people to talk about their past—people they once loved or hated, events that once mattered so much, emotions that were once so intense—is often ridiculed or ignored as an irrelevancy, a sign that memory for recent events is fading, a wish to bring back the lost years of youth. Yet psychiatrist Robert N. Butler, former director of the National Institute on Aging and now professor of geriatrics and adult development at Mount Sinai Medical School in New York, maintains that such reminiscences are an essential part of a normal life review process. By going over their lives mentally, people often deal with conflicts that they didn't resolve earlier and give new significance and meaning to their lives. They can expiate guilt they may have carried for years, become reconciled with estranged family or friends, and express their views to younger people who will then be able to carry on their values. The sense of completion felt after accomplishing these tasks can be a comfort as they round out the time that still remains to them. Thus the old can prepare themselves to face their own death, freer from the fears that had gripped them earlier.

While few people openly review their sexual histories as such, more would benefit from doing so. From time to time someone who had heard about my work on this book and the interviews I was conducting would ask with much bewilderment, ''Why would anyone *want* to talk about their sexual experiences? Are these people exhibitionists?'' While I don't pretend to know all the complexities that motivate people, some of the reasons behind the willingness to come forward emerged during the interviews as my informants expressed them in their own words.

Some people are so happy, proud, and fulfilled in their sexual experiences that they want to share them, but for reasons of propriety or modesty are usually reticent. Guaranteed confidentiality, they welcome the opportunity to discuss the loves of their lives with someone they're not likely to bump into socially. Laurence, an urbane sixty-five-year-old publishing executive, regaled me with stories about people and events that had been major sexual influences in his life, harking back to the years of World War II when he had been an army lieutenant stationed in Europe. Among the insights engendered by these experiences, for example, was a completely altered view of female sexuality.

"This was the first time in my life that I realized—really realized—that women wanted sex and enjoyed sex just as much as men did," Laurence told me. "Getting to know some of these European women helped me become more honest about my own sexual needs and more understanding of women's. From that time on, I looked at women in a very different way." After our two-hour lunch at one of Manhattan's literary watering places, Laurence said, "I've had a wonderful time talking about all of this. Who else would listen to me tell stories about things that happened almost forty years ago?"

Others have been troubled about one or another aspect of their sexual lives, and as they talk they sometimes get a new perception of themselves that they find helpful in resolving problems. "I jumped at the chance to talk to you," Steven told me as he was talking about his life, especially with regard to the changes that contracting genital herpes had brought. "I don't particularly like the stage my life is in. I have never felt so stuck, and I thought that talking about where I am might help me get my thoughts in order."

A number of interviewees told me how satisfying they found it to structure their thinking about their sexual attitudes and activities, to probe for the influences in their lives that affected their sexuality, to focus on those events and experiences that served as turning points in their sexual development. "I've never thought about these things in quite this way before" has been a common refrain.

Such focusing can be especially valuable for the elderly, to put this aspect of their lives in perspective, along with their feelings about their relationships, their achievements, their place in history. Providing a forum for older people to acknowledge their sexuality may well be a more valuable service than teaching them how to glaze pottery, write poetry, or do many of the other activities commonly encouraged at senior citizens centers.

Eva, seventy-five, offers me this kind of sexual life review when we speak in her home, just outside of Albuquerque. When I had called her the day before, at the suggestion of a colleague of mine who's a friend of hers, Eva told me that she didn't know whether she'd be able to meet with me today, because these are difficult days for her. She's receiving chemotherapy for leukemia, which leaves her feeling weak and sick. Today she is having new carpeting installed in her home. Perhaps the excitement will be too much. Perhaps we can meet next week. When she learns that I have to leave Albuquerque tomorrow night, she says, "Well, then, call me in the morning." When I do, she asks me to call later in the day, in the hopes that she'll be feeling strong enough to see me in the evening. When I call again, she says, "Come right over."

I'm surprised, then, to be greeted at the front door by a woman who looks surprisingly healthy and vigorous in her deep-red jogging suit, one more splash of bright color in a home that is a paean to the Southwest. Before we sit down to talk, I take her up on her offer to show me around, since my interest was whetted by the lush profusion of cactus plants welcoming visitors to her front door and then heightened by the abundance of art on every plane.

The house is full of Eva's work. Her paintings cover the walls. Clay sculptures, many of them family groupings (molded by this woman who has lived alone for many years, even while she was married, and who never had nor wanted children), dot the furniture and floor. Smiling as she points out various items, she shows her zest for her life and her pride in her work.

As we walk back into the living room, Eva apologizes: "I hope this will be worth your while. I don't know what I can give you, because sex is not the major thing in my life." She sweeps the room with her hand. "This is—my work. My plants. My home. But let's see whether I can tell you anything. You just ask me your questions."

For a woman to whom sex has not been "that important," Eva has lived a celebration of sex, from an inauspicious beginning when she was seventeen to a richly passionate series of encounters up to the present. "My first sexual experience was horrible." She shakes her head at the memory. "My sister was marrying a man I was in love with—or thought I was in love with. I was terribly jealous, so I had made up my mind that when she has her wedding night I would rid myself of my virginity. I wanted to have love that night. I picked out a sculptor who was very strong and very marvelous and I liked his work. And all what I felt was pain. It was not done on romance, it was done out of madness. I didn't really feel anything."

A few days later, Eva became what she calls "the first hippie in Europe." While her parents were out of town, she emptied out the bank account that held her dowry, ran away from Vienna to Paris, and became a stage designer. She fell in with the avant-garde of the theatrical world, seeking out men who would be leaving town within days.

"I had been brought up to believe that sex is something you shouldn't do, so I couldn't let loose. But if I knew I would never see the guy again, I figured the heck with it, tomorrow he's in Africa, so tonight I can let myself go. There was a wildness in me. I was a specialist at biting, which I did because I was always mad. I always wanted to say, 'I'm the stronger one.' It was not until I was over forty that I had my first orgasm. It was in a very romantic setting, and I really awoke then as a woman and wanted more from sex and from men."

What Eva attributes to "normal maturity" mellowed her, made her kinder and softer. "I had already enough experience to get the wildness out of me, the wildness that was really fighting sex." Only then was Eva able to develop close relationships with the men she went to bed with. And although sex was an integral part of these relationships, she says to me more than once, "I see now that sex is not that important to me, because it's very hard for me to answer these questions. I can say that I had some wonderful men, that there was especially one or two in my life which I loved and they loved me. But I wouldn't say that the sex part was overbearing. Sex is only for me a little part of all the wonderful things we are doing in life. I think when we went outside together and photographed and painted and walked, it was just as beautiful as when we were in bed. So I can't separate it. And I don't think I was ever oversexed."

Eva's marriage was a union not of passionate lovers but of good friends. "The best friend I ever had until he died twelve years ago," she says of Will, whom she married when she was twenty-seven. After he proposed by mail—he had become an American citizen and she was still in Europe—she wrote him a long letter telling him that she liked him very much but did not return his love. When Will repeated his offer of marriage, which would enable her to immigrate to the United States, she accepted.

"My husband was a brilliant and wonderful guy, and it was a fabulous adventure being married to him. I think it was on a higher standard than most marriages. He was living in Washington and I was living in New York and we only saw each other every once in a while, but when we did it was marvelous. But I wouldn't say I took it that serious that I didn't think of going to the left or to the right. And he didn't mind it, either. We never talked about it. See, I am a very free spirit all my life. I do exactly as I want, and that has helped me over many frustrations."

While Eva and Will were well matched intellectually, they were not in close sexual harmony. "He was a scientist, and his approach to love was a little too scientific for my taste," Eva says. "I was rather passionate and liked to be all caught up in whatever I was doing at the time without thinking of anything else, but he would plan things, say, to do the whole thing starting at seven thirty and stopping at eight fifteen so he could listen to a scientific radio program. So that wasn't my style and we never clicked in that direction. But we clicked as human people, and I would say he was the finest person I have ever met."

Sex with a man she admires has been Eva's greatest relaxation. During those periods when she was immersed in a burst of intense creativity, she would think of sex as an interruption and would not want to take the time or the energy away from her work. But when she had finished a group of pictures or a sculpture or fabric design, she would celebrate by pouring her energies into an intense sexual relationship.

"I was never interested in sex for sex," she says, waving her arm in the air to dismiss all those poor benighted souls who are content with little. "If I couldn't talk to the man afterwards, he can go in the ashcan. I don't believe in the sex-and-goodbye. It has to be with somebody you can laugh with, you can discuss with, you can cry with. And then sex is an explosion, it's beautiful. And you feel respect and you feel much better and you work much better. I have to be with a man I respect. He has to be intelligent, witty, and sensitive. If he has a little bit of brain and a certain sense of humor and a sense of timing, then the technique comes automatically. You don't have to go to a school to learn it. You know. You know each other and respect each other and you know what the other person needs.

"I am a very lucky person. I attract a certain type of person, a give-and-take type of person. All right, it's not pure luck. I think if you give enough, then the other person will give, too. This is true for when I give to another sick person—and then when I am sick, that person will give to me. And I think that is connected the same as sex. If you give a little more than you take, just a little more, then you are going to be happy. Then you win!

"Still, with the kindness, you need to keep some wildness, too. You have to be able, in sex, to be a little wild animal and let go. Forget you had any bit of makeup on you, that your hair looked a certain way. For me, I would like to take an oil bath and make sex in that. You know, get oily together and not worry about it. I think someday I will still get to do that. Because even though I'm seventy-five and I'm sick I think I can go on and have a sex life, every once in a while, until I'm eighty. Or maybe eighty-five. I don't see anything bad about getting older. I think it's fascinating. I was very pretty a long time ago and I don't have that anymore. But I have things to make up for that. I have changed my whole lookout on life, and I have more young friends now than I ever had. I understand them better than their own parents do. If I didn't have all those years behind me, I wouldn't be who I am now."

"Whenever I felt like having somebody I was lucky, I had somebody. And if I didn't, I pushed my luck and found somebody. Like, I just ended a relationship with a thirty-eight-year-old man, a handsome, brilliant scientist. He is my style, the personality I like—my husband was a scientist, too. If I have somebody who's very calm and logical thinking, it excites me. Because I'm just the opposite. I'm buzzing all over the place. And these calm guys, they seem to like that. So there was a clicking here with this man and our ages were never discussed.

285

And we went together quite a bit. But then I just decided, as much as I like him, it has to stop, because one of these days—you see, I'm now very old and tired and it hurts me here and it hurts me there, and then he suddenly will wake up and say, 'Eh, she's an old crow and I don't want that.' So now he remembers it's wonderful between us.

"It was a little painful to break it off, but I don't spend time thinking about the past. I think about tomorrow. I just had this carpeting installed—" Eva points to the carpeting, the color of desert sand, the perfect backdrop for the vivid splashes of color all about. "And I bought forty yards of watercolor paper because I have a series I want to do. I switched from oils to watercolors, because they take less strength. And then I just bought some Christmas wrappings on sale, to be ready for next year, so I intend to live next year. And I just met a man about my age who I thought would be good to get to know better, so I called him up and he's coming over for coffee tomorrow."

Eva does not look like an aging sex kitten, like a woman who would be either interested in or attractive to a man almost forty years her junior. Her short gray hair is unstyled, simply cut. Her nails are blunt cut, unpolished, short. Her face is bare of any cosmetics other than a light touch of color on her lips. In this way Eva is like the other sexually active women over fifty whom I've spoken to. They accept themselves for the women they are today, which bespeaks a comfortable sense of self-esteem. None of these women—not Eva, not Liz, not Mae, not Nora—tries to call up earlier days through elaborate makeup, trendy hair coloring or styling, artful corseting, youthful styles of dress.

For these women, their sexuality is neither the central focus of their lives nor a badge that's been imposed on them by outside forces, by advertising and media pressures that try to tell women how they should look, how they should be. Nor is it something they feel obliged to cast out in the later decades of their lives. Instead, they, like millions of other women and men, wear their sexuality easily as an inner force that informs the way they think, the way they feel, the way they act in all the corners of their lives.

The men and women profiled in this chapter are not typical of most of their contemporaries. Still, the fact that they are unrepresentative is less important than the fact that they represent possibilities. We need to remember that in the realm of sexuality, no one is "typical." Everyone is unique. The direction any individual's sexual path will take depends on a unique combination of genetic disposition and the combined influences of specific people and events. The possibilities exemplified in these five lives—the sexual awakening of a man in his eighties, the new-found love of a woman almost eighty, the frenetically active liaison between a man and a woman both in their seventies, the continuing sexual appeal that a seventy-five-year-old woman holds for men (including at least one much younger than herself)—all indicate that the sexual palette of late life holds many hues that can be painted into a gallery of living masterworks.

The sexual force can remain in the soul as long as there is breath, as long as there is life. Even though one may choose, at various times in one's life, to invest this sexual energy in work or in nonsexual relationships or in play, it is still there. Even when the day comes when the flesh is uninterested in carrying out the sexual imperatives of earlier days, that force remains. Even if, in illness or in late life, most of one's sexual expression takes the form of reminiscing about the past, sexual vigor bubbles under the surface, fueling the surge of memories and infusing the psyche with remembered joys. This is why we need never stop being sexual beings, no matter how much or how little we express our sexuality in actions or in words. This is why we can continue to draw strength from the vitality that flows from our sexuality throughout all our years on this earth.

Notes

SOME READERS MAY want to delve further into a particular topic or to take issue with some of my statements. The following notes, which document references to research findings, quotations, and theories referred to throughout this book, should help either of these efforts. The citations are keyed to the pages on which the referred-to statements appear. Whenever a quotation is not referenced in these notes, it means that the statement was voiced during a personal interview with me. When an observation or conclusion is not referenced, this indicates that it is attributable to me. Complete publishing information is in the Bibliography.

Introduction

p. 5 Sigmund Freud: Although I refer to Freud's concepts in several places, I barely scratched the surface of his complex theories on sexual development. The papers and lectures that explain his theories in detail can be found in the collection listed in the Bibliography. A good one-chapter summary is given in Hall and Lindzey's *Theories of Personality,* and a briefer summary is given in Papalia and Olds's *Psychology.* Erik H. Erikson: The basic outline of his eight crises in development can be found in *Childhood and Society*.

p. 6 Descriptions of these and other studies of adult development can be found in *Human Development* by Papalia and Olds, in *Passages* by Sheehy, and in the Gould, Levinson, and Vaillant works cited in the Bibliography.

Chapter 1: Sowing and Gleaning

p. 25 The Reverend Stayton spoke on "Advances in Sexology" before the annual conference of the Eastern Region of the Society for the Scientific Study of Sex (SSSS) in Philadelphia on April 16, 1982. Dr. Calderone made these points in an article in the January 1982 issue of *SIECUS Report*.

Chapter 2: The Sensual Seedling

p. 30 A woodcut showing the Christ Child's grandmother fondling his penis is reproduced in Steinberg's book. Calderone's article, "Fetal Erection and Its Message to Us," is illustrated by a photograph of a fetal erection.

pp. 30–31 "No one has made systematic, direct observations . . ." J. S. Hyde, *Understanding Human Sexuality*, p. 257.

p. 33 Calderone and Johnson, p. 262.

p. 34 Among the works that deal with this controversy are Masson's book and Triblich's and Klein's paper.

p. 35 Spitz's work is still classic.

pp. 36–37 Simon's book recommends a number of touching exercises to be done within the family. Schneider's book, *Infant Massage,* focuses on the baby. Prescott, p. 65.

p. 37 The finding about deprivation of physical affection during childhood is in Steele and Pollock. Steele's statement about the sex lives of abusing parents is cited by Prescott.

pp. 37–38 During the 1970s the American Academy issued several statements favoring breastfeeding, following the lead of the mothers who were putting more pressure on their doctors to help them succeed in this skill. As documented by Martinez and Dodd, 1971 marked a turning point for

American women, when the decline in breastfeeding rates was reversed. The latest figures, as reported by *The New York Times* (1984a), indicate that for the first time in years more American women are nursing their newborns than giving them bottles.

p. 39 Gadpaille's book about sexual development throughout the life span is especially informative about the early years of childhood and adolescence. While he offers standard psychoanalytic viewpoints and a traditional view of male and female roles within the family, his commonsense approach puts theories and facts into perspective. This quote is on p. 58. On p. 75 he cites a 1949 paper by René Spitz on the prevalence of masturbation among well-cared-for infants.

p. 40 Kinsey's books on the sexuality of women and men are still the most extensive sources of information on sexual behavior. The "Cleveland study" of parental attitudes and practices toward sex (Roberts) is one of the studies that have found that parents find masturbation harder to talk about or deal with than anything else of a sexual nature.

p. 41 Gadpaille, p. 75. The follow-up of O'Connor's workshop participants is reported by Kuriansky, Sharpe, and O'Connor.

p. 42 Some of Dr. Calderone's suggestions are elaborated in Calderone and Ramey.

p. 43 Zilbergeld, *Male Sexuality.*

pp. 45–46 Psychiatric second thoughts about parental nudity were reported in *Medical Aspects of Human Sexuality.* Gadpaille's statement is on p. 101.

pp. 46–47 During 1979 and 1980, Richard B. Hartley, professor of psychology at the University of Puget Sound in Tacoma, Washington, collected some 250 sexual autobiographies from students in his classes in human sexuality. The anonymity of all the writers was preserved, giving the students the freedom to be honest. Dr. Hartley graciously allowed me access to these autobiographies, which, at his request, I will send on to the Kinsey Institute for Sex Research in Bloomington, Indiana. The autobiographies have been a valuable resource for all chapters up through the twenties. Borneman's research underlying his concept of pubertal amnesia was presented to the 6th World Congress of the World Association of Sexology in 1983 and was reported in *Sexuality Today.*

p. 49 These findings on girls' ignorance about their own body parts are summarized by Pogrebin (1980) in the excellent chapter "Nonsexist Sexuality."

pp. 52–53 Figures on the prevalence of incest are cited in a paper issued by the American Psychological Association, and in Collins, 1982. Some views of those who maintain that children sometimes benefit from sexual relationships with adults are presented in Constantine and Martinson. The statements on the relative harm from different kinds of incest are cited from Brody, 1979; those on the long-term effects are from APA, 1983 (citing research by Courtois and Meiselman); those on the prevalence of incest among prostitutes from a *Sexuality Today* article citing the work of Jayne Hynes; and those on the experiences of mothers in incestuous families from APA, 1983 (citing research by Johnston and Stone, 1983).

p. 55 The Incest Survivors Resource Network, International offers emotional support, advocacy, and education to those who have experienced incest. Information can be obtained by writing to the network at Friends Meeting House, 15 Rutherford Place, New York, N.Y. 10003.

p. 55 The figures on the prevalence of childhood abuse in the history of rapists were cited in the workshop "Rape: Victims and Offenders," presented in New York City on August 13, 1982, by A. Nicholas Groth, Ph.D., and Ann W. Burgess, R.N.

p. 56 Descriptions of different types of rapists (anger, power, and sadistic) are in Groth, Burgess, and Holmstrom.

Chapter 3: The Budding Bough

p. 61 "Romeo and Juliet" effect is described in Driscoll, Davis, and Lipetz.

pp. 64–65 The progression of stages in adolescent sexual activity is described in Gagnon and Simon, pp. 75-76. References for adolescence are as follows: Earlier age of first intercourse: Dreyer; Zelnik and Shah. Rarity of promiscuity: Zelnik, Kantner, and Ford. Girls' first intercourse with a steady boyfriend, while boys' is with a more casual date: Zelnik and Shah. Rarity of boys' involvement with prostitutes: Sorensen, 1973. Lowering of double standard: Mahoney, 1983. Projections for teen pregnancy are in the Alan Guttmacher Institute report.

p. 65 Statistics on virginity in Zelnik and Shah; Chilman; and Lewis and Lewis. Erikson, p. 263.

p. 66 Information on Ohio State University students is in Clatworthy. Similar patterns showed up among the University of Puget Sound students whose autobiographies I read.

p. 67 Dr. Gordon received the award of the American Association of Sex Educators, Counselors and Therapists (AASECT) at its national conference in New York City, March 13, 1982.

pp. 67–68 Goodman, p. 40. The Emory/Grady program is described in Howard.

p. 68 Most pregnancies occur in the first six months in Zabin, Kantner, and Zelnik; relationship between sex guilt and failure to use birth control in Bishop and in Herold and Goodwin; almost 90 percent of boyfriends leave their pregnant girlfriends in Gordon, 1982; the first time is worth waiting for in Weis, 1983.

pp. 68–69 Corroboration of Weis in Murphy.

p. 70 The sensate focus technique pioneered by Masters and Johnson is described in *Human Sexual Inadequacy*.

p. 70 Gardner, p. 98.

p. 77 Bell, Weinberg, and Hammersmith.

p. 79 Dr. Bell voiced these conclusions in a talk given at the 1982 AASECT conference in New York City; the essence of the talk was then published in *SIECUS Report*.

p. 80 Gadpaille, p. 343.

Chapter 4: *Groves of Nubility*

p. 89 Dr. Caplan's workshop on "Developing Relationships Through the Life Cycle" was held April 19, 1983, in Philadelphia at the conference "Sexuality Through the Life Cycle," co-sponsored by the Junior League of Philadelphia and Planned Parenthood, Southeastern Pennsylvania.

p. 90 As many as 70 percent of women do not climax from intercourse alone, according to Hite.

p. 92 Increased frequency of oral sex in Mahoney, 1983, pp. 196-197.

pp. 92–93 Figures on participation by women are in Kinsey, 1953, and Tavris and Sadd, 1977; figures for teenagers are in Hass, 1979. Traditional sexual scripts are in Gagnon and Simon. These research findings are borne out by the sexual autobiographies of the University of Puget Sound students.

pp. 95–96 The relationship between guilt and contraception is in Bishop and in Herold and Goodwin. The need to be "swept away" is described in Cassell.

p. 96 The figures for abortions are in Henshaw and O'Reilly.

p. 100 Decline of the double standard is documented in Mahoney, pp. 207-210. The 1959 study by Erhmann was cited by Mahoney, p. 208.

Chapter 5: *Vales of Venus*

p. 104 Ages for first marriage are from the National Center for Health Statistics.

p. 105 "Miss Manners's" description of the backward courtship is in Martin, 1983.

pp. 105–106 News reports of the rise in the reported rates of venereal diseases are in Lyons, 1983, and Brody, 1984.

p. 110 Levinson *et al.*

p. 115 This is true of Kinsey's 1948 and 1953 books and of Masters and Johnson's 1966 and 1970 books. Masters and Johnson did go on to write another book (with professional writer Robert J. Levin), *The Pleasure Bond,* in which they explored the interweaving of sex, love, and commitment. The value of love in sex therapy is reported by Cookerly and McClaren.

pp. 115–116 The results of the *Psychology Today* surveys are in Rubenstein, and the relationship between sex and love is reported by Cargan. Figures on couples who live together are in Roy Watson.

p. 116 Evidence that married people are more sexually active is cited by Hunt and the *Playboy* 1983 survey (March). An exception to this is reported by Blumstein and Schwartz, who found cohabiting couples to be more sexually active than married ones.

pp. 116–117 Gadpaille, p. 378.

p. 118 The finding that people who've lived together before marriage are no happier afterward is reported by Jacques and Chason; Roy Watson, and DeMaris and Leslie found that they are, in fact, less happy.

p. 118 Dr. Gaylin's comments to me are presented at greater length in his 1982 paper.

pp. 119–120 Blumstein and Schwartz, p. 37; Gadpaille, p. 365.

p. 120 Levinson *et al.*, p. 55.

p. 122 Among the few studies of sex in marriage are those by Persky *et al.*; Myers; Greenblat; Frank, Anderson, and Rubinstein; and Blumstein and Schwartz. Information about frequency after ten years is in Blumstein and Schwartz.

p. 125 Studies of the effect of pregnancy on a couple's sexual relationship include those by Brenner and Greenberg; May; and Bittman and Zalk.

pp. 125–126 The effects of pregnancy on the father are cited by Liebenberg; Bittman and Zalk; Zalk; and Hartman and Nicolay. Findings about husbands' extramarital sex during their wives' pregnancy were reported by Masters and Johnson, 1966.

p. 126 The relationship between pregnancy and physical abuse by husbands was reported by Gelles.

Chapter 6: Fertile Forests

p. 129 Levinson and Sheehy both treat this transition extensively.

p. 134 Axelrod wrote *The Seven Year Itch*. The 1977 report of the ages of couples coming for marriage counseling was written by Berman, Miller, Vines, and Lief. More recent studies, including the one by the Institute for Advanced Study of Human Sexuality in San Francisco, are cited by Lacayo. *Playboy*'s January 1983 report on the magazine's sex survey gave figures for first extramarital sex.

pp. 136–137 Figures for reported extramarital sex are in Kinsey, 1948 and 1953, and in Hunt and Wolfe. The national opinion polls were reported by the National Opinion Research Center. Weis (1976) analyzed survey data.

pp. 137–138 Healthy and disturbed reasons are in Ellis. The *Playboy* reports are in issues of January and March 1983; a previous study about the positive relationship between premarital and extramarital sex was

Notes

Athanasiou and Sarkin. Thompson also reported this link. Affairs don't break up marriages in March 1983 *Playboy*.

p. 138   Eleanor Macklin described conjoint therapy at a workshop at the 1978 conference of the National Council on Family Relations in Philadelphia. Silverman's workshops were reported by McGarry.

p. 140   For information on breastfeeding and female sexuality, see Olds and Eiger; Masters and Johnson, 1966; and Fisher and Gray.

pp. 141–142   Frank, Anderson, and Rubinstein; Blumstein and Schwartz, p. 204; *Playboy*, March 1983, p. 184. Studies showing the negative impact children have on the marital relationship include Feldman and Feldman; Belsky, Spanier, and Rovine; Blumstein and Schwartz; and Harriman. Difficulties after childbirth are reported by Fischman and Rankin and by Blumstein and Schwartz.

p. 143   The Study Group's report is in *Children and Sex: The Parents Speak*.

pp. 144–145   Infertility figures are in Bouton. Dr. Toth is quoted in Bouton.

p. 145   Liebmann-Smith elaborated on her comments to me in her article in *Self*.

pp. 147–148   Bird; Levinson *et al*.

p. 148   Rohrlich, p. 65.

pp. 152–153   The study of women's lives is reported by Baruch, Barnett, and Rivers.

p. 153   Blumstein and Schwartz, pp. 173-174.

pp. 153–154   The survey of married couples is reported by White. Leiblum discussed the problems of time in a session on "State of the Science: Sex Therapy" at a conference of the Eastern Region of SSSS, April 17, 1982.

pp. 154–155   Bird, p. 69. Women who make more money have better sex lives in Baruch, Barnett, and Rivers, p. 53. Assertive women have better sex lives than passive ones in Sheppard and Seidman. Divorce rate among two-paycheck couples in Bird, p. 83.

p. 156   Goode; men's and women's friendship patterns in Lowenthal and Haven and in Powers and Bultena.

p. 157 For a fuller description of marriage enrichment programs, see Olds and Olds, and Collins, 1983.

Chapter 7: Blooming Again

p. 165 Segraves is quoted in Brody, 1983(b).

p. 167 Ephross and Weiss described the plight of divorced parents over thirty-five.

pp. 167–168 The stress of divorce is discussed by Brody, 1983(b); Holmes and Rahe; Hetherington, Cox, and Cox; and Reed, in his writings and in his workshop on "Newly Single Adults," held April 19, 1983, in Philadelphia at the conference "Sexuality Through the Life Cycle," co-sponsored by the Junior League of Philadelphia and Planned Parenthood, Southeastern Pennsylvania.

p. 169 *Playboy*'s figures on divorced men are in March 1983 issue.

p. 169 Reed reported that women suffer more from divorce.

pp. 172–173 Ephross and Weiss discussed the problems of single parents.

p. 173 The discussion group whose meetings I attended (typical of many around the country) is SPAN (Single Parents Action Network), sponsored by the North Shore Child Guidance Association in Manhasset, New York.

pp. 174–175 Eakin is quoted in Greenberg.

Chapter 8: The Amatory Thicket

p. 176 The age-forty, or midlife, transition is discussed extensively by Gould, Levinson, Sheehy, and Vaillant.

p. 179 Sexual metaphors at midlife are discussed by Rohrlich.

p. 180 Erikson wrote about identity as a prerequisite for intimacy; Gilligan has questioned this sequence among women.

pp. 180–181 Sheppard and Seidman, p. 82.

pp. 181–182 The positive relationship between body image and sexual assertiveness was reported by Levitan.

p. 182 Figures on hysterectomy were reported by Harrison, p. ix.

p. 183 Women's feelings about sex after hysterectomy were reported by Zussman *et al.* and by Morgan and Bjornson.

p. 183 Figures on prevalence of breast cancer from American Cancer Society.

pp. 185–186 The British study was cited by Bennetts; the study of Hawaiian women was reported by Gerard. Kriss was quoted by Bennetts.

pp. 188–189 I have been unable to track down the quote from Auden and would be grateful if any reader could supply it. The basis for the statements about good sex in long-term relationships is in Zilbergeld, 1983; Hunt; Wolfe; and Tavris and Sadd.

p. 191 Pogrebin wrote about marriage in *The New York Times*, 1983.

pp. 198–199 The follow-up study of O'Connor's workshop participants is reported by Kuriansky, Sharpe, and O'Connor.

p. 199 Kaplan, 1979, pp. 38-39.

p. 200 Lieblum: See note for p. 151.

Chapter 9: Greener Grass

p. 203 Rose, p. 166.

p. 204 Sprenkle and Weis.

p. 205 Neugarten, 1968(a), p. 97.

pp. 208–209 Dr. McGinnis presented a workshop, "Extramarital Therapy: The New 'Third Dimension' of Marital and Sex Therapy," at the meeting of the Eastern Region of SSSS, April 15, 1983, in Philadelphia.

pp. 224–227 The studies of swingers are reported by Bartell, Gilmartin, Karlen, Levitt and Duckworth, Murstein, and Varni.

Chapter 10: Bowers in Bloom

p. 230 Bernard A. Eskin, M.D., gave the average menopausal age as fifty-one during his presentation on the panel "Sexuality and the Menopause" on March 13, 1982, at the AASECT annual meeting in New York City.

pp. 230–231 The studies of the impact of the menopause on female sexuality were reported by Purifoy, Martin, and Tobin and by Starr and Weiner.

pp. 231–232 The study of forty-two sexually active postmenopausal women was reported by Gloria Bachmann, M.D., during the AASECT panel "Sexuality and the Menopause" cited above. Evidence for the relationship between estrogen and cancer was reported by Hoover, Gray, and Fraumeni, and by Judd *et al.* Recent research on the beneficial effects of estrogen in combination with progestin has been reported by Bush *et al.,* Hammond *et al.,* Judd *et al.,* and Nachtigall *et al.* Data on postmenopausal hormone levels were given by Dr. Eskin at the AASECT panel cited above.

p. 233 The effects of illness and medications on male potency are described by Kaplan, 1979, pp. 211-222, and by Slag *et al.*

p. 233 Figures on the relationship between health and sexuality are in Brecher *et al.*, p. 267.

pp. 234–235 The study of sexual activity in postmenopausal women was reported by Sandra Leiblum, Ph.D., at the AASECT panel cited above. The relationship between sexual activity in earlier years and that in later life was established by Kinsey, 1948; Brecher *et al.*; and Masters and Johnson, 1966.

p. 235 Factors that cause sexual dysfunction in middle and old age are cited by Masters and Johnson, 1966.

p. 236 Leiblum made this statement during the presentation of the AASECT panel cited above.

p. 237 Research showing the absence of the "empty nest syndrome" is reported by Sheppard and Seidman; Rubin; and Harkins.

pp. 240–241 O'Neill and O'Neill, 1972. Quote from O'Neill and O'Neill, 1984, pp. xii and xv. In addition to the research studies cited by them, a 1984 report by Adams and Rubin found no significant differences between sexually open and sexually exclusive couples.

p. 241 Mary Ann Watson, 1981.

p. 242 Information about heart rates during sex came from Dr. Stein.

p. 243 The Japanese report was by Ueno. The drop in extramarital sex after heart problems was reported by Kavich-Sharon.

pp. 243–244 Hott, 1980; Holy Cross Hospital.

p. 245 One study showing that doctors rarely discuss sexuality with their heart patients is that done by James Cripton of the University of Calgary and reported in *Sexuality Today*, March 22, 1982.

p. 247 Dr. Michela's study was described in *TC Today*.

Chapter 11: Perennial Passions

p. 248 Neugarten (1975) described such people in their sixties as the "young-old."

p. 249 Levinson *et al.*; Erikson. The survey showing people feel younger than their true age was done by Cadwell Davis Partners, pp. 26-28.

pp. 253–254 O'Neill and O'Neill (1984) maintain that most people cannot handle sexually open marriage. Figures on extramarital sex past fifty in Brecher *et al.*, pp. 110-124.

pp. 253–254 The high incomes of people aged fifty-five to sixty-five are cited by *The New York Times*, 1984(b). Statistics on happiness of marriages are in Brecher *et al.*, pp. 56, 104-105. They quote the fifty-seven-year-old wife on p. 115.

p. 258 Findings about retired persons are in Starr and Weiner, pp. 198-203; Brecher *et al.*, pp. 62-64; Streib and Schneider; and Barfield and Morgan.

p. 259 Quote is in Starr and Weiner, p. 204. Figures on the increase of young adults living with their parents are given by Lindsey.

p. 261 Figures on the imbalance between the sexes are given by Brecher *et al.*

p. 261 The quote from Brecher *et al.* is on p. 153.

pp. 263–264 Sontag, p.11. de Beauvoir, pp. 348-349.

p. 266 People describing their ideal lovers are quoted in Starr and Weiner, p. 115.

pp. 266–267 The quote from Aristophanes' *Lysistrata*, translated by Donald Sutherland, in *Greek Comedy* (New York: Dell Books, 1974), p. 50. A discussion of May-December relationships is in Berardo *et al.*

p. 267 "Equity theory" is described by Walster, Walster, and Berscheid.

pp. 267–268 Berardo *et al.*, p. 11; Neugarten is interviewed in Hall.

Chapter 12: Stands of Evergreens

pp. 273–274 The decade-by-decade declines in male orgasmic experience are documented in Brecher *et al.*, pp. 326-327; those in the female experience are on pp. 325-326.

p. 274 The tendency of many women to reach orgasm more often through masturbation than with a partner is reported by Hite and by Masters and Johnson, 1966.

p. 275 The seventy-two-year-old man is quoted by Brecher *et al.*, p. 372. The sixty-seven-year-old woman is quoted by Starr and Weiner, p. 150. Their statement is on p. 151.

pp. 275–276 This segment of the *Phil Donahue Show* was broadcast in New York on February 26, 1982.

p. 277 Brecher *et al.*, pp. 200-201.

p. 280 Butler explained the concept of the life review in 1968.

Bibliography

Adams, James R., and Arline M. Rubin. (1984). "Outcomes of Sexually Open Marriages: A Five Year Follow-up." Paper presented at meeting of Eastern Region of the Society for the Scientific Study of Sex, (SSSS), Philadelphia, April 7.

Staff. (1981). *Teenage Pregnancy: The Problem That Hasn't Gone Away.* New York: Alan Guttmacher Institute.

American Academy of Pediatrics Committee on Nutrition. (1982). The promotion of breast-feeding: Policy statement based on task force report. *Pediatrics, 69,* 654–661.

American Academy of Pediatrics Committee on Nutrition and Nutrition Committee of the Canadian Pediatric Society. (1978). Breast Feeding. *Pediatrics, 62,* 598.

American Cancer Society. (1983). *Cancer Facts and Figures 1984.* New York: American Cancer Society.

Staff. (1983, January 3). Incest: Now easier to prevent, identify, treat? American Psychological Association.

301

Athanasiou, R., and R. Sarkin. (1974). Premarital sexual behavior and post-marital adjustment. *Archives of Sexual Behavior, 3,* 207–224.

Axelrod, G. (1953). *The Seven Year Itch.* New York: Random House.

Barfield, R. E., and J. N. Morgan. (1974). *Early Retirement: The Decision and the Experience and a Second Look.* Ann Arbor, Mich.: Institute for Social Research.

———. (1978). Trends in satisfaction with retirement. *The Gerontologist, 18,* 19–23.

Bartell, Gilbert D. (1971). *Group Sex: A Scientist's Eyewitness Report on the American Way of Swinging.* New York: Wyden.

Baruch, Grace, Rosalind Barnett, and Caryl Rivers. (1983). *Lifeprints: New Patterns of Love and Work for Today's Women.* New York: McGraw-Hill.

Beauvoir, Simone de. (1972). *The Coming of Age.* New York: Putnam's.

Bell, Alan P. (1982). Sexual preference: A postscript. *SIECUS Report, 11*(2), 1–3.

———, Martin S. Weinberg, and Sue K. Hammersmith. (1981). *Sexual Preference: Its Development in Men and Women.* Bloomington: Indiana University Press.

Belsky, Jay, Graham B. Spanier, and Michael Rovine. (1983). Stability and change in marriage across the transition to parenthood. *Journal of Marriage and the Family, 45,* 567-577.

Bennetts, Leslie. (1982, March 1). Breast cancer and sexuality. *The New York Times,* p. B6.

Berardo, Felix M., Hernan Vera, and Donna H. Berardo. (1981). "Age-Discrepant Marriages." Paper presented at National Council on Family Relations (NCFR) annual meeting, Milwaukee, October.

Berman, Ellen M., William R. Miller, Neville Vines, and Harold I. Lief. (1977). The age 30 crisis and the 7-year-itch. *Journal of Sex and Marital Therapy, 3,* 197–204.

Bird, Caroline. (1979). *The Two-Paycheck Marriage.* New York: Rawson, Wade.

Bishop, Paul. (1983). "Parental Disapproval of Sex, Mother-Daughter Closeness, and Sex Guilt as Obstacles to Contraceptive Use." Unpublished paper, Department of Psychology, Northern Kentucky University.

Bibliography

Bittman, Sam and Sue Rosenberg Zalk. (1978). *Expectant Fathers.* New York: Ballantine.

Bjornson, Edith. (1984). "Sex after hysterectomy-oopherectomy: An old wives' tale revisited." *National Women's Health Network News, 9*(2), 5, 15.

Blumstein, Philip, and Pepper Schwartz. (1983). *American Couples: Money, Work, Sex.* New York: Morrow.

Bouton, Katherine. (1982, June 13). Fighting male infertility. *The New York Times Magazine,* pp. 86–88, 91, 100.

Brecher, Edward M., and The Editors of Consumer Reports Books. (1984). *Love, Sex, and Aging: A Consumers Union Report.* Boston: Little, Brown.

Brenner, Paul, and Martin Greenberg. (1977, July). The impact of pregnancy on marriage. *Medical Aspects of Human Sexuality,* pp. 15–22.

Brody, Jane E. (1979, June 13). Personal health. *The New York Times,* p. C8.

———. (1983, December 13). Divorce's stress exacts long-term health toll. *The New York Times,* pp. C1, C5.

———. (1984, June 5). Infection linked to sex surpasses gonorrhea. *The New York Times,* pp. C1, C11.

Bush, Trudy L., Linda D. Cowan, Elizabeth Barrett-Connor, Michael H. Criqui, John M. Karon, Robert D. Wallace, H. Al Tyroler, and Basil M. Rifkind. (1983). Estrogen use and all-cause mortality. *Journal of the American Medical Association, 249,* 903–906.

Butler, Robert N. (1968). "The life review: An interpretation of reminiscence in the aged." In B. Neugarten, ed., *Middle Age and Aging.* Chicago: University of Chicago Press.

Cadwell Davis Partners. (1982). *Age Perception Survey.* New York: Cadwell Davis, pp. 26–28.

Calderone, Mary, S. (1982). Sex doesn't bear thinking of . . . or does it? *SIECUS Report,* 1, 4.

———. (1983, May–July). Fetal erection and its message to us. *SIECUS Report,* 9–10.

———and Eric W. Johnson. (1981). *The Family Book about Sexuality.* New York: Harper and Row.

———and James W. Ramey. (1982). *Talking with Your Child about Sex.* New York: Random House.

303

Cargan, Leonard. (1981). Singles: An examination of two stereotypes. *Family Relations, 30,* 377–385.

Cassell, Carol. (1984). *Swept Away: Why Women Fear Their Own Sexuality.* New York: Simon & Schuster.

Chilman, Catherine S. (1980). *Adolescent Sexuality in a Changing American Society: Social and Psychological Perspectives.* Bethesda, Md.: U.S. Department of Health, Education and Welfare, Public Health Service, National Institute of Health, NIH Publication No. 80-1426.

Clatworthy, Nancy M. (1980). ''Morals and the Ever Changing College Student.'' Paper presented at the North Central Sociological Meeting, Dayton, Ohio, May 1.

Collins, G. (1982, May 13). Studies find sexual abuse of children is widespread. *The New York Times,* pp. C1, C10.

———. (1983, November 14). 50 years of keeping couples together. *The New York Times,* p. B9.

Constantine, Larry L., and F. M. Martinson, eds. (1981). *Children and Sex: New Findings, New Perspectives.* Boston: Little, Brown.

Cookerly, J. Richard, and Kathleen A. McClaren. (1982). Sex therapy with and without love: An empirical investigation. *Journal of Sex Education and Therapy, 8*(2), 35–38.

DeMaris, Alfred, and Gerald R. Leslie. (1984). Cohabitation with the future spouse: Its influence upon marital satisfaction and communication. *Journal of Marriage and the Family, 46,* 77–84.

Dreyer, Philip H. ''Sexuality during adolescence.'' In Benjamin B. Wolman, ed., *Handbook of Developmental Psychology.* Englewood Cliffs, N. J.: Prentice-Hall, pp. 559–601.

Driscoll, Richard, Keith E. Davis, and Milton E. Lipetz. (1972). Parental interference and romantic love: The Romeo and Juliet effect. *Journal of Personality and Social Psychology, 24,* 1–10.

Ellis, Albert. (1968). Healthy and disturbed reasons for having extramarital relations. *Journal of Human Relations, 16,* 490–501.

Ephross, Paul H., and Joan C. Weiss. (1983). ''Sex and Single Parents: Issues Current and Future.'' Paper presented at annual meeting of Eastern Region of SSSS, Philadelphia, April 16.

Bibliography

Erikson, Erik H. (1950, 1963). *Childhood and Society*. New York: Norton.

Feldman, Harold, and Margaret Feldman. (1977). "Effect of Parenthood at Three Points in Marriage." Unpublished manuscript.

Fischman, Susan, and Elizabeth Rankin. (1983). "Changes in Intimate and Sexual Relationships in Postpartum Couples." Paper presented at conference of the Eastern Region of SSSS, Philadelphia, April 15.

Fisher, William A., and Janice Gray. (1983). "Erotophobia—Erotophilia and Couples' Sexual Behavior during Pregnancy and after Childbirth." Paper presented at annual meeting of SSSS, Chicago, November 18.

Frank, Ellen, Carol Anderson, and Debra Rubinstein. (1978). Frequency of sexual dysfunction in 'normal' couples. *New England Journal of Medicine, 299,* 111–115.

Freud, Sigmund. (1938). *The Basic Writings of Sigmund Freud.* New York: Modern Library.

Gadpaille, Warren J., M.D. (edited by Lucy Freeman). (1975). *The Cycles of Sex.* New York: Scribner's.

Gagnon, John H., and William Simon. (1973). *Sexual Conduct: The Social Sources of Human Sexuality.* Chicago: Aldine.

Gardner, James E. (1982). *The Turbulent Teens.* Los Angeles: Sorrento Press.

Gaylin, Ned. (1982). Trust: The overlooked essential of marriage. *Medical Aspects of Human Sexuality, 16*(11), 50–57.

Gelles, Richard J. (1975). Violence and pregnancy: A note on the extent of the problem and needed services. *Family Coordinator, 24,* 81–86.

Gerard, Dianne. (1982). "Sexual Functioning after Mastectomy: Physiological and Subjective Indices." Paper presented at American Association of Sex Educators, Counselors and Therapists (AASECT) meeting, New York City, March.

Gilligan, Carol. (1982). *In a Different Voice: Psychological Theory and Women's Development.* Cambridge, Mass.: Harvard University Press.

Gilmartin, Brian G. (1975, February). Suburban mate-swapping. *Psychology Today,* pp. 54–58.

———. (1977). "Swinging: Who gets involved and how?" In Roger W. Libby and Robert N. Whitehurst, eds., *Marriage and Alternatives: Exploring Intimate Relationships.* Glenview, Ill.: Scott, Foresman.

305

Goode, William J. (1978). "The Male Sex Role: An Insider's View." Speech given at Northwestern University, May.

Goodman, Ellen. (1983, July). The turmoil of teenage sexuality. *Ms.*, pp. 37–41.

Gordon, Sol. (1982). "Text of Gordon's 1982 acceptance speech: AASECT Outstanding Contributions Award." *Impact '82-83*, pp. 5–6.

———— and Judith Gordon. (1983). *Raising a Child Conservatively in a Sexually Permissive Society.* New York: Simon & Schuster.

Gould, Roger L. (1978). *Transformations: Growth and Change in Adult Life.* New York: Simon & Schuster.

Greenberg, Diane. (1982, January 3). When single parents have a date. *The New York Times*, p. 6LI.

Greenblat, Cathy S. (1983). The salience of sexuality in the early years of marriage. *Journal of Marriage and the Family, 45,* 289–299.

Groth, A. Nicholas, Ann W. Burgess, and Lynda L. Holmstrom. (1977). Rape: Power, anger, and sexuality. *American Journal of Psychiatry, 134,* 1239–1243.

Hall, Calvin S., and Gardner Lindzey. (1978). *Theories of Personality.* 3rd ed. New York: Wiley.

Hall, Elizabeth. (1980, April). Acting one's age: new rules for old. Bernice Neugarten interviewed. *Psychology Today*, pp. 66–80.

Hammond, Charles B., Frederick R. Jelovsek, Kerry L. Lee, William T. Creasman, and Roy T. Parker. (1979). Effects of long-term estrogen replacement therapy. *American Journal of Obstetrics and Gynecology, 133,* 537–547.

Harkins, Elizabeth Bates. (1978). Effects of empty nest transition on self-report of psychological and physical well-being. *Journal of Marriage and the Family, 40,* 549–556.

Harlow, Harry, and Margaret Harlow. (1962). The effect of rearing conditions on behavior. *Bulletin of the Menninger Clinic, 26,* 213–224.

Harriman, Lynda C. (1983). Personal and marital changes accompanying parenthood. *Family Relations, 32,* 387–394.

Harrison, Michelle, M.D. (1982). Foreword to Susanne Morgan, *Coping with a Hysterectomy.* New York: Dial.

Bibliography

Hartman, A., and R. Nicolay. (1966). Sexually deviant behavior in expectant fathers. *Journal of Abnormal and Social Psychology, 71,* 232–234.

Hass, Aaron. (1979). *Teenage Sexuality.* New York: Macmillan.

Henshaw, Stanley K., and Kevin O'Reilly. (1983). Characteristics of abortion patients in the U.S., 1979–1980. *Family Planning Perspectives, 15,* 6, Table 1.

Herold, Edward S., and Marilyn S. Goodwin. (1981). Premarital sexual guilt and contraceptive attitudes and behavior. *Family Relations, 30,* 247–253.

Hetherington, E. Mavis, Martha Cox, and Roger Cox. (1976). "The Aftermath of Divorce." Paper presented at meeting of American Psychological Association, Washington, D.C., September.

———. (1978). "Family Interaction and the Social, Emotional and Cognitive Development of Children Following Divorce." Paper presented at the Symposium on the Family: Setting Priorities. Sponsored by the Institute for Pediatric Service of Johnson & Johnson Baby Co., Washington, D.C., May 17-20.

Hite, Shere. (1976). *The Hite Report.* New York: Macmillan.

Holmes, Thomas L., and R. H. Rahe. (1976). The social readjustment rating scale. *Journal of Psychosomatic Research, 11,* 213.

Staff. (1984). Guidelines for sexual intercourse: Cardiac patients. Fort Lauderdale: Holy Cross Hospital.

Hoover, Robert, Laman A. Gray, and Joseph F. Fraumeni, Jr. (1977, September 10). Stilboestrol (Diethylstilbestrol) and the risk of ovarian cancer. *Lancet,* pp. 533–534.

Hott, Jacqueline. (1980). Sex and the heart patient: A nursing view. *Topics in Clinical Nursing, 1,* 75–84.

Howard, Marion. (1983). Postponing sexual involvement: A new approach. *SIECUS Report, 11*(4), 5–8.

Hunt, Morton. (1974). *Sexual Behavior in the 1970s.* Chicago: Playboy Press.

Hyde, Janet Shibley. (1979). *Understanding Human Sexuality.* New York: McGraw-Hill.

Jacques, Jeffrey M., and Karen J. Chason. (1979). Cohabitation: Its impact on marital success. *Family Coordinator, 28,* 35–39.

Judd, Howard L., Robert E. Cleary, William T. Creasman, David C. Figge,

Nathan Kase, Zev Rosenwaks, and George E. Tagatz. (1981). Estrogen replacement therapy. *Journal of the American College of Obstetricians and Gynecologists, 58,* 267–275.

Kaplan, Helen Singer. (1974). *The New Sex Therapy.* New York: Quadrangle.

———. (1979). *Disorders of Sexual Desire.* New York: Simon & Schuster.

Karlen, Arno. (1980, May). Swingers: The conservative hedonists. *Sexology,* pp. 13–18.

Kavich-Sharon, Richard. (1981). ''Sexual Behavior of Men, Women and Their Spouses Before and After Coronary Events.'' Paper presented at meeting of SSSS, New York City, November 21.

Kinsey, Alfred C., Wardell B. Pomeroy, and Clyde E. Martin. (1948). *Sexual Behavior in the Human Male.* Philadelphia: Saunders.

——— and Paul H. Gebhart. (1953). *Sexual Behavior in the Human Female.* Philadelphia: Saunders.

Kuriansky, Judith B., Lawrence Sharpe, and Dagmar O'Connor. (1982). The treatment of anorgasmia: Long-term effectiveness of a short-term behavioral group therapy. *Journal of Sex & Marital Therapy, 8,* 29–43.

Lacayo, Richard. (1983, November). The new 4 year itch: A different timetable for the straying urge. *Self,* pp. 130–131.

Levinson, Daniel J., with Charlotte N. Darrow, Edward B. Klein, Maria H. Levinson, and Braxton McKee. (1978). *The Seasons of a Man's Life.* New York: Ballantine.

Levitan, Jean. (1983). ''Relationship between Body Image and Sexual Control, Sexual Anxiety and Sexual Assertiveness in a Selected Group of College Women.'' Paper presented at meeting of Eastern Region of SSSS, Philadelphia, April 15.

Levitt, Eugene, and Jane Duckworth. (1982). ''A Personality Analysis of a 'Swinger' Club.'' Paper presented at meeting of Eastern Region of SSSS, Philadelphia, April 17.

Lewis, Howard R., and Martha E. Lewis. (1980). *The Parent's Guide to Teenage Sex and Pregnancy.* New York: St. Martin's Press.

Libby, Roger W., and Robert N. Whitehurst, eds. (1973). *Renovating Marriage: Toward New Sexual Life-Styles.* Danville, Calif.: Consensus Publishers.

———. *Marriage and Alternatives: Exploring Intimate Relationships.* Glenview, Ill.: Scott, Foresman.

Liebenberg, Beatrice. (1967). "Expectant Fathers." Paper presented at the American Orthopsychiatric Association annual meeting, Washington, D.C., March. Subsequently published in *Child & Family,* Summer 1969, pp. 265–278.

Liebmann-Smith, Joan. (1984, May). Making babies, not love. *Self,* pp. 146–150.

Lindsey, Robert. (1984, January 15). A new generation finds it hard to leave the nest. *The New York Times,* p.18.

Lowenthal, Marjorie F., and Clayton Haven. (1968). "Interaction and Adaptation: Intimacy as a Critical Variable." In Bernice L. Neugarten, ed., *Middle Age and Aging.* Chicago: University of Chicago Press, pp. 390–400.

Lyons, Richard D. (1983, October 4). Sex in America: Conservative attitudes prevail. *The New York Times,* pp. C1, C4.

Mahoney, E. R. (1983). *Human Sexuality.* New York: McGraw-Hill.

Martin, Judith. (1983, October 2). Miss Manners: Etiquette for all occasions: The backward courtship. *LI Newsday Sunday Magazine,* p. 6.

Martinez, Gilbert A., and David A. Dodd. (1983). 1981 milk feeding patterns in the United States during the first 12 months of life. *Pediatrics, 71,* 166–170.

Masson, Jeffrey M. (1983). *The Assault on Truth: Freud's Suppression of the Seduction Theory.* New York: Farrar, Straus and Giroux.

Masters, William H., and Virginia E. Johnson. (1970). *Human Sexual Inadequacy.* Boston: Little, Brown.

———. (1966). *Human Sexual Response.* Boston: Little, Brown.

———and Robert J. Levin. (1975). *The Pleasure Bond.* Boston: Little, Brown.

May, Katharyn A. (1982). Factors contributing to first-time fathers' readiness for fatherhood: An exploratory study. *Family Relations, 31,* 353–361.

McGarry, T. W. (1984, February 1). Counseling to help married women enjoy their affairs. *Philadelphia Inquirer,* p. 4-D.

McGinnis, Tom. (1981). *More Than Just a Friend: The Joys and Disappointments of Extramarital Affairs.* Englewood Cliffs, N.J.: Prentice-Hall.

Staff. (1979). Sexual survey #20: Current thinking on children's sexuality. *Medical Aspects of Human Sexuality, 13,* 120–121.

Morgan, Susanne. (1982). *Coping with a Hysterectomy.* New York: Dial.

Murphy, Daniel P. (1982). "Reactions of Men and Women to Their First Act of Sexual Intercourse: The Times They Ain't A-Changin'!" Paper presented at national conference of the American Association of Sex Educators, Counselors & Therapists (AASECT), New York City, March 14.

Murstein, Bernard I., ed. (1978). "Swinging." In *Exploring Intimate Life Styles.* New York: Springer, pp. 109–130.

Myers, Jennifer G. (1981). "An Investigation of the Relationship between Marital and Sexual Satisfaction." Paper presented at national meeting of SSSS, New York City, November.

Nachtigall, Lila E., Richard H. Nachtigall, Robert D. Nachtigall, and E. Mark Beckman. (1979). Estrogen replacement therapy I: A 10-year prospective study in the relationship to osteoporosis. *Journal of the American College of Obstetricians and Gynecologists, 53,* 277–281.

Staff. (1981). *Monthly Vital Statistics Report,* July 31. (From 1980 census.) National Center for Health Statistics.

National Opinion Research Center. (1977). *General Social Surveys Codebook for 1972-1977.* Chicago: University of Chicago Press.

Neugarten, Bernice L. (1975, January 18). The rise of the young-old. *The New York Times,* p. 29.

———. (1968). "The Awareness of Middle Age." In Bernice L. Neugarten, ed. *Middle Age and Aging.* Chicago: University of Chicago Press, pp. 93–98.

———. (1968). "Adult Personality: Toward a Psychology of the Lifecycle." In Bernice L. Neugarten, ed., *Middle Age and Aging.* Chicago: University of Chicago Press, pp. 137–147.

Staff. (1984, February 23). Catering to older age groups. *The New York Times,* pp. D1, D3.

———. (1984, March 25). Study cites sharp increase in breast feeding. *The New York Times,* p. 31.

Olds, Mark, and Sally Wendkos Olds. (1973, January 21). The weekend that changes marriages. *LI Newsday Sunday Magazine,* pp. 9, 18–20.

Bibliography

Olds, Sally Wendkos. (1980, June 10). When parents divorce. *Woman's Day,* pp. 70, 108–110.

—— and Marvin S. Eiger. (1972). *The Complete Book of Breastfeeding.* New York: Workman Publishing. (Bantam paperback, 1973).

O'Neill, Nena, and George O'Neill. (1984). *Open Marriage.* New York: Evans. (A reissued edition of the book first published in 1972, with a new foreword, update, and bibliography.)

Papalia, Diane E., and Sally Wendkos Olds. (1978, 1981). *Human Development.* New York: McGraw-Hill.

——. (1985). *Psychology.* New York: McGraw-Hill.

Persky, Harold, Natalie Charney, Dorothy Strauss, William R. Miller, Charles P. O'Brien, and Harold I. Lief. (1982). The relationship of sexual adjustment and related sexual behaviors and attitudes to marital adjustment. *American Journal of Family Therapy, 10,* 38–49.

The Playboy readers' sex survey. (1983). *Playboy,* Part one: January, pp. 108, 241–250. Part two: March, pp. 90–92, 178–184. Part three: May, pp. 126–128, 136, 210–220. Part four: July, pp. 130–132, 192–203. Part five: October, pp. 92–96, 182–189.

Pogrebin, Letty Cottin. (1980). *Growing Up Free: Raising Your Child in the 80's.* New York: Bantam.

——. (1983, September 1). Hers: Couples who hide their happiness. *The New York Times,* p. C2.

Powers, E., and G. Bultena. (1976). Sex differences in intimate friendships of old age. *Journal of Marriage and the Family, 38,* 739–747.

Prescott, James W., Ph.D. (1975). Body pleasure and the origins of violence. *The Futurist, ix,* 64–80.

Purifoy, Frances E., Clyde E. Martin, and Jordan D. Tobin. (1983). "Age-Related Variation in Female Sexual Arousal and Orgasmic Response." Paper presented at annual meeting of SSSS, Chicago, November 18–20.

Reed, David. (1976). "Sexual Behavior in the Separated, Divorced, and Widowed." In Benjamin Sadock, Harold Kaplan, and Alfred Freedman, eds., *The Sexual Experience.* Baltimore: Williams & Wilkins Co., pp. 249–255.

Roberts, E. J., David Kline, and John Gagnon. (1978). *Family Life and Sexual*

Learning: A Study of the Role of Parents in the Sexual Learning of Children. New York: Project on Human Sexual Development, Population Education, Inc.

Rohrlich, Jay B. (1980). *Work and Love: The Crucial Balance.* New York: Summit Books.

Rose, Phyllis. (1983). *Parallel Lives: Five Victorian Marriages.* New York: Knopf.

Rubenstein, Carin. (1983, July). The modern art of courtly love. *Psychology Today,* pp. 42–49.

Rubin, Lillian. (1979). *Women of a Certain Age.* New York: Harper & Row.

Sadock, Benjamin, Harold Kaplan, and Alfred Freedman, eds. (1976). *The Sexual Experience.* Baltimore: Williams & Wilkins Co.

Schneider, Vimala. (1979). *Infant Massage.* New York: Bantam.

Staff. (1983). Austrian researcher: Pubertal amnesia blocks out early sexual activities. *Sexuality Today, 6,* 1, 3.

Staff. (1983). Prostitution: Creative programming for a vulnerable population. *Sexuality Today, 6,* 1.

Sheehy, Gail. (1976). *Passages: Predictable Crises of Adult Life.* New York: Dutton.

Sheppard, Samona, and Sylvia Seidman. (1982). "Midlife Women, the Women's Movement, and Sexuality." Paper presented at annual meeting of AASECT, New York City, March 12.

Simon, Sidney B. (1976). *Caring, Feeling, Touching.* Niles, Ill.: Argus Communications.

Slag, Michael F. *et al.* (1983). Impotence in medical clinic outpatients. *Journal of the American Medical Association,* 249, 1736-40.

Sorensen, Robert C. (1973). *Adolescent Sexuality in Contemporary America.* New York: World.

Spitz, René. (1945). "Hospitalism: An Inquiry into the Genesis of Psychiatric Conditioning in Early Childhood." In D. Fenschel *et al.,* eds., *Psychoanalytic Studies of the Child.* Vol. 1. New York: International Universities Press, pp. 53–74.

———. (1964). "Hospitalism: A Follow-up Report." In D. Fenschel *et al.,* eds., *Psychoanalytic Studies of the Child*. Vol. 2. New York: International Universities Press, pp. 113–117.

Sprenkle, Douglas H., and David L. Weis. (1978). Extramarital sexuality: Implications for marital therapists. *Journal of Sex and Marital Therapy*, 4, 279–291.

Starr, Bernard D., and Marcella Bakur Weiner. (1981). *The Starr-Weiner Report on Sex and Sexuality in the Mature Years*. New York: Stein & Day.

Steele, Brandt F., and C. B. Pollock. (1968). "A Psychiatric Study of Parents Who Abuse Infants and Small Children." In Ray E. Helfer and C. Henry Kempe, eds., *The Battered Child*. Chicago: University of Chicago Press, pp. 103–147.

Steinberg, Leo. (1983). *The Sexuality of Christ in Renaissance Art and in Modern Oblivion*. New York: Pantheon.

Streib, G. F., and C. J. Schneider. (1971). *Retirement in American Society: Impact and Process*. Ithaca, N. Y.: Cornell University Press.

Study Group of New York. (1983). *Children and Sex: The Parents Speak*. New York: Facts on File.

Tavris, Carol, and A. Sadd. (1977). *The Redbook Report on Female Sexuality*. New York: Delacorte.

Staff. (1983). Psychologist finds marriages improve after heart attack. *TC Today, 12,* 3.

Thompson, Anthony P. (1983). Extramarital sex: A review of the research literature. *Journal of Sex Research, 19,* 1–22.

Today's Child (1979, May). "When Child Catches You Au Naturel, In Flagrante." Report of study by Maria Paluszny, published in *Medical Aspects of Sexuality.*

Tribich, David, and Milton Klein. (1981). On Freud's 'blindness.' *Colloquium, 4,* 52–59.

Ueno, M. (1963). The so-called coition death. *Japanese Journal of Legal Medicine, 17,* 330–340.

Vaillant, George, and Charles McArthur. (1972). Natural history of male psychologic health. I. The adult life cycle from 18–50. *Seminars in Psychiatry, 4,* 415–427.

Varni, Charles A. (1973). "Contexts of Conversion: The Case of Swinging." In Roger W. Libby and Robert N. Whitehurst, eds., *Renovating Marriage: Toward New Sexual Life-Styles*. Danville, Calif.: Consensus Publishers, pp. 166–181.

Walster, Elaine, G. William Walster, and Ellen Berscheid. (1978). *Equity Theory and Research*. Boston: Allyn & Bacon.

Watson, Mary Ann. (1981). Sexually open marriage: Three perspectives. *Alternative Lifestyles, 4,* 3–21.

Watson, Roy L. (1983, January). Premarital cohabitation vs. traditional courtship: Their effects on subsequent marital adjustment. *Family Relations, 32,* 139–147.

Weis, David L. (1976). "An Analysis of American Attitudes toward Extramarital Sexual Relations: Survey Research Utilizing N.O.R.C. Data." Paper presented at annual convention of National Council on Family Relations, New York City, October 21.

———. (1983). Affective reactions of women to their initial experience of coitus. *Journal of Sex Research, 19,* 209–237.

White, Lynn K. (1983). Determinants of spousal interaction: Marital structure or marital happiness. *Journal of Marriage and the Family, 45,* 511–519.

Wolfe, Linda. (1981). *The Cosmo Report*. New York: Arbor House.

Zabin, Laurie S., John F. Kantner, and Melvin Zelnik. (1979). The risk of adolescent pregnancy in the first months of intercourse. *Family Planning Perspectives, 11,* 215–222.

Zalk, Sue R. (1981). "Transition from Son to Father: Unresolved Psychosexual Conflicts in Expectant Fathers." Paper presented at annual convention of APA, Los Angeles, August.

———. (1983). "Expectant Fathers and Sex during Pregnancy." Mimeographed paper.

Zelnik, Melvin, John F. Kantner, and Kathleen Ford. (1981). *Sex and Pregnancy in Adolescence*. Beverly Hills, Calif.: Sage Publications.

——— and Farida K. Shah. (1983). First intercourse among young Americans. *Family Planning Perspectives, 15,* 64–72.

Zilbergeld, Bernie. (1978). *Male Sexuality*. New York: Bantam.

———. (1983). "Is There Sex after the Honeymoon? Eroticism in Long-Term Relationships." In *Sexuality and the Family Life Span. Proceedings, Changing Family Conference XI.* Iowa City: University of Iowa Press.

Zussman, Leon, Shirley Zussman, Robert Sunley, and Edith Bjornson. (1981). Sexual response after hysterectomy–oophorectomy: Recent studies and reconsideration of psychogenesis. *American Journal of Obstetrics and Gynecology, 140,* 725–729.

Index

Note: First names appearing in the index are pseudonyms referring to cases in the text.

Index

318

Index

321

INDEX

Index

INDEX

Index

love and sex, 114–15
marriage, 115–27
  committed love and companionship and,
    119–20
  communication and, 119–20
  divorce, 117, 118
  faith and, 118–19
  intimacy and, 120–22
  living together compared to, 116
  parents and, 120
  pregnancy and, 122–27
  rationale for, 116–17
  sex and, 116, 122
  success of, and previous cohabitation, 118
  time and, 119
monogamy, 107–108
1960s, 104
sexual goals of, 103
sexual revolution, 104–106
  casualty of, 114–15
singles, 104–106
venereal disease, 105–10
women, 111–12
"Twenty-four-hour syndrome," 113
Two-income couples, 147, 148, 153–57
  divorce and, 155
  male "centrality" and, 156
  problems between partners, 155–57
  quality vs. quantity of sex, 154–55
  time and, 153–54
Two-Paycheck Marriage, The (Bird), 147

U.S. Naval Station, Honolulu, 185–86
University of Chicago, 165
University of Colorado, 37
University of Florida, 267
University of Maryland, 118
University of Massachusetts, 36
University of Puget Sound, 46–47, 86, 101, 105
University of Virginia, 167
Unmarried older women, *see* Sixties, the,
  unmarried older women

Vahanian, Tilla, 111–12, 147, 210, 258
Values, 85–86
Variations, 221

Vasectomy, 141
Venereal disease, 105–10
  chlamydia, 105–106
  genital herpes, 105, 108–10, 226, 251, 281
  gonorrhea, 106–108
  swingers' clubs and, 226
Vibrators, 178, 198, 272
Vince, 218, 219, 222, 224
Violence, 37
Virginity
  first intercourse, *see* Adolescent years,
    first intercourse
  maintaining, as a mature decision, 86–88
  marriage and, 9
  sexual revolution and, 104
  statistics on, 65, 66

Walden, Flo, 48–49, 176, 178
Washington Post, The, 105
Watson, Mary Ann, 241, 242
Weinberg, Martin S., 77
Weiner, Marcella Bakur, 248–49, 258
Weis, David L., 68–69, 204
Wendy, 128–29
Widowhood, 250, 260–62, 269–72, 284
"Wild oats" philosophy, 191
Will, 284
Win, 132–34
Women's liberation movement, 179–81
  aging and, 237–38
  body image and, 181
  development as individuals and, 180
  liberalization of age norms and, 267–68
  middle-aged women and, 180–81
  sex and, 179–80, 181
Work and Love: The Crucial Balance (Rohrlich),
  148
Wright State University, 115

Yale University, 6, 110, 120, 144

Zack, 234
Zalk, Sue Rosenberg, 126
Zaslow, Stephen L., 173
Zilbergeld, Bernie, 43

325

.